The
Australia
Book

The Australia Book

The Portrait of a Nation
By our Greatest Writers

Edited by T. Inglis Moore

Currey O'Neil

A CURREY O'NEIL BOOK
John Currey, O'Neil Publishers Pty Ltd
56 Claremont Street,
South Yarra, Victoria
First published 1961
© 1982 Collection, Currey O'Neil
© Individual writers in collection
Set by Procomp Productions Pty Ltd, South Australia
Printed and bound at Griffin Press Limited, Netley, South Australia
ISBN 0 85902 248 X

CONTENTS

History

Pastoral

People, Great and Small

Humour and Sentiment

Customs and Sports

Poems, Songs and Ballads

Traditions and Beliefs

INTRODUCTION

English, Scottish, Irish and Welsh folk, migrating to the antipodes in the late eighteenth and nineteenth centuries, combined to form the distinctive amalgam of the Australian people. If the English patterns of life and social institutions predominated in the new country, its literature has also owed much to the Celtic strains. When the poet was not a Brennan or FitzGerald, he was probably a McCrae or Neilson, while the outstanding critic, A. G. Stephens, was of Welsh descent.

In selecting the historical material I am indebted to the expert aid given by my colleague Mr D. W. A. Baker, Senior Lecturer in History, Australian National University. I also wish to express my thanks to the staffs of the National Library, Canberra, and the Mitchell Library, Sydney, for research services.

The special character of our history and literature, determined by the comparatively short term of Australian society, has meant inevitably that the bulk of the selection here had to be taken from modern and contemporary sources. It is true that the first-known European discovery of Australia was made in 1606, the year when Shakespeare was busy writing *Macbeth* or *King Lear*. British settlement did not come, however, until 1788, and for the next hundred years the creative writing in the various Australian colonies was written either by emigrants with a British outlook, such as Gordon and Kingsley, or by native-born writers who, even when they were passionately Australian in sentiment like the poets Harpur and Kendall, still followed English modes. It was not until the 1880s and 1890s, when the nationalist *Bulletin* sponsored an indigenous literature, that the writing emerged from its colonial stage to become exuberantly, often aggressively, Australian in its themes, outlook, and language. A national tradition was established in the bush ballads of 'Banjo' Paterson, the poetry of Bernard O'Dowd, the short stories of Henry Lawson, and the novels of Joseph Furphy and Miles Franklin. Australian creative literature as a national form of expression is thus essentially modern. Its growth from colonialism through a self-conscious, assertive nationalism to an independent maturity parallels, of course, a similar development in other countries which began as colonies, including the United States.

One marked characteristic of the literature has been its dominance by the Bush, a broad term for the inland, with a relative neglect of the cities. This offers a curious paradox, since Australia today is highly urbanised, with more than four-fifths of the population living in cities and towns. Yet it is only in the last three decades that attention has been paid to urban and industrial subjects, and many creative writers in prose or verse still tend to follow the tradition, formed in the nineties, of 'going bush'. Not only do commercial novelists exploit the outback, but the more imaginative novelists like Patrick White have sent their heroes into the desert to seek the salvation of their souls. The people as a whole cherish the legend of the bushman as the highest and most distinctive type of national character. The last few years have seen a popular revival of bush folklore and the old bush songs and ballads.

This book has drawn freely upon these folk songs since they present the popular spirit in a form which, however limited in literary quality, is often vigorous, racy and of the soil. They are the voice, crude and realistic, of the people themselves. On the other hand, space has been found for a few of the sophisticated visitors from overseas, such as Mark Twain and Trollope, D. H. Lawrence, and Dr Thomas Wood, who saw the Australian scene freshly and perceptively.

Like the old bush songs, the literature deals mainly with the workers and rarely with the great middle class of business and professional people. This feature, shaped in the nineties, still prevails to a great extent, along with the working-class point of view. The hero of the unofficial national song, *Waltzing Matilda*, is the swagman, set against the opposing forces of property and the law represented by the squatter and the police troopers. He is allied to the bushranger celebrated in the ballads as a Robin Hood of the bush.

This book is not a literary anthology, although it includes most of the leading authors of our past. Rather, it attempts to give a representative picture of Australia, of the country itself, the people and its history, and the national ways of life and thought. Such a picture must be necessarily incomplete as a personal choice must be made. I hope, however, that readers will not only enjoy the picture for its own sake but also gain a richer understanding of our national spirit and the unique qualities distinguishing the land and the people of Australia.

T. INGLIS MOORE

Prologue

NATIONALITY

I have grown past hate and bitterness,
I see the world as one;
Yet, though I can no longer hate,
My son is still my son.

All men at God's round table sit,
And all men must be fed;
But this loaf in my hand,
This loaf is my son's bread.

MARY GILMORE (1865–1962)

2

PLACES

MY COUNTRY

The love of field and coppice,
Of green and shaded lanes,
Of ordered woods and gardens
Is running in your veins.
Strong love of grey-blue distance,
Brown streams and soft, dim skies—
I know, but cannot share it,
My love is otherwise.

I love a sunburnt country,
A land of sweeping plains,
Of ragged mountain ranges,
Of droughts and flooding rains.
I love her far horizons,
I love her jewel-sea,
Her beauty and her terror—
The wide brown land for me!

The tragic ring-barked forests,
Stark white beneath the moon,
The sapphire-misted mountains,
The hot gold hush of noon,
Green tangle of the brushes
Where lithe lianas coil,
And orchids deck the tree-tops,
And ferns the warm dark soil.

Core of my heart, my country!
Her pitiless blue sky,
When, sick at heart, around us
We see the cattle die—
But then the grey clouds gather,
And we can bless again
The drumming of an army,
The steady soaking rain.

Core of my heart, my country!
Land of the rainbow gold,
For flood and fire and famine
She pays us back threefold.
Over the thirsty paddocks,
Watch, after many days,
The filmy veil of greenness
That thickens as we gaze . . .

An opal-hearted country,
A wilful, lavish land—
All you who have not loved her,
You will not understand—
Though Earth holds many splendours,
Wherever I may die,
I know to what brown country
My homing thoughts will fly.

                    DOROTHEA MACKELLAR (1885–1968)

THE AUSTRALIAN ALPS

A new heaven and a new earth! Tier beyond tier, height above height, the great wooded ranges go rolling away westward, till on the lofty skyline they are crowned with a gleam of everlasting snow. To the eastward they sink down, breaking into isolated forest-fringed peaks, and rock-crowned eminences, till with rapidly straightening lines they fade into the broad grey plains, beyond which the Southern Ocean is visible by the white sea-haze upon the sky.

All creation is new and strange. The trees, surpassing in size the largest English oaks, are of a species we have never seen before. The graceful shrubs, the bright-coloured flowers, ay, the very grass itself, are of species unknown in Europe; while flaming lories and brilliant parakeets fly whistling, not unmusically, through the gloomy forest, and overhead in the higher fields of air, still lit up by the last rays of the sun, countless cockatoos wheel and scream in noisy joy, as we may see the gulls do about an English headland.

4

To the northward a great glen, sinking suddenly from the saddle on which we stand, stretches away in long vista, until it joins a broader valley, through which we can dimly see a full-fed river winding alone in gleaming reaches, through level meadow land, interspersed with clumps of timber.

We are in Australia. Three hundred and fifty miles south of Sydney, on the great watershed which divides the Belloury from the Maryburnong, since better known as the Snowy River of Gippsland.

HENRY KINGSLEY (1830–1876)
The Recollections of Geoffry Hamlyn

AUSTRALIA

Last sea-thing dredged by sailor Time from Space,
Are you a drift Sargasso, where the West
In halcyon calm rebuilds her fatal nest?
Or Delos of a coming Sun-God's race?
Are you for Light, and trimmed, with oil in place,
Or but a Will o' Wisp on marshy quest?
A new demesne for Mammon to infest?
Or lurks millennial Eden 'neath your face?
The cenotaphs of species dead elsewhere
That in your limits leap and swim and fly,
Or trail uncanny harp-strings from your trees,
Mix omens with the auguries that dare
To plant the Cross upon your forehead sky,
A virgin helpmate Ocean at your knees.

BERNARD O'DOWD (1866–1953)

BOTANY BAY

Farewell to old England for ever,
Farewell to my rum culls as well;
Farewell to the well-known old Bailee,
Where I used for to cut such a swell.

5

Chorus
Singing too-ral li-oor-al li-ad-dity
Singing too-ral li-oor-al li-ay;
Singing too-ral li-oor-al li-ad-dity
Singing too-ral li-oor-al li-ay;

There's the Captain as is our Commander,
There's the bo'sun and all the ship's crew,
There's the first and second-class passengers,
Knows what we poor convicts go through.

'Taint leavin' old England we cares about,
'Taint cos we mispels what we knows,
But becos all we light-fingered gentry
Hops around with a log on our toes.

Oh, had I the wings of a turtle-dove!
I'd soar on my pinions so high,
Slap bang to the arms of my Polly love,
And in her sweet presence I'd die.

Now, all my young Dookies and Duchesses,
Take warning from what I've to say,
Mind all is your own as you touchesses,
Or you'll find us in Botany Bay.

Folk Song

SYDNEY IN THE NINETIES

Sydney had grown up with the growing up of the young people of my generation. The city had advanced rapidly in population and in prosperity— causing some anxiety to the extreme protectionists in Victoria, who had taken it for granted that with Sydney's outmoded attachment to free trade she would sink permanently into the second place, leaving Melbourne as the great emporium for the east of Australia—and Sydney had developed a character of its own, as described by Kipling:

The first flush of the tropics in my blood
And at my feet Success.

Her citizens preserved an easy-going, light-hearted temperament and did not take themselves too seriously. A visiting journalist from England—I think it was Foster Fraser—summed up the three chief cities in Australia in the words, 'Sydney for pleasure, Melbourne for business, Adelaide for culture'. This little epigram made him unpopular in all three cities. It was not what he credited each of them with, but what by implication he excluded. Each city thought itself entitled to honourable mention in all three categories. Like Bottom the weaver, each fancied itself in all the roles.

And Sydney, in spite of its growth, had not yet developed that huge unwieldiness—that form of gigantism—which it shows to-day. Nor was it yet in the grip of all the devastating mechanical gadgets of the twentieth century, and it was a pleasant place to live in. I always feel when I visit Sydney now that its growth has been too uncontrolled, and that it would profit by a great fire like that of London, followed by a great planner like Paris's Haussmann who would make order out of chaos, give the city impressive exits and entrances, open up a scenic drive along the harbour foreshores, and provide a fair allowance of stately boulevards. As it is, Sydney always strikes me as a careless beauty who has neglected her appearance, whilst Melbourne has made up for her comparative lack of natural advantages by careful grooming.

Added to this, Sydney's manner of enjoying itself has always been more informal and hearty than Melbourne's. There has always been more of the open-air amusements, yachting, surfing and picnicking and so forth, which are favoured by the climate, the harbour, and the unlimited supply of sandy beaches.

SIR ROBERT RANDOLPH GARRAN (1867–1957)
Prosper the Commonwealth

A STRANGE, INVISIBLE BEAUTY

The train ran for a long time through Sydney, or the endless outsides of Sydney. The town took almost as much leaving as London does. But it was different. Instead of solid rows of houses, solid streets like London, it was mostly innumerable detached bungalows and cottages, spreading for great distances, scattering over hills, low hills and shallow inclines. And then waste marshy places, and old iron, and abortive corrugated iron 'works'—all like the Last Day of creation, instead of a new country. Away to the left they saw the shallow waters of the big opening where Botany Bay is: the sandy shores, the factory chimneys, the lonely places where it is still Bush. And the weary half-established straggling of more suburb.

'Como,' said the station sign. And they ran on bridges over two arms of water from the sea, and they saw what looked like a long lake with wooded shores and bungalows: a bit like Lake Como, but, oh, so unlike. That curious sombreness of Australia, the sense of oldness, with the forms all worn down low and blunt, squat. The squat-seeming earth. And then they ran at last into real country, rather rocky, dark old rocks, and sombre bush with its different pale-stemmed dull-leaved gum-trees standing graceful, and various healthy-looking undergrowth, and great spiky things like zuccas. As they turned south they saw tree-ferns standing on one knobbly leg among the gums, and among the rocks ordinary ferns and small bushes spreading in glades and up sharp hillslopes. It was virgin bush, and as if unvisited, lost, sombre, with plenty of space, yet spreading grey for miles and miles, in a hollow towards the west. Far in the west, the sky having suddenly cleared, they saw the magical range of the Blue Mountains. And all this hoary space of bush between. The strange, as it were, *invisible* beauty of Australia, which is undeniably there, but which seems to lurk just beyond the range of our white vision. You feel you can't *see*—as if your eyes hadn't the vision in them to correspond with the outside landscape. For the landscape is so unimpressive, like a face with little or no features, a dark face. It is so Aboriginal, out of our ken, and it hangs back so aloof. Somers always felt he looked at it through a cleft in the atmosphere; as one looks at one of the ugly-faced, distorted Aborigines with his wonderful dark eyes that have such an incomprehensible ancient shine in them, across gulfs of unbridged centuries. And yet, when you don't have the feeling of ugliness or monotony, in landscape or in nigger, you get a sense of subtle, remote, *formless* beauty more poignant than anything ever experienced before.

D. H. LAWRENCE (1885–1930)
Kangaroo

9

WESTERN AUSTRALIAN OUTPOST

There is a church in Derby, and a post office and a school, a couple of hotels, a police station and some houses—all built of planks and corrugated iron. When a ship puts in a horse-tram comes to life; and seated on its hard wooden benches you can see a foreshore dried like crocodile skin, some gnarled old baobab trees, and sand—tan, grey, and coppery bronze—whose glare makes you screw up your eyes. No fruit grows in Derby; no vegetables. Seats in the school are petrol cases with the ends knocked out. The constable's beat is as big as Yorkshire. Iron is hot to the touch even when the sun is off it, and the white ant eats wood to powder. After dark every light is a misty haze dimmed by swirling insects; sandflies bite like needles; mosquito nets are a burden; sleep is coma. Such is Derby, W.A., and one hundred and ninety people live there.

We saw most of them.

The traveller's impressions of a place are necessarily different from those of its inhabitants. Beauties stir him, or austerities depress him because he sees them once and is gone; the keen edge both of admiration and of rebellion is generally blunted in those who have to see them every day. The Derby that I saw and have described, an outpost in an empty land, cannot be the same Derby to the men I met over its curry and strong tea. Outpost? they say—what about the places over the Fitzroy, or up in the Territory? This is a centre, a gathering place; warmish, perhaps, in a dry spell, and you can't get new books and you get tired of beef (what's a salad taste like nowadays?), but Derby is *home*. Very well. I shall not try to reconcile two opposites at this conference, but instead, I will say from the chair that hearts in Derby are as warm as the sunshine, and the talk out-values many a novel.

THOMAS WOOD (1892–1950)
Cobbers

SURF BEACH, MANLY

The summer was embalmed those last few days in a heavy atmosphere which slightly blurred the sun while augmenting its power. The Sunday crowd composed of all possible varieties of the city's people sat and lay,

10

walked and tottered about the sands, a dense swarm clad in flannels and thin brightly coloured frocks, shirt sleeves and braces, bathing costumes abbreviated to the extremity of contemporary defiance of regulation. This profusion of colours and hot male and female flesh was not all overwhelming as it might have been in any other place, because the pines and the ocean diminished it and reduced it into insignificance.

Between the dressing sheds above the declivity near South Steyne and the beach, the free figures of men, women and children rushed to and fro. In the shallow water between the green curve of the next breaker and the narrow stretch of churned yellow sand another thick swarm bobbed and ducked. The continuous human cry, heightened by the predominant pitch of the women and children, blended above that long curve of beach with the noise of the tumbling ocean into one incessant meaningless sound. Along the asphalt path by the low sea wall saunterers passed before the critical eyes of the people in the chairs beneath the Norfolk Island pines. Beyond the inner bathers young men and women more expert and more venturesome swam out and rode the breakers until they came in danger of collision with the legs and bodies of the splashing mob in the foam. A few, emboldened by the knowledge that on this beach there had for a long time been no attacks by sharks, swam out afar, their heads bobbing spots in the swell, waiting for that occasional especially big purler which would bear them rigid, triumphant from their fearful loneliness, to the safety of the infested sands. . . .

The heavy heat, like an ointment percolating through the skin and flesh into the centres of nervous life, produced a lethargy out of which their utterances came slowly, each syllable weighed equally with the others. The sun beat them almost into insensibility. The ocean quivered ceaselessly and violently in the universal undulation and the pines writhed ceaselessly upwards, their writhing motions more passionate because confined like those of dark equatorial men and women bound and burning at the stakes. All this rapid movement and glare charged in with violet and purple patterns through their half-closed eyelids.

LEONARD MANN (1895–1981)
A Murder in Sydney

EARLY MELBOURNE

One night, in 1858, a man and his horse were drowned in Elizabeth Street, under 'the miserable dark lanterns that disgraced the metropolis'. At about the same time, a horse and dray were carried down Swanston Street, past where Young and Jackson's now stands, into the river. These happenings afforded a chance to some sardonic joker, who wrote to the mayor, John Thomas Smith, suggesting he should set up lifebuoys 'the whole length of the post office coast'. During summer, instead of floods, the inhabitants suffered dust-storms, full of specks and straws, so that it became difficult to breathe. The sky like London fog; the atmosphere that of a lighted oven. . . .

In 1841 Georgiana, trudging from Spencer Street to Russell Street (then a name only), covered five blocks before she came to Swanston Street, and in that space measured, east to west, all the town there was. Her most difficult passage would be across Elizabeth Street, once a tributary to the Yarra, and, during bad weather, unfordable, except high up along the ridge of Lonsdale Street. Another thoroughfare, baulked at one end by thick forest, had become crooked through recoil, losing its likeness to a road, so much, as to necessitate the use of a board inscribed:

THIS IS GREAT BOURKE STREET EAST

On the north, the occupied part of the settlement began to thin away towards Lonsdale Street, and, six blocks south, wilted again to Flinders Street. Here a few houses stayed, fastened to the first firm ground emergent from the river; beyond them, all was bog, a number of planks set end to end showing the way to the punt on the Yarra.

HUGH McCRAE (1876–1958)
Georgiana's Journal

THE VICTORIA MARKET RECOLLECTED
IN TRANQUILLITY

Winds are bleak, stars are bright,
Loads lumber along the night:
Looming, ghastly white,
A towering truck of cauliflowers sways
Out of the dark, roped over and packed tight
Like faces of a crowd of football jays.

The roads come in, roads dark and long,
To the knock of hubs and a sleepy song.
Heidelberg, Point Nepean, White Horse,
Flemington, Keilor, Dandenong,
Into the centre from the source.

Rocking in their seats
The worn-out drivers droop
When dawn stirs in the streets
And the moon's a silver hoop;
Come rumbling into the silent mart,
To put their treasure at its heart,
Waggons, lorries, a lame Ford bus,
Like ants along the arms of an octopus
Whose body is all one mouth; that pays them hard
And drives them back with less than a slave's reward.
When Batman first at Heaven's command
Said, 'This is the place for a peanut-stand',[1]

It must have been grand!

. . . . . .

Along the shadows, furtive, lone,
The unwashed terrier carried his week-end bone,
An old horse with a pointed hip
And dangling disillusioned under-lip

---

[1] This combines satiric references to the first line of *Rule Britannia* and to the historic remark made by John Batman in 1835 when he sailed up the river Yarra, and contemplated the site of Melbourne: 'This will be the place for a village'.

Stands in a harvest-home of cabbage-leaves
And grieves.
A lady by a petrol case,
With a far-off wounded look in her face
Says, in a voice of uncertain pitch,
'Muffins', or 'crumpets', I'm not sure which.
A pavement battler whines with half a sob,
'Ain't anybody got a bloody bob?'
Haunted by mortgages and overdrafts
The old horse droops between the shafts.

.   .   .   .   . ′ .

When Batman first at Heaven's command
Stuck flag-staffs in this sacred strand . . .
We'll leave all that to the local band.

> FURNLEY MAURICE (FRANK WILMOT) (1881–1942)
> *Melbourne Odes*

CONTRASTS IN CITIES

Indeed, it is one of the slightly depressing features to the stranger that men
and women wear the same clothes, build the same houses, eat the same
food and sing the same songs—or, rather, listen to the same records—from
one end of the continent to the other. Still, certain differences can be
observed. Australians themselves have a saying that when a stranger
arrives in Perth, the first question he is asked is, 'Where do you come
from?'; in Adelaide, 'What Church do you belong to?'; in Melbourne,
'What school were you at?'; in Sydney, 'How much money have you got?';
while in Brisbane they merely say, 'Come and have a drink'. This jest has a
certain rough truth. Perth is kindly and easy-going, with even now
something of the air of a frontier town. Adelaide, prim and staid, often
seems dominated by that Puritanical, Protestant, almost Victorian middle-
class respectability which elsewhere exists only as a vociferous but fading
minority. Melbourne is outwardly by far the most English and class-con-
scious of Australian cities, though it also has the most violent criminals
and the biggest Italian community. Sydney, which is regarded by the rest of

Australia with something of the same half-amused, half-shocked disapproval with which a citizen of Boston regards Chicago or an Edinburgh man regards Glasgow, is turbulent, crude, vital and grossly materialist. Here, too, the Irish element is more noticeable. Pitt Street may be like Manchester, but the pubs of Pyrmont or Balmain take you back with a rush to Glasgow or Belfast. In Brisbane the heat of a tropical climate has slowed down the Australian character without substantially changing it. Indeed, for all these shades of distinction the difference between the countryman and the townsman is everywhere more noticeable than the difference between the citizen of Sydney and the citizen of Perth.

JOHN DOUGLAS PRINGLE (1912–   )
Australian Accent

CANBERRA FROM RED HILL

Below them lay a great valley with a level floor, as if it had once been a lake rimmed about with mountains. It might have remained a lost valley, a forgotten strong-hold of peace where nothing changed in centuries, one of those idyllic worlds that still survive here and there; but a great city had been built across it. Canberra was laid out beneath them in its geometrical design, in oblongs, ellipses, and circles, as if the architect had taken his set-square and compasses and worked directly upon the plain. It was much more like architectural rendering, an idealisation done to scale, than a happy-go-lucky Australian town. Even the colours carried distinctly in the clear air, into which no factories smoked—the snow-white blocks of Government buildings, with Parliament House like a giant wedding-cake in the centre; the creamy cubes with red or green roofs that were private houses; an occasional mass of dark brick and dark lines of exotic ever-greens to accent the scene. The evergreens showed small, black, compact, like the trees of some super Noah's ark, while lines of pale, feathery green marked avenues of oaks and elms bursting into their spring leaf. The Molonglo River looped and twisted across the city, pale blue from the sky.

The city was sharply determined. Beyond it the plain stretched, empty, a perfect *tabula rasa* showing from this height a hundred delicate, blending shades of colour—paddocks of sun-baked grass smeared with the greyish mauve of a weed; fawn smudged with rust of sorrel; pale sage-green; the

15

gamboge of the soil filmed with green of springing grass; windy silver of dry, bleached grass. All—city, plain, mountains—were steeped in the light of an October morning, a beautiful, fearless light that lay like a delicate bloom over the landscape—golden bloom of sunlight on walls, grape-coloured shadows, blue distances.

M. BARNARD ELDERSHAW
(MARJORIE BARNARD, 1897–   *and* FLORA ELDERSHAW, 1897–1956)
Plaque with Laurel

HOME LAND

This is the naked and Aboriginal feel
Of Nobody's Land for which my dreaming flesh—
Speeding to dine in wildernesses of suburb,
Hiring trunks at a roofed-in swimming-pool,
Touring with crowds to recommended mountains—
Ached for long years. Wild rocks and rag-like trees
Crossfaded hourly with the orthodox town,
The formal field. But it is active joy,
Pushing through scrub, to feel the bush no ghost—
An angular presence, elbowy, lean as famine,
Dry-rasping, hot with prickles; topping a crag,
To greet the satin sea where one white sail

Glides like a fin; rolling in sand as fine
As table salt, or inland on a desert
Standing at midnight opposite the moon
To find afresh that the elements are four,
Not ninety-two. I count them by their feel,
Think with my nose and skin, alive not dying.

JOHN THOMPSON (1907–1968)
from *The Traveller*

THE OLD BARK HUT

Oh, my name is Bob the Swagman, before you all I stand,
And I've had my ups and downs while travelling through the land.
I once was well-to-do, my boys, but now I am stumped up,
And I'm forced to go on rations in an old bark hut.

Chorus
In an old bark hut, in an old bark hut,
I'm forced to go on rations in an old bark hut.

Ten pounds of flour, ten pounds of beef, some sugar and some tea,
That's all they give to a hungry man, until the Seventh Day.
If you don't be moighty sparing, you'll go with a hungry gut—
For that's one of the great misfortunes in an old bark hut.

Chorus
In an old bark hut, in an old bark hut,
For that's one of the great misfortunes in an old bark hut.

The bucket you boil your beef in has to carry water, too,
And they'll say you're getting mighty flash if you should ask for two.
I've a billy, and a pint pot, and a broken-handled cup,
And they all adorn the table in the old bark hut.

Chorus
In an old bark hut, in an old bark hut,
And they all adorn the table in the old bark hut.

Faith, the table is not made of wood, like many you have seen—
For if I had one half so good, I'd think myself serene;
'Tis only an old sheet of bark—God knows when it was cut—
It was blown from off the rafters of the old bark hut.

Chorus
In an old bark hut, in an old bark hut,
It was blown from off the rafters of the old bark hut.

18

And of furniture, there's no such thing, 'twas never in the place.
Except the stool I sit upon—and that's an old gin case.
It does us for a safe as well, but you must keep it shut,
Or the flies would make it canter round the old bark hut.

Chorus
In an old bark hut, in an old bark hut,
Or the flies would make it canter round the old bark hut.

If you should leave it open, and the flies should find your meat,
They'll scarcely leave a single piece that's fit for man to eat.
But you musn't curse, nor grumble—what won't fatten will fill up—
For what's out of sight is out of mind in an old bark hut.

Chorus
In an old bark hut, in an old bark hut,
For what's out of sight is out of mind in an old bark hut.

I've seen the rain come in this hut just like a perfect flood,
Especially through that great big hole where once the table stood.
There's not a blessed spot, me boys, where you could lay your nut,
But the rain is sure to find you in the old bark hut.

Chorus
In an old bark hut, in an old bark hut,
But the rain is sure to find you in the old bark hut.

So beside the fire I make my bed, and there I lay me down,
And think myself as happy as the king that wears a crown.
But as you're dozing off to sleep a flea will wake you up,
Which makes you curse the vermin in the old bark hut.

Chorus
In an old bark hut, in an old bark hut,
Which makes you curse the vermin in the old bark hut.

Faith, such flocks of fleas you never saw, they are so plump and fat,
And if you make a grab at one he'll spit just like a cat.
Last night they got my pack of cards, and were fighting for the cut—
I thought the devil had me in the old bark hut.

Chorus
In an old bark hut, in an old bark hut,
I thought the devil had me in the old bark hut.

So now, my friends, I've sung my song, and that as well as I could,
And I hope the ladies present won't think my language rude;
And all ye younger people, in the days when you grow up,
Remember Bob the Swagman, and the old bark hut.

Chorus
In an old bark hut, in an old bark hut,
Remember Bob the Swagman, and the old bark hut.

Old Bush Song

THE DEVIL'S BLOW-HOLE

This great tunnel-spout is near Port Arthur, Tasmania, the notorious prison in the transportation period, from which the convict John Rex was making a desperate escape at night.

The darkness had increased with the gale. The wind, ravaging the hollow heaven, had spread between the lightnings and the sea an impenetrable curtain of black cloud. . . . The shrieking which he had heard a few moments ago had ceased, but every now and then dull but immense shocks, as of some mighty bird flapping the cliff with monstrous wings, reverberated around him, and shook the ground where he stood. He looked towards the ocean, and a tall misty Form—white against the all-pervading blackness— beckoned and bowed to him. He saw it distinctly for an instant, and then, with an awful shriek, as of wrathful despair, it sank and vanished. . . .

With a fierce thrill of renewed hope, he ran forward; when at his feet, in his face, arose that misty Form, breathing chill warning, as though to wave him back. The terror at his heels drove him on. A few steps more, and he should gain the summit of the cliff. He could *feel* the sea roaring in front of him in the gloom. The column disappeared; and in a lull of wind, uprose from the place where it had been, such a hideous medley of shrieks, laughter, and exultant wrath, that John Rex paused in horror. Too late. The ground gave way—it seemed—beneath his feet. He was falling—clutching, in vain, at rocks, shrubs, and grass. The cloud-curtain lifted, and by the lightning that leaped and played about the ocean, John Rex found an explanation of his terrors, more terrible than they themselves had been. The track he had followed led to that portion of the cliff in which the sea had excavated the tunnel-spout known as the Devil's Blow-Hole.

Clinging to a tree that, growing half way down the precipice, had arrested his course, he stared into the abyss. Before him—already high above his head—was a gigantic arch of cliff. Through this arch he saw, at an immense distance below him, the raging and pallid ocean. Beneath him was an abyss splintered with black rocks, turbid and raucous with tortured water. Suddenly the bottom of this abyss seemed to advance to meet him; or, rather, the black throat of the chasm belched a volume of leaping, curling water, which mounted to drown him. . . .

The roaring column mounted with hideous swiftness. Rex felt it rush at him and swing him upward. With both arms round the tree, he clutched the sleeves of his jacket with either hand. Perhaps if he could maintain his hold, he might outlive the shock of that suffocating torrent. He felt his feet rudely seized, as though by the hand of a giant, and plucked upwards. Water gurgled in his ears. His arms seemed about to be torn from their sockets. Had the strain lasted another instant, he must have loosed his hold; but, with a wild hoarse shriek, as though it was some sea-monster baffled of its prey, the column sank, and left him gasping, bleeding, half drowned, but alive.

MARCUS CLARKE (1846–1881)
For the Term of His Natural Life

MACQUARIE HARBOUR

Macquarie Harbour jailers lock
the sullen gates no more . . .
but lash-strokes sound in every shock
of ocean on the dismal rock
along that barren shore.

21

No more the bolters[1] hear the hound
that bays upon the wind,
and terror-spurred keep onward bound
until they drop upon the ground,
starved and terror-pinned . . .

but gales that whine among the hills
sniff at the savage tracks
the hopeless took. The snowfall fills
bleak ranges; then the moonlight spills
broad arrows on their backs.

REX INGAMELLS (1913–1955)

THE KARRI FOREST

Sunshine, where it pierced the trees, quivered in brilliant restless patches over dry leaves on the ground, ruddy and green rosettes of sundew, figured by the tall stalks of winged white flowers, fading rose and mauve, and the mustard yellow primroses of hibbertia.

Through the smoke which went up from Deb's fire Red saw them, and across the leaves and Tom Colburn lying stretched beside the dead tree. He might have been a branch of it, in his worn white moleskins and washed-out shirt.

'Milkin' twenty cows, these days', Red heard Deb say. 'Up at daybreak . . . and when it's hot and still like this smoke about . . . I can't keep my eyes open.'

After a while she drowsed too. Sun-dazed and sleepy himself in the heat and stillness, Red saw Deb lying on the dry leaves, an arm's length from him. She had turned her back and flung an arm over her face. Her limbs twined over each other, brown legs and long brown arms, bare from under her blue cotton dress.

Red thought of a young tree fallen there beside him as he took Deb in. His sleep-stricken brain tore the blue rags of dress from her young strong body, and it gleamed against the dark foliage and through the haze of the forest, as trunks of the karri gleamed, mellow ivory, with the glamour of

[1] Escaped convicts.

22

parchment, the lustre of silk. Dreaming, afraid to stir, disturb or change the half-waking, strange soaking joyousness he lay in, Red wondered vaguely whether he was asleep or awake. He was conscious only of wandering in misty depths of the forest.

Bone-white and silver in high light against the leafage, the dead tree caught and held his brain. Abysses of trees fell away from the dead tree and surrounded him. Red could not see far for tapestry of the leaves, and the smoke bush fires in the distance put among them.

There was a faint dry ticking as if the pulse of every living thing in the forest was vibrating. Life was suspended; yet Red heard that ticking, the rattle of frail shells, innumerable infinitesimal insect castanets clicking, as an assurance that the transfixed world about him was not the world of a dream. He could almost hear sap flowing in the trees, electric currents circulating among roots of the plants; the soil stir and move to its nitrogen, potassium and phosphates. The air he breathed was undulating with rarefied elixirs. He seemed to be drifting away on them, absorbing subtle magnetisms of the air, the earth, insects and trees.

KATHARINE SUSANNAH PRICHARD (1883–1969)
Working Bullocks

OUT BACK

Draw a wire fence and a few ragged gums, and add some scattered sheep running away from the train. Then you'll have the bush all along the New South Wales western line from Bathurst on.

The railway towns consist of a public house and a general store, with a square tank and a school-house on piles in the nearer distance. The tank stands at the end of the school and is not many times smaller than the building itself. It is safe to call the pub 'The Railway Hotel', and the store 'The Railway Stores', with an 's'. A couple of patient, ungroomed hacks are probably standing outside the pub, while their masters are inside having a drink—several drinks. Also it's safe to draw a sundowner sitting listlessly on a bench on the veranda, reading the *Bulletin*.

. . . We crossed the Macquarie—a narrow, muddy gutter with a dog swimming across, and three goats interested.

. . . Somebody told me that the country was very dry on the other side of Nevertire. It is. I wouldn't like to sit down on it anywhere. The least

23

horrible spot in the bush, in a dry season, is where the bush isn't—where it has been cleared away and a green crop is trying to grow. They talk of settling people on the land! Better settle *in* it. I'd rather settle on the water; at least, until some gigantic system of irrigation is perfected in the West.

. . . Somebody said to me 'Yer wanter go out back, young man, if yer wanter see the country. Yer wanter get away from the line'. I don't wanter; I've been there.

You could go to the brink of eternity so far as Australia is concerned and yet meet an animated mummy of a swagman who will talk of going 'out back'. Out upon the out-back fiend!

. . . At 5.30 we saw a long line of camels moving out across the sunset. There's something snaky about camels. They remind me of turtles and goannas.

Somebody said, 'Here's Bourke'.

HENRY LAWSON (1867–1922)
In a Dry Season

THE SPEEWAH

Yes, Old-timer, strange things happened on the Speewah. The kangaroos there were as tall as mountains and the emus laid eggs that men blew and used for houses.

But where the Speewah is, no one knows. The men from the Darling said it was back o' Bourke and the men of Bourke said it was out West and the men of the West pointed to Queensland and in Queensland they told you the Speewah was in the Kimberleys.

Tom Ronan, a bushman of Katherine, N.T., told me in a letter:

'It was, I think, originally, the place a bit "farther out", "over the next range" where cattle were a bit wilder, horses a bit rougher and men a bit smarter than they were anywhere else. With the growth of backblocks folk lore, its position in the scheme of things became more definite: It was the land of running creeks and shady trees and good, green horse feed, the bushman's "Field of Asphodel", the place where all good bagmen—and some that weren't so good—went when they died. . . .'

Whatever its origin, it is possible, from the stories told about it, to get a picture of this mythical station and of some of the men who ran it . . .

First there is 'Crooked Mick' who tried to strangle himself with his

24

own beard in the Big Drought. He was a gun shearer; 500 a day was nothing to him. Once, the boss, annoyed because of Crooked Mick's rough handling of some wethers, strode up to him on the board and barked, 'You're fired'. Crooked Mick was shearing flat out at the time. He was going so fast that he shore fifteen sheep before he could straighten up and hang his shears on the hook. . . .

Big Bill, who built the barbed wire fence, was the strongest man on the Speewah, they say. He made his fortune on the Croydon goldfields cutting up mining shafts and selling them for post holes. He was originally put on to fence the Speewah but gave it up after a day digging post holes. He left his lunch at the first hole when he started in the morning, then at midday he put down his crowbar and set off to walk back for his lunch. He had sunk so many holes he didn't reach his lunch till midnight. That finished him.

'A bloke'd starve going at that rate', he said.

ALAN MARSHALL (1902–   )
They were Tough Men on the Speewah

WHERE THE DEAD MEN LIE

Out on the wastes of the Never Never—
That's where the dead men lie!
There where the heat waves dance for ever—
That's where the dead men lie!
That's where the Earth's loved sons are keeping
Endless tryst: not the west wind sweeping
Feverish pinions can wake their sleeping—
Out where the dead men lie!

Where brown Summer and Death have mated—
That's where the dead men lie!
Loving with fiery lust unsated—
That's where the dead men lie!
Out where the grinning skulls bleach whitely
Under the saltbush sparkling brightly;
Out where the wild dogs chorus nightly—
That's where the dead men lie!

Deep in the yellow, flowing river—
That's where the dead men lie!
Under the banks where the shadows quiver—
That's where the dead men lie!
Where the platypus twists and doubles,
Leaving a train of tiny bubbles;
Rid at last of their earthly troubles—
That's where the dead men lie!

Only the hand of night can free them—
That's when the dead men fly!
Only the frightened cattle see them—
See the dead men go by!
Cloven hoofs beating out one measure,
Bidding the stockmen know no leisure—
That's when the dead men take their pleasure!
That's when the dead men fly!

BARCROFT BOAKE (1866–1892)

CATTLE STATION,
NORTHERN TERRTORY

Oscar held dominion over six hundred square miles of country, which extended east and west from the railway to the summit of the Lonely Ranges, and north and south from the horizons, it might be said, since there was nothing to show where the boundaries lay in those directions.

Jasmine had said that he worshipped property. It was true. But he did not value Red Ochre simply as a grazing-lease. At times it was to him six hundred square miles where grazing grew and brolgas danced in the painted sunset and emus ran to the silver dawn—square miles of jungle where cool deep billabongs made watering for stock and nests for shouting nuttagul geese—of grassy valleys and stony hills, useless for grazing, but good to think about as haunts of great goannas and rock-pythons—of swamps where cattle bogged and died, but wild hog and buffalo wallowed in happiness—of virgin forests where poison weed lay in wait for stock, but where possums and kangaroos and multitudes of gorgeous birds dwelt as from time immemorial. At times he loved Red Ochre.

26

27

At times he loved it best in Wet Season—when the creeks were running and the swamps were full—when the multi-coloured schisty rocks split golden waterfalls—when the scarlet plains were under water, green with wild rice, swarming with Siberian snipe—when the billabongs were brimming and the water-lilies blooming and the nuttaguls shouting loudest—when bull-grass towered ten feet high, clothing hills and choking gullies—when every tree was flowering and most were draped with crimson mistletoe and droning with humming-birds and native bees—when cattle wandered a land of plenty, fat and sleek, till the buffalo-flies and marsh-flies came and drove them mad, so that they ran and ran to leanness, often to their death—when mosquitoes and a hundred other breeds of maddening insects were there to test a man's endurance—when from hour to hour luke-warm showers drenched the steaming earth, till one was sodden to the bone and mildewed to the marrow and moved to pray, as Oscar always did when he had had enough of it, for that which formerly he had cursed—the Dry! the good old Dry—when the grass yellowed, browned, dried to tinder, burst into spontaneous flame—when harsh winds rioted with choking dust and the billabongs became mere muddy holes where cattle pawed for water—when gaunt drought loafed about a desert and exhausted cattle staggered searching dust for food and drink, till they fell down and died and became neat piles of bones for the wind to whistle through and the gaunt-ribbed dingo to mourn—then one prayed for the Wet again, or if one's heart was small, packed up and left this Capricornia that fools down South called the Land of Opportunity, and went back and said that nothing was done by halves up there except the works of puny man.

XAVIER HERBERT (1901–   )
Capricornia

A HOMESTEAD IN THE NEVER-NEVER

The homestead is that of Elsey Station, Northern Territory, in 1902.

The homestead, standing half-way up the slope that rose from the billabong, had, after all, little of that 'down-at-heels, anything'll do' appearance that Mac had so scathingly described. No one could call it a 'commodious station home', and it was even patched up and shabby; but, for all that, neat and cared for. An orderly little array of one-roomed buildings, mostly built of sawn slabs, and ranged round a broad oblong space with a precision that suggested the idea of a section of a street cut out from some neat compact little village.

The cook's quarters, kitchens, men's quarters, store, meat-house, and waggon-house, facing each other on either side of this oblong space formed a short avenue—the main thoroughfare of the homestead—the centre of which was occupied by an immense wood-heap, the favourite gossiping place of some of the old black fellows, while across the western end of it, and looking down it, but a little aloof from the rest of the buildings, stood the House, or, rather, as much of it as had been rebuilt after the cyclone of 1897. As befitted their social positions the forge and black boys' 'humpy' kept a respectful distance well round the south-eastern corner of this thoroughfare; but, for some unknown reason, the fowl-roosts had been erected over Sam Lee's sleeping-quarters. That comprised this tiny homestead of a million and a quarter acres, with the Katherine Settlement a hundred miles to the north of it, one neighbour ninety miles to the east, another, a hundred and five to the south, and others about two hundred to the west.

Unfortunately, Mac's description of the House had been only too correct. With the exception of the one roughly finished room at its eastern end, it was 'mostly verandas and promises'.

MRS AENEAS GUNN (1870–1961)
We of the Never-Never

THE BLUE MOUNTAINS

These lines have a special interest in that Wentworth as a youth took part with Blaxland and Lawson in the historic crossing of the Blue Mountains in 1813. The poem *Australasia* won second prize for the Prize Poem for the Chancellor's Medal at Cambridge University in 1823. Wentworth later became an Australian statesman and constitution-maker.

> Hail, mighty ridge! that from thy azure brow
> Survey'st these fertile plains, that stretch below . . .
> Vast Austral Giant of these rugged steeps,
> Within those secret cells rich glitt'ring heaps
> Thick piled are doom'd to sleep, till some one spy
> The hidden key that opes the treasury;

How mute, how desolate thy stunted woods,
How dread thy chasms, where many an eagle broods,
How dark thy caves, how lone thy torrents' roar,
As down thy cliffs precipitous they pour,
Broke on our hearts, when first with vent'rous tread
We dared to rouse thee from thy mountain bed!

WILLIAM CHARLES WENTWORTH (1790–1872)
Australasia

EUREKA PARK, BALLARAT

The brief rebellion of the gold-diggers at the Eureka Stockade in 1854 against the licence system and the official use of repression by the police and soldiers has become a legend of Australian radicalism.

They left the car outside the white paling fence round the Eureka Park enclosure, and walked to the monument.

The blue-stone monolith stuck up against a golden sky. Firs, dark and mysteriously shadowed, backed flower-beds lit by more dahlias, superb, crimson and blood-red, white, flesh-pink and golden. Four little guns on guard below the monolith, above the eight corners of the wide base, stood like toys on white-painted wooden mounts.

Sevarrin walked up the steps and read the inscription:

EUREKA STOCKADE

SUNDAY MORNING DEC. 3RD 1854

TO THE HONOURED MEMORY OF THE HEROIC PIONEERS WHO FOUGHT AND FELL ON THIS SACRED SPOT IN THE CAUSE OF LIBERTY, AND THE SOLDIERS WHO FELL AT DUTY'S CALL. . . .

'Here Lalor had the Stockade built, slabs and old broken carts and ropes and whatever they could find—I think they made it too big—there was a store here inside and a butcher's shop and diggers who went on working on their own claims all the time—perhaps they couldn't help but make the Stockade too big. I don't know. And then everybody started to drill, and a blacksmith set to work to make pikes—' . . .

'But the captain in charge of the military, Captain Thomas, he had trained troops and courage. He heard there were not many diggers in the Stockade on Saturday night—told so by a spy called Goodenough—so Thomas didn't wait, as Lalor expected him to wait, for the force from Melbourne. He attacked at dawn on Sunday.'

30

'And caught them unawares?'

'Yes. That's what really beat them. A sentry posted at the barricades saw a red dot in the shadowy bush. He fired his rifle to give the alarm, and he was right—the soldiers came out of their cover and began to advance. I forget, but I think all the Californians were down there in front of us, they had rifles and pits were dug for them. Captain Ross commanded one flank—but all the diggers inside the Stockade, there can't have been more than a hundred and fifty, leapt up to the defence. They fired a volley, and killed some of the soldiers. Some people say the soldiers hesitated, but Captain Wise—remember his name on the tablet?—called on them to advance, and a little bugler sounded the "Charge", and kept on sounding it again and again. Not a digger picked him off, either. They just went on firing at the oncoming soldiers so long as they had ammunition. Wise himself was shot down. But the soldiers surrounded the Stockade, and the cavalry came in, galloping in over the barricades, leaping the pike-men, cutting them down, and the soldiers charged with their bayonets. The diggers had no hope. Lalor was down, shot in the shoulder or arm. Vern cleared out. A ring of poor diggers, with only their pikes left, fell in round the flag. Captain Ross called on them to make a stand. They stood—faithful to their oath to the end. As the sun came up, the soldiers went off carting their own wounded, dragging the beautiful flag in the dirt, driving off more than a hundred prisoners, many wounded and bloody . . . There was nothing left here but the dead and dying, charred ruins of fired tents, women crying over their men, and one poor little dog who sat and howled by his dead master . . . Lalor was bleeding quietly to death, hidden underneath some slabs—until some mate found him, and bound him up and dragged him off to hide in a cottage nearby till a surgeon could be got to amputate his arm.'

HENRIETTA DRAKE-BROCKMAN (1901–1968)
The Fatal Days

COOBER PEDY

Night in a cave, deep down in a maze of grave-holes.

Walls of pink and white sandstone closed in on me, ghostly in the fire-light, gleaming with snake-trails of gypsum, and scraps of jewel that shone like cat's eyes in the glim. Now and again I could hear the muffled coughs and dragging footsteps of men that moved about me in the hill, unseen and unknown, and I was alone in the desert, 2000 miles from home . . . It was my first night at Coober Pedy.

Six hundred miles from the sea and eight feet below its level, in the Stuart Ranges, South Australia, lies Coober Pedy, where the opal gougers live in caverns of the hills, like the robbers in Gil Blas.

One of the most remarkable communities of white men in the world, you will find it only on the most comprehensive of maps, and you could pass right through it in a motor-car, daytime or night-time, and not know it existed. To believe it true, you must travel out across 200 miles of mostly saltbush, and sleep in a cave as I did.

Coober Pedy. Coober = man. Pedy = hole in the ground. Deep in the hills, away from the blinding glare and a torment of flies, I found a hundred men and eight women, Slaves of the Ring, condemned to eternal digging. Never a gleam of sunshine penetrated their dug-outs. Hardly a straggler was seen by day, threading the tracks of its thousand graves, graves of lost hope, or a fortune. There is no geological logic of opal, no reef to follow, as in gold. You dig and dig, and give up digging in despair, and the next man takes on the hole and digs two feet further and finds £1000 worth.

ERNESTINE HILL (1899–1972)
The Great Australian Loneliness

TANGMALANGALOO

The bishop sat in lordly state and purple cap sublime,
And galvanized the old bush church at Confirmation time;
And all the kids were mustered up from fifty miles around,
With Sunday clothes, and staring eyes, and ignorance profound.
Now was it fate, or was it grace, whereby they yarded too
An overgrown two-storey lad from Tangmalangaloo?

A hefty son of virgin soil, where nature has her fling,
And grows the trefoil three feet high and mats it in the spring;
Where mighty hills uplift their heads to pierce the welkin's rim,
And trees sprout up a hundred feet before they shoot a limb;
There everything is big and grand, and men are giants too—
But Christian Knowledge wilts, alas, at Tangmalangaloo.

The bishop summed the youngsters up, as bishops only can;
He cast a searching glance around, then fixed upon his man.
But glum and dumb and undismayed through every bout he sat;
He seemed to think that he was there, but wasn't sure of that.
The bishop gave a scornful look, as bishops sometimes do,
And glared right through the pagan in from Tangmalangaloo.

'Come, tell me, boy', his lordship said in crushing tones severe,
'Come, tell me why is Christmas Day the greatest of the year?
How is it that around the world we celebrate that day
And send a name upon a card to those who're far away?
Why is it wandering ones return with smiles and greetings, too?'
A squall of knowledge hit the lad from Tangmalangaloo.

He gave a lurch which set a-shake the vases on the shelf,
He knocked the benches all askew, up-ending of himself.
And oh, how pleased his lordship was, and how he smiled to say,
'That's good, my boy. Come, tell me now; and what is Christmas Day?'
The ready answer bared a fact no bishop ever knew—
'It's the day before the races out at Tangmalangaloo.'
                    JOHN O'BRIEN (REV. FATHER P. J. HARTIGAN) (1879–1952)
                                                    Around the Boree Log

BROKEN HILL—SCHOOL OF THE AIR

When we reached the square modern building at the north end of town, set in a corner of a public school playground, lessons had already started. Mrs Gibb was on the air, so we tiptoed past the control cabin and into the inviting modern classroom that gave us a cool and restful welcome. Bowls of fresh flowers stood about, the lime-green walls contrasted with the white, grey and yellow curtains. Much to my surprise I noticed polished oak desks which ran the length of the room; there was a soft grey carpet on the floor. Everything was immaculate—only one thing was missing. The children. They were all hundreds of miles away.

The teacher's desk was dominated by an imposing microphone. Behind this sat the woman who controls the largest schoolroom in the world, with her ninety-three unseen pupils scattered over 200 000 square miles. Mrs Gibb was speaking over the microphone when we came in, and we sat down quietly to listen and watch. She is a tall, middle-aged woman, this unusual school-mistress, with attractively greying hair bound in braids round her head, smiling grey-blue eyes and a wide, expressive mouth. We realised as we watched that she possessed three essential characteristics: humour, kindliness and strength.

The radio control-room was at the far end, and the general activity of this nerve centre of the school could be seen through a large plate-glass window.

'Calling 8RH, calling 8RH. Tell me something about the weather in your part of the country, Johnnie', said Mrs Gibb. 'Over to you.' Some static followed, then a small voice from more than two hundred miles away began to describe the weather conditions at his own homestead. . . .

We were very fortunate, while at Broken Hill, to witness the most unusual activity of the School of the Air—a play-reading; simple, perhaps under ordinary circumstances, but imagine a play being performed while the characters are separated from each other by hundreds of miles.

Each child took his or her correct cue over the radio, and dressed for the part, although unseen by anyone other than their own family. Before the play took place each child gave a description of his or her costume—while the rest of the cast listened at their radio receivers.

CHARLES CHAUVEL (1897–1959) *and* ELSA CHAUVEL (1898–   )
Walkabout

THE MUSGRAVE RANGE,
CENTRAL AUSTRALIA

The peculiar feature of the Musgrave landscapes is the great development of grasslands. In amongst the hills, and frequently enclosed on all sides, and accessible only through rocky passes, are little plains of varying extent, and broad valleys, entirely free from bush growth, but with an even carpet of grasses and herbs.

The large open space of true 'waving in the wind' sort of grass is a rare feature in this country of scrubs and thickets; and when they are backed by long vistas of blue hills falling away with a gently graded softening of

34

outline into the distance, a combination is presented which stirs memories of a softer clime.

To Giles the Englishman—after weeks of bush-whacking in the mulga farther north—these views appealed with special force, and his descriptions of them are pathetically filled with a homesick longing which found expression in the nomenclature of the place. His maps are studded with glens and passes, tarns and vales.

. . . Basedown, in the winter of 1903, was similarly impressed by the 'unaustralian' character of many of its views—if one may put it so un-patriotically. Writing of Glen Ferdinand he states:

> When the mists of evening rose and the light in the Glen grew dim, the blue-black thickets of mulga on the plain could no longer be distinguished from the pines on the hills, and I could scarce persuade myself to believe that the landscape before me was part of arid Central Australia, and not Thuringia or Tyrol.

I saw it all in the height of midsummer, when the green swards and wild flowers were no longer there to help the illusion, but even so the old-worldliness of the place was very evident.

H. H. FINLAYSON (1895–   )
The Red Centre

STEEL MILLS

The slag was satisfactory, the temperature right. Was the heat ready to tap?

No matter how often he watched a tapping, it never ceased to move him. You sensed that the open-hearth crew felt the same. There was a mounting excitement towards the end of a heat. You had made your decision. Had you succeeded or failed? Once the furnace was tapped, it was too late. Your chance to avert failure was over.

Bar often wondered at the apparent calmness with which the shop manager decided on just the moment for tapping. He himself always felt tense. Once you tapped there was no possibility of remedying any of your mistakes. Up to then there had still been a chance of correcting the ratio of the new mixture, but no more. You had made your decision, and you had to abide by it whether the steel was good or bad. The crew were apparently

35

self-assured as they went about their job, but he knew that this coolness was assumed: no one could tap a furnace with calmness and indifference!

Rowley gave a signal. Bar moved round to the casting pit behind the furnaces where the heats were teemed into ingots. The furnace helpers were waiting at the teeming bay for the shop manager's order to tap. Bar couldn't have told how often he'd watched this, yet it never failed to thrill him. It all looked so easy on the surface, the furnace helpers waiting to prick out the fireclay plug with a long iron rod, to plunge it into the tap-hole and release the molten metal, the others in readiness along the box, where everything was waiting to receive the steel. He watched a furnace helper drive the rod against the plug, seeing the muscles ripple in his hairy forearms. They were men all right! Standing opposed to the full fury of the released steel, they didn't even bother to put on their protective garments, but worked in their ordinary flannels.

The rod pierced the tap-hole. Flame burst out with a dull roar. Sparks filled the teeming bay. The cascade of white-hot steel gushed forth.

This was the moment for which the whole vast complex of works existed. This was the thing for which you studied, planned and worked. Here, Bar exulted, here in the dazzling flood that lit the whole building, showing up the girders of the crane tracks, filling the high roof with leaping light and shadow, silhouetting the dark figure of the helper in an aura like the sun—here was the source of world-power to-day. Steel, his steel.

The gush of molten metal ceased. The shop manager gave a signal to the crane driver. Enormous hooks clinked into place and the ladle moved slowly towards the teeming bay.

DYMPHNA CUSACK (1904–1981)
Southern Steel

POEMS FROM THE COALFIELDS

Air Shaft

The hearts are pumping—feel!—the air
Flows down from such an open place,
Flows down the bratticed windpipes
To the face.

36

The air is flowing—sweet, its breath;
But flows grimly, for the lungs
Are dusted with the particles of death.

Advice from a Nightwatchman

This is no place for lovers;
Find a park.
All I'm afraid this offers
Is the dark—
The dark reminder of a hooter's blow,
The dark adventure of a day below,
The dark and silent outline of a wheel
Against the sky, the dark and clammy feel
Of what can happen down there
In the dark
To him who holds your hand; go
Find a park.

IAN HEALY (1919–   )

WITTENOOM—MIGRANT TOWN

It is the blue asbestos town, a mining community fostered by the Colonial Sugar Refinery in the heart of the great scenic gorges of central Western Australia. Here, a couple of hundred miles inland from Roebourne, hundreds of New Australians from Hungary, Poland, Germany, the Baltic States and other countries are doing a major pioneering job for this country.

In fact, migrants now form a majority of the whole community at Wittenoom. Engineers, surveyors, metallurgists, miners and others from the mines of central and eastern Europe are applying the skills and knowledge acquired in their apprenticeship days and early manhood in the Old World to digging out this precious blue commodity worth £100 a bag f.o.b. Fremantle . . .

To these people from the great cities and highly-developed communities of Europe, the prospect of life in the huts and tents of Wittenoom with live theatre and major concerts 1000 miles away in Perth must often have seemed something like a sentence to a desert island. But they did not allow themselves to be deterred. Thanks to their own efforts and those of the company responsible they are fast making Wittenoom a little oasis in the desert. . . .

They are making their own flower and vegetable gardens in the desert, organising their own clubs, dances, picture nights, barbecues, concert parties and picnics, developing centres for sport and recreation. They are making an up-to-date community in an out-of-the-way corner of Australia which we have long neglected. No railway runs to Wittenoom. The sea is 200 miles away. . . . But if you can find a livelier, healthier more zestful community in Australia to-day you are indeed fortunate. Here are our new pioneers in a mining and mechanical adventure of the mid-twentieth century.

ROHAN RIVETT (1917–1977)
The Migrant and the Community

NEW GUINEA

In Memory of Archbishop Alain de Boismenu, M.S.C.

Bird-shaped island, with secretive bird-voices,
Land of apocalypse, where the earth dances,
The mountains speak, the doors of the spirit open,
And men are shaken by obscure trances.

The forest-odours, insects, clouds and fountains
Are like the figures of my inmost dream,
Vibrant with untellable recognition;
A wordless revelation is their theme.

The stranger is engulfed in those high valleys
Where mists of morning linger like the breath
Of Wisdom moving on our specular darkness.
O regions of prayer, of solitude, and of death!

Life holds its shape in the modes of dance and music,
The hands of craftsmen trace its patternings;
But stains of blood, and evil spirits, lurk
Like cockroaches in the interstices of things.

We in that land begin our rule in courage,
The seal of peace gives warrant to intrusion;
But then our grin of emptiness breaks the skin,
Formless dishonour spreads its proud confusion.

Whence that deep longing for an exorciser,
For Christ descending as a thaumaturge
Into his saints, as formerly in the desert,
Warring with demons on the outer verge.

Only by this can life become authentic,
Configured henceforth in eternal mode:
Splendour, simplicity, joy—such as were seen
In one who now rests by his mountain road.

JAMES McAULEY (1917–1976)

40

HISTORY

THE CHIEFEST NOVELTY

Australian history is almost always picturesque and indeed, it is so curious and strange, that it is itself the chiefest novelty the country has to offer, and so it pushes other novelties into second and third places. It does not read like history, but like the most beautiful lies. And all of a fresh, new sort, no moldy old stale ones. It is full of surprises, and adventures, and incongruities, and contradictions, and incredibilities; but they are all true; they all happened.

MARK TWAIN (S. L. CLEMENS) (1835–1910)
Following the Equator

CAPTAIN COOK

Cook was a captain of the Admiralty
When sea-captains had the evil eye,
Or should have, what with beating krakens off
And casting nativities of ships;
Cook was a captain of the powder-days
When captains, you might have said, if you had been
Fixed by their glittering stare, half-down the side,
Or gaping at them up companionways,
Were more like warlocks than a humble man—
And men were humble then who gazed at them,
Poor horn-eyed sailors, bullied by devils' fists
Of wind or water, or the want of both,
Childlike and trusting, filled with eager trust—
Cook was a captain of the sailing-days
When sea-captains were kings like this,
Not cold executives of company-rules
Cracking their boilers for a dividend
Or bidding their engineers go wink
At bells and telegraphs, so plates would hold

41

Another pound. Those captains drove their ships
By their own blood, no laws of schoolbook steam,
Till yards were sprung, and masts went overboard—
Daemons in periwigs, doling magic out,
Who read fair alphabets in stars
Where humbler men found but a mess of sparks,
Who steered their crews by mysteries
And strange, half-dreadful sortilege with books,
Used medicines that only gods could know
The sense of, but sailors drank
In simple faith. That was the captain
Cook was when he came to the Coral Sea
And chose a passage into the dark.

How many mariners had made that choice
Paused on the brink of mystery. 'Choose now!'
The winds roared, blowing home, blowing home,
Over the Coral Sea. 'Choose now!' the trades
Cried once to Tasman, throwing him for choice
Their teeth or shoulders, and the Dutchman chose
The wind's way, turning north. 'Choose, Bougainville!'
The wind cried once, and Bougainville had heard
The voice of God, calling him prudently
Out of a dead lee shore, and chose the north,
The wind's way. So, too, Cook made choice,
Over the brink, into the devil's mouth,
With four months' food, and sailors wild with dreams
Of English beer, the smoking barns of home.
So Cook made choice, so Cook sailed westabout,
So men write poems in Australia.

KENNETH SLESSOR (1901–1971)
Five Visions of Captain Cook

CAPTAIN COOK DESCRIBES THE
EAST COAST OF AUSTRALIA

The Coast of this Country, at least so much of it as lays to the Northward of 26° of Latitude abounds with a great Number of fine Bays and Harbours, which are shelter'd from all Winds. But the Country itself so far as we know doth not produce any one thing that can become an article in trade to invite Europeans to fix a settlement upon it. However, this Eastern side is not that barren and Miserable Country that Dampier and others have described the Western Side to be. We are to Consider that we see this Country in the pure state of Nature the Industry of man has had nothing to do with any part of it and yet we find all such things as nature hath bestowed upon it in a flourishing state. In this Extensive Country it can never be doubted but what most sorts of Grain, Fruits, Roots, etc. of every kind would flourish here were they once brought hither, planted and cultivated by the hand of Industry and here are Provender for more Cattle at all seasons of the year than can be brought into this Country— When one considers the Proximity of this Country with New Guineay, New-Britain and several other Islands which produce Cocoa-nutts and many other fruits proper for the Support of Man, it seems strange that they should not long ago have been transplanted here . . .

From what I have said of the Natives of New-Holland they may appear to some to be the most wretched people upon the earth: but in reality they are far more happier than we Europeans; being wholly unacquainted not only with the superfluous but the necessary Conveniences so much sought after in Europe, they are happy in not knowing the use of them. They live in a Tranquillity which is not disturbed by the Inequality of Condition: The Earth and sea of their own accord furnishes them with all things necessary for life; they covet not Magnificent Houses, Household-stuff etc. they live in a warm and fine Climate and enjoy a very wholsome Air: so that they have very little need of Clothing and this they seem to be fully sensible of for many to whome we gave Cloth etc. to, left it carelessly upon the Sea beach and in the woods as a thing they had no manner of use for. In short they seem'd to set no value upon anything we gave them nor would they ever part with any thing of their own for any one article we could offer them this in my opinion argues that they think themselves provided with all the necessarys of Life and that they have no superfluities. . . .

JAMES COOK (1728–1779)
Journal of the First Voyage of Captain James Cook

44

TAKING POSSESSION OF THE NEW COLONY

Owing to the multiplicity of pressing business necessary to be performed immediately after landing, it was found impossible to read the public commissions and take possession of the colony, in form, until the 7 February. On that day all the officers of guard took post in the marine battalion, which was drawn up, and marched off the parade with music playing, and colours flying, to an adjoining ground, which had been cleared for the occasion, whereon the convicts were assembled to hear His Majesty's commission read, appointing his Excellency Arthur Phillip, Esq., Governor and Captain General in and over the territory of New South Wales, and its dependencies; together with the act of parliament for establishing trials by law within the same; and the patents under the Great Seal of Great Britain, for holding the civil and criminal courts of judicature, by which all cases of life and death, as well as matters of property, were to be decided. When the Judge Advocate had finished reading, his Excellency addressed himself to the convicts in a pointed and judicious speech, informing them of his future intentions, which were, invariably, to cherish and render happy those who shewed a disposition to amendment; and to let the rigour of the law take its course against such as might dare to transgress the bounds prescribed. At the close three vollies were fired in honour of the occasion, and the battalion marched back to their parade, where they were reviewed by the Governor, who was received with all the honours due to his rank. His Excellency was afterwards pleased to thank them, in public orders, for their behaviour from time of their embarkation; and to ask the officers to partake of a cold collation, at which it is scarce necessary to observe, that many loyal and public toasts were drank in commemoration of the day.

WATKIN TENCH (*c*.1759–1833)
A Narrative of the Expedition to Botany Bay . . .

GOVERNOR PHILLIP FORESEES THE FUTURE

What was it which kept burning in him this flame of faith in a land of which, after all, he knew next to nothing? More than once he had found himself writing words in his dispatches which had surprised himself. He remembered a letter to Lord Sydney: '*. . . nor do I doubt that this country* *will prove the most valuable acquisition Great Britain ever made'*. Even at the time he had felt a faint astonishment at his own conviction, and he felt it again now, and threw the bedclothes back restlessly and got out of bed. '... *nor do I doubt* ...' Why such certainty? On what was it based? He went across to the doorway and outside into the clear night and looked up at the sky. He felt again the sense which had so often troubled him before, of the utter strangeness of this land in which he found himself, and he remembered the name given to it by earlier explorers, and said under his breath, looking at the gaunt, still branches of a gum-tree outlined against the sky: '*Terra Australis Incognita*'. *Incognita*, indeed! What did he know of it? A little of a seemingly endless coastline, a fringe of an apparently endless interior, a glimpse of those blue mountains which he had called the Carmarthen Hills. Beyond them? Beyond them the *terra Australis incognita*! And he had written: '... *nor do I doubt* ...'

There came over him as he stood there, with an influence sobering and steadying rather than alarming, a sense of deep responsibility. To whom, to what? But of course to his country, his homeland, that far, green island on the other side of the world. Those words of his— had they been, perhaps, misleading? He had no grounds for so high, so extravagant a claim. Had he not— he to whom they looked for faithful intelligence of this new venture— painted a picture more cheerfully coloured than the facts of their present existence warranted?

He breathed deeply. There was something rather refreshing, he thought, in the smell of these queer forests. Looking over the settlement with eyes now growing accustomed to the darkness, he could see the lines of the convicts' huts, and his mind, the mind of the administrator, began to consider their occupants with intentness and detachment. It had been his habit, all his life, to perform such tasks as lay to his hand, thinking not overmuch of them and saying less; but he had not been able to subdue the gnawing sense of dissatisfaction which, from the beginning of their sojourn in this place, had gone hand in hand with his rigid performance of duty. The seed of it lay there, in those convict huts. This was no place for them; they were the product of a different world from this ...

Suddenly illumination came to him, and a deep relief. Here, buried in him and unsuspected till now, was the knowledge which had lent him that seemingly irrational confidence. He was a practical man, a stranger to all mysticism and introspection. He believed, as all good Englishmen did, that his race was Heaven-favoured, Heaven-guided, sent to be a builder in strange lands and a teacher of strange peoples. But now he felt a power which was even stronger than the power of his race, an influence from the land itself—the strange land, the *terra incognita*—which human folly and human brutality could not harm, could not even touch. He saw now that they had delivered themselves up to it, that no word or deed or authority of his could stay its quiet, unhurried processes of envelopment and absorption. '*Acquisition!*' The ageless silence swallowed the presumptuous word. What had been thrust upon it as shame and degradation and hypocrisy became merely human life; the overlying, man-made creeds and customs and conceptions fell from it, leaving it nakedly re-born.

Here, indeed, was value, here indeed was wealth, and hope and rich justification for confidence! Phillip's sigh was half weariness and half relief for an uneasiness allayed. '. . . *nor do I doubt* . . .' They had been the right words after all. He went slowly back to bed, walking with less than his usual alertness, for he was very tired.

ELEANOR DARK (1901–   )
The Timeless Land

OLD BOTANY BAY

'I'm old
Botany Bay;
Stiff in the joints,
Little to say.

I am he
Who paved the way,
That you might walk
At your ease to-day;

I was the conscript
Sent to hell
To make in the desert
The living well;

47

I bore the heat,
I blazed the track—
Furrowed and bloody
Upon my back.

I split the rock;
I felled the tree:
The nation was—
Because of me!'

Old Botany Bay
Taking the sun
From day to day . . .
Shame on the mouth
That would deny
The knotted hands
That set us high!

MARY GILMORE (1865–1962)

CONDITIONS ON CONVICT TRANSPORT SHIPS

The writer of this letter was the first Anglican Chaplain in New South Wales. The ships arrived in Port Jackson in June 1790.

There were on,

The *Neptune*	520 convicts, but 163 died on board, and 269 landed sick
The *Scarborough*	252 convicts, but 68 died on board, and 96 landed sick
The *Surprise*	211 convicts, but 42 died on board, and 121 landed sick

This short calculation given me will support what I am going to relate.

'I have been on board these different ships—was first on board the *Surprise*—went down amongst the convicts, where I beheld a sight truly shocking to the feelings of humanity, a great number of them lying, some

48

half and others nearly quite naked, without either bed or bedding, unable to turn or help themselves. Spoke to them as I passed along; but the smell was so offensive, I could scarcely bear it.'

'I then went on board the *Scarborough*, proposed to go down among them but was dissuaded from it by the Captain. The *Neptune* was still more wretched and intolerable, therefore never attempted it.'

'Some of these unhappy people died after the ships came into the harbour, before they could be taken on shore; part of these had been thrown into the harbour, and their dead bodies cast upon the shore, and were seen lying naked upon the rocks; took an occasion to represent this to his Excellency, in consequence of which immediate orders were sent on board, that those who died on board should be carried to the opposite North Shore to be buried.'

'The landing of these people was truly affecting and shocking, great numbers were not able to walk, nor to move hand or foot. Such were slung over the ship's side in the same manner as they would sling a cask or box, or anything of that nature. Upon their being brought up to the open air, some fainted, some died upon deck, and others in the boat before they reached the shore.'

'When come on shore, many were not able to walk, to stand, or to stir themselves in the least. Hence some were led by others while some crept upon their hands and knees, and some were carried on the back of others.'...

'The complaints they had to make were not less affecting to the ear than their outward condition was to the eye. The usage they met with on board, according to their own story, was truly shocking. Sometimes for days, nay, for a considerable time together, they had been to the middle in water, chained together, hand and leg—even the sick not exempted—nay, many died with the chains upon them. Promises, entreaties, were all in vain, and it was not till a very few days before they made the harbour, that they were released out of irons.'

'The greatest complaints by far, were from those persons who had come in the *Neptune*. No wonder that they should be so afflicted—no wonder to hear them groaning, and crying, and making the most bitter lamentations.'

REV. RICHARD JOHNSON (1753–1827)

49

THE PUNISHMENT OF CONVICTS

These convicts were Irish rebels transported after the 1798 rising in Ireland whose further unrest in the colony was regarded by the authorities as a public danger. The gentlemanly Joseph Holt, known as the former General of the rebels, was not implicated.

I did attend to the minute and we march'd up to Towngabby where all the Government men was, and this was the plan to give them the opportunity of seeing the punishment inflicted on several. There was one man of the Name of Morris Fitzegarrel and he was ordered to Receive three Hundred lashes.

The way they floged them was theire armes pulled Round a large tree and their breasts squezed against the tree so the men had no power to cringe or stir. Father Harrel was ordered to lay his hand against the tree by the hand of the man that was floging. There was two flogers, Richard Rice and John Jonson, the Hangman from Sidney. Rice was a left handed man and Jonson was Right handed so they stood at each side and I never saw two trashers in a barn moove there stroakes more handeyer then those two man killers did.

The moment they begun I turn my face Round towards the other side and one of the Constibles came and Desired me to turn and look on. I put my hand in my pocket and pulled out my pen knife and swore I Rip him from the navil to the Chin. They all gather Round me and would have ill used me but Mr Smith came over and ask'd them who gave them any orders about me so they wore oblige to walk off. I cud compare them to a pack of hands at the death of hair, all yelping. I turned once about and as it happened I was to leew'rd of the flogers and I protest, tho' I was two perches from them, the flesh and skin blew in my face as they shooke off the cats.

Fitzegarrel Recaiv'd his 300 lashes. Doctor Mason (I never will forget him) use to go to feel his pulls and he smiled and sayd 'this man will tire you before he will fail, — go on'. It is against the law to flog a man past 50 lashes without a Doctor, and during the time he was geting his punishment he never gave as much as a word: only one and that was saying, 'Don't strike me on the Nick, flog me fair'. When he was let loose two of the Constibles went and tuck hould of him by the arms to help him in the Cart. I was standing by he said to them, 'let my arms go', struck both of them with his elbows in the pit of the somack and nock them boath down and

50

then step in the Cart. I herd Doctor Mason say 'that man had strength in nuff to bear two hundredd more'.

JOSEPH HOLT (1756–1826)

JIM JONES

Oh, listen for a moment, lads,
And hear me tell my tale;
How, o'er the sea from England's shore,
I was compelled to sail.
The jury says, 'He's guilty, sir!'
And says the judge, says he—
'For life, Jim Jones, I'm sending you
Across the stormy sea.

'And take my tip, before you ship
To join the iron gang,
Don't be too gay at Botany Bay,
Or else you'll surely hang.
Or else you'll hang', he says, says he,
'And after that, Jim Jones,
High up upon the gallows tree
The crows will pick your bones.

'You'll have no chance for mischief then—
Remember what I say:
They'll flog the mischief out of you
When you get to Botany Bay!'
The waves were high upon the sea,
The winds blew up in gales;
I'd rather be drowned in misery
Than go to New South Wales.

For night and day the irons clang,
And, like poor galley slaves,
We toil and moil and when we die

Must fill dishonoured graves.
But by and by I'll break my chains;
Into the bush I'll go;
And join the brave bushrangers there—
Jack Donahoe and Co.

And some dark night when everything
Is silent in the town
I'll shoot the tyrants one and all
And shoot the floggers down.
I'll give the law a little shock—
Remember what I say,
They'll yet regret they sent Jim Jones
In chains to Botany Bay.

Folk Song

JOHN MACARTHUR INTRODUCES
MERINO SHEEP

In the year 1792 or 1793, a few English sheep, which had been accidentally carried out from Ireland, were landed in New South Wales; and the late John Macarthur, Esq., who was then resident in the colony as captain and paymaster of the New South Wales Corps, observing the effect produced by their accidental crossing with the sheep of the hair-bearing breeds from the Cape of Good Hope and Bengal, of which there was then a considerable number in the colony, his attention was strongly directed to the subject of the improvement of coarse-woolled sheep, and the growth of wool in New South Wales. The effect of the crossing was a decided improvement of the animals—the hairy coat of the progeny of the Cape and Bengal breeds being gradually converted into wool—while the influence of the climate on the fleece of sheep generally was decidedly favourable. Shortly after this interesting fact had been ascertained, Captain Waterhouse, a naval officer who was then in the colony, having been ordered to proceed to the Cape in command of a vessel in His Majesty's service, Captain Macarthur requested him particularly to endeavour to procure a few sheep of improved breed in that colony, and to bring them to New South Wales; offering to share with him in the cost and in the general result of the speculation. Captain Waterhouse never returned to the colony; but the commission with which he had been charged by Captain Macarthur was duly executed by Captain Kent, who, on his return to the colony in charge of the vessel previously under the command of Captain Waterhouse, in the year 1796, brought along with him a few sheep of the pure Merino breed, which he had purchased at the Cape, at the sale of the property and effects of Colonel Gordon, an officer of Scotch extraction in the Dutch service, then recently deceased. On their arrival in the colony, these sheep were equally divided between Captain Macarthur, Captain Kent, Captain Cox (afterwards paymaster of the New South Wales Corps), and the Rev. Mr Marsden; Captain Macarthur obtaining five ewes and one ram. It appears, however, that Captain Macarthur alone paid the requisite attention to these valuable animals, which it seems were made little account of and neglected by the other gentlemen; and his perseverance in the matter not infrequently exposed him to no small degree of ridicule on the part of his contemporaries. By his persevering attention Captain Macarthur at length formed a considerable flock, which was afterwards greatly increased about the year 1803, by his purchase of the whole of the sheep and other stock of Colonel (afterwards General) Foveaux. . . .

The discouragements, however, with which Mr Macarthur—who now retired from the army, and settled in the colony, as a merchant and stockholder—had to struggle through a long series of years, in demonstrating the practicability of producing fine wool in New South Wales to an unlimited extent, were sufficient to have paralyzed the energies of a less energetic mind; and the obligations under which he has consequently laid the colony in all time coming, through his unremitted perseverance and unexampled success, are great beyond calculation. The peculiar adaptation of the climate of New South Wales to the constitution and habits of fine woolled sheep, and the capabilities of the colony for the production of that valuable article of export to any conceivable extent, would doubtless have been discovered sooner or later by some other inhabitant of the colony, even if they had not been ascertained and demonstrated by Mr Macarthur: but this possibility does not in the least detract from the merit of that gentleman as a real benefactor of his adopted country; for the very same remark is applicable in the very same manner to the noble invention of Guttenberg, and the splendid discoveries of Columbus.

JOHN DUNMORE LANG (1799–1878)
An Historical and Statistical Account of New South Wales

THREE CULTURAL FORCES

By 1817, too, the main ideas which were to mould the minds of Australians in the nineteenth and twentieth centuries had been transplanted from Europe. The early Church of England chaplains, Johnson and Marsden, had sowed the seeds of the Protestant view of the world—the connexion in their minds between liberty, material well-being, and the Protestant religion, the Bible and sabbatarian values. With the Irish convicts in 1791 came the Catholic view of the world, as moulded to meet conditions in Ireland. Thus even before 1800, the contenders in the great conflicts in the nineteenth century on religion, education, and politics had arrived on the shores of Australia. So, indeed, had the third force—the ideas of the Enlightenment on liberty, equality, happiness, and progress. And though the men on the front of the stage in our documents speak of food, of shelter, of loneliness and isolation, and squabble over trifles, this is the period in which the shape of things to come is first formed.

MANNING CLARK (1915–   )
Sources of Australian History

THE ARREST OF GOVERNOR BLIGH
IN THE RUM REBELLION

The following is from the evidence given by Bligh himself at the Court Martial of Major Johnston.

The regiment marched down from the barracks, led on by Major Johnston and the other officers, with colours flying and music playing as they advanced to the house. Within a few minutes after, the house was surrounded; the soldiers quickly broke into all parts of it, and arrested all the magistrates, Mr Gore, the provost-marshal, Mr Griffin, my secretary, and Mr Fulton, the chaplain. I had just time to call to my orderly sergeant to have my horses ready, while I went up stairs to put on my uniform, the family being then in deep mourning; when, on my return, as I was standing on the staircase waiting for my servant with my sword, I saw a number of soldiers rushing up stairs with their muskets and fixed bayonets, as I conceived to seize my person. I retired instantly into a back room, to defeat their object, and to deliberate on the means to be adopted for the restoration of my authority, which in such a critical situation could only be accomplished by my getting into the interior of the country adjacent to the Hawkesbury, where I knew the whole body of the people would flock to my standard. To this situation I was pursued by the soldiers, and after experiencing much insult was conducted below by Lieutenant Minchin, who told me that Major Johnston was waiting for me. We passed together into the drawing-room, every part being crowded with soldiers under arms, many of whom appeared to be intoxicated.

I then received a letter, brought by Lieutenant Moore, and signed by Major Johnston (calling himself Lieutenant-Governor), requiring me to resign my authority, and to submit to the arrest under which he placed me; which I had scarcely perused, when a message was delivered to me, that Major Johnston wished to speak to me in the adjoining room, at the door of which he soon after appeared, surrounded by his officers and soldiers; and in terms much to the same effect as his letter, he there verbally confirmed my arrest. Martial law was proclaimed, my secretary and my friends were prevented from seeing me, and I was left only with my daughter and another lady.

By Major Johnston's orders several persons seized my cabinet and papers, with my commission, instructions, and the great seal of the colony. These were locked up in a room, guarded by two sentinels, and several others were placed round the house to prevent my escape.

On the following day Lieutenant Moore came with Major Johnston's orders, and carried away my swords and what fire-arms he found in the house.

WILLIAM BLIGH (1754–1817)

GOVERNOR MACQUARIE DEFENDS HIMSELF

From 1810 to 1821 the infant colony of New South Wales prospered under the conscientious and benevolent autocracy of Governor Lachlan Macquarie, but his enlightened policy of treating the emancipists (ex-convicts) on social equality with the free immigrants aroused bitter criticism from army officers and landowners. Macquarie here defends his policy in a report to Earl Bathurst on his return to London in 1822.

I found the colony barely emerging from infantile imbecility, and suffering from various privations and disabilities; the country impenetrable beyond forty miles from Sydney; agriculture in a yet languishing state; commerce

55

in its early dawn; revenue unknown; threatened with famine; distracted by faction; the public buildings in a state of dilapidation and mouldering to decay; the few roads and bridges formerly constructed rendered almost impassable; the population in general depressed by poverty; no public credit nor private confidence; the morals of the great mass of the population in the lowest state of debasement, and religious worship almost totally neglected. . . .

Such was the state of New South Wales when I took charge of its administration on the 1 January 1810. I left it in February last, reaping incalculable advantages from my extensive and important discoveries in all directions, including the supposed insurmountable barrier called the Blue Mountains, to the westward of which are situated the fertile plains of Bathurst; and, in all respects, enjoying a state of private comfort and public prosperity which I trust will at least equal the expectation of His Majesty's Government. . . .

Finding on my arrival many persons free, who had come out originally as convicts, and sustaining unblemished characters since their emancipation, but treated with rudeness, contumely, and even oppression, as far as circumstances permitted, by those who had come out free, and viewed with illiberal jealousy the honest endeavours of the others to attain and support a respectable station in society, I determined to counteract this envious disposition in one class, by admitting, in my demeanour and occasional marks of favour to both, no distinction where their merits, pretensions and capacities were equal. I considered this as the first step towards a general reformation of the manners and habits of the motley part of the population of New South Wales as it then existed, and I am happy to add that twelve years experience of its effects has fully justified my most sanguine anticipations. . . .

That the colony has, under my orders and regulations, greatly improved in agriculture, trade, increase of flocks and herds, and wealth of every kind; that the people build better dwelling-houses, and live more comfortably; that they are in a very considerable degree reformed in their moral and religious habits; that they are now less prone to drunkenness, and more industrious; and that crimes have decreased, making due allowance for the late great increase of convict population; every *candid, liberal minded* man, at all acquainted with the history of the colony for the last twelve years, will readily attest.

LACHLAN MACQUARIE (1761–1824)

SOCIAL DIFFICULTIES IN A
CONVICT COLONY

An agreeable society had been then (1829) formed in Sydney . . .

Yet with much that was then pleasant in colonial society, it had its severe aspect. It must not be forgotten that my remarks apply to a convict settlement, in which the possession of wealth afforded but dubious evidence of a previous career of respectability. Many persons, originally transported for crime, had displayed the recuperative energy that is in man, by which though he sinks he but sinks to rise again, and resume the position that in early life he had forfeited. No doubt, the easy acquisition of property by convicts on their becoming free, and the circumstance of becoming heads of families, largely contributed to this happy consummation. It is obvious we cannot judge of motives; and whether principle or self-interest be the cause of reformation, society is the gainer when a bad man is transformed into a well-conducted one.

When, therefore, amendment in the mode of life was accomplished, charity and policy united in recommending the formation of the whole free community into an equal and united people. So thought not 'society' in those days: not only were persons who had been transported excluded from the upper circle of the place, be their wealth or worth what it might, but the exclusion extended, at least partially, to their connexions. In the few instances with regard to them in which this too rigid rule of exclusion was relaxed, it was painful to witness the averted eye and the unwelcome shrug of the shoulders that the young and blameless relations of the strictly-excluded class had to encounter on appearing, as if they were intruders, at places of evening entertainment. The term *pure merino*, a designation given to sheep where there is no cross-blood in the flocks, was applied to mark a class who were not only free and unconvicted, but who could boast of having no collateral relationship or distant affinity with those in whose escutcheon there was a blot. These *pure merinos* formed the topmost round in the social ladder. The inequitableness of this rule of judgment may be seen by a simple illustration. Tried by such a test, a most estimable man, a late cabinet minister of England, and through a long and useful public life the representative of one of the finest counties in England, would have been deemed unfit for admission to a Sydney ball; and a late very learned and eminent bishop would have been a *tabooed* member of the 'upper circle' in Sydney at this period, because they both happened to have near relations who by their misconduct brought disgrace, not on these excellent and eminent persons, but *on themselves.* The rule of disfavour did not end even here; for some against whom no social objection could be raised were designated a 'convict-ridden set', because they did not adopt this doctrine of exclusion to an extent that appeared to them impolitic and indefensible.

R. THERRY (1800–1874)
Reminiscences of Thirty Years' Residence in New South Wales and Victoria

THE OPERATION OF THE LAND LAWS
IN THE 1830s

. . . the Land Regulations . . . That these are the most excellent things in theory that statesmanship ever imagined, I am not prepared to dispute. That they suit pretty well the highest class, those who legislate in the colony, those from whom the legislators of the colony are drawn, those from whom emanate the representations which by one means and another are rendered so influential in the Imperial legislature, may also be true. But they suit nobody else. Their effect is principally two-fold. They entirely prevent persons of small property from becoming landholders and agriculturists; by which again they coercively construct an immensely larger labouring class than otherwise would exist in the colony. Consequently the rich landholder both keeps the produce markets to himself; and again procures labourers at a vastly lower rate of wages. He diminishes the competition with himself in the produce market, and just so much increases the competition among the labourers in the labour market.

ALEXANDER HARRIS (1805–1874)
Settlers and Convicts

A CAROL ON CAROLINE CHISHOLM

Beyond the roaring ocean, beneath the soil we tread,
You've English men and women well housed and clothed and fed
Who but for health and guidance to leave our crowded shores
Would now be stealing, begging, or be starving at our doors.

58

Who taught them self-reliance and stirred them to combine
And club their means together to get across the brine?
Who led their expeditions and under whose command
Through dangers and through hardships sought they the promised land?
A second Moses, surely, it was who did it all
It was a second Moses in bonnet and in shawl.
By means of one good lady were all these wonders wrought,
By Caroline Chisholm's energy, benevolence and thought.

Punch (1853)

THE WARADGERY TRIBE

Harried we were, and spent,
  Broken and falling,
Ere as the cranes we went,
  Crying and calling.

Summer shall see the bird
  Backward returning;
Never shall there be heard
  Those, who went yearning.

Emptied of us the land,
  Ghostly our going,
Fallen, like spears the hand
  Dropped in the throwing.

We are the lost who went
  Like the cranes, crying;
Hunted, lonely, and spent,
  Broken and dying.

MARY GILMORE (1865–1962)

A GOVERNOR'S DESPATCH ON THE
GOLD RUSHES

It is quite impossible for me to describe to your Lordship the effect which these discoveries have had upon the whole community, and the influence which their consequences exercise at this time upon the position and prospects of every one, high and low. The discoveries early in the year in the Bathurst district of New South Wales unsettled the public mind of the labouring classes of all the Australian colonies to a certain extent, and had a marked and immediate influence upon the labour market, and the price of provisions in this colony; still both the distance from the scene of the discovery and the approach of winter were in our favour, a journey to the Bathurst district requiring a degree of decision and preparation which few comparatively of the labouring classes were in a position to meet. The discoveries within our bounds, coming as they do at the close of the wet season, in localities in comparative proximity to our towns, exercise a far wider influence upon our excitable population than did the discoveries in New South Wales upon that colony, under the advantages of a larger population and the greater remoteness of the gold field. Within the last three weeks the towns of Melbourne and Geelong and their large suburbs have been in appearance almost emptied of many classes of their male inhabitants; the streets which for a week or ten days were crowded by drays loading with the outfit for the workings are now seemingly deserted. Not only have the idlers to be found in every community, and day labourers in town and the adjacent country, shopmen, artisans, and mechanics of every description thrown up their employments, and in most cases, leaving their employers and their wives and families to take care of themselves, run off to the workings, but responsible tradesmen, farmers, clerks of every grade, and not a few of the superior classes have followed; some, unable to withstand the mania and force of the stream, or because they were really disposed to venture time and money on the chance, but others, because they were, as employers of labour, left in the lurch and had no other alternative. Cottages are deserted, houses to let, business is at a stand-still, and even schools are closed. In some of the suburbs not a man is left, and the women are known for self-protection to forget neighbours jars, and to group together to keep house. The ships in the harbour are, in a great measure, deserted; and we hear of instances, where not only farmers and respectable agriculturists have found that the only way, as those employed by them deserted, was to leave their farms, join them, and form a band, and go shares, but even masters of vessels, foreseeing the impossibility of maintaining any control over their men otherwise, have made up parties among them to do the same. Fortunate the family, whatever its position, which retains its servants at any sacrifice, and can further secure the wonted supplies for their households from the few tradesmen who remain, and retain the means of supplying their customers at any augmentation of price. Drained of its labouring population, the price of provisions in the towns is naturally on the increase, for although there may be an abundant supply within reach, there are not sufficient hands to turn it to account. Both here and at Geelong all buildings and contract works, public and private, almost without exception, are at a stand-still. No contract can be insisted upon under the circumstances.

C. J. LA TROBE (1801–1875)

BEHAVIOUR ON THE GOLDFIELDS

. . . While we were returning through Forest Creek we came up with a party of fellows who bore unmistakable traces of the sly-grog shop in their gait and appearance, and who shouted to us as we rode by, 'Who stole the donkey?' a favourite piece of chaff here directed against white hats—on what grounds I do not know. This was the only piece of incivility I met with while at Mount Alexander. I was often in one part or other of the diggings and I never met with any sort of rudeness, and frequently with singular civility. Sir Montagu, who from his Irish connections was still more among them than I was, gave exactly the same account. My black coat, which by the account of so many—even of diggers—was to procure me so much hooting, never excited the slightest notice. Strange that people should take such trouble to tell lies. I likewise observed that throughout the diggings the orderly quiet with which the Sunday was kept was very remarkable and very creditable. There was less noise and less apparent (more I cannot speak to) revelry than a passing stranger would notice in the town of Hatfield. The reverent demeanour of those who attended our service this morning was also very noticeable.

LORD ROBERT CECIL (1830–1903)
Gold Fields Diary

LOOK OUT BELOW!

A young man left his native shores,
For trade was bad at home;
To seek his fortune in this land
He crossed the briny foam;
And when he went to Ballarat,
It put him in a glow,
To hear the sound of the windlass,
And the cry 'Look out below'.

Wherever he turned his wandering eyes,
Great wealth he did behold
And peace and plenty hand in hand,
By the magic power of gold;
Quoth he, as I am young and strong,
To the diggings I will go,
For I like the sound of the windlass,
And the cry 'Look out below'.

Amongst the rest he took his chance,
And his luck at first was vile;
But he still resolved to persevere,
And at length he made his pile.
So says he, I'll take my passage,
And home again I'll go,
And I'll say farewell to the windlass,
And the cry 'Look out below'.

Arrived in London once again,
His gold he freely spent,
And into every gaiety
And dissipation went.
But pleasure, if prolonged too much,
Oft causes pain, you know,
And he missed the sound of the windlass,
And the cry 'Look out below'.

And thus he reasoned with himself—
Oh, why did I return,
For the digger's independent life
I now begin to yearn.
Here purse proud lords the poor oppress,
But *there* it is not so;
Give me the sound of the windlass,
And the cry 'Look out below'.

So he started for this land again,
With a charming little wife;
And he finds there's nothing comes up to
A jolly digger's life.
Ask him if he'll go back again,
He'll quickly answer, no;
For he loves the sound of the windlass,
And the cry 'Look out below'.

CHARLES R. THATCHER (1831–1882)

AUSTRALIAN ARISTOCRACY

In 1853 it was proposed by W. C. Wentworth and others to establish an Australian hereditary aristocracy and an equivalent of the English House of Lords. This speech was fairly typical of the colonial attitude to the proposal.

Because it was the good pleasure of Mr Wentworth, and the respectable toil of that puissant legislative body whose serpentine windings were so ridiculous, we were not permitted to form our own Constitution, but instead we were to have one and an Upper Chamber cast upon us, built upon a model to suit the taste and propriety of certain political oligarchs, who treated the people at large as if they were cattle to be bought and sold in the market, as indeed they were in American slave states, and now in the Australian colonies, where we might find bamboozled Chinese and kidnapped Coolies. And being in a figurative humour, he might endeavour to cause some of the proposed nobility to pass before the stage of our imagination as the ghost of Banquo walked in the vision of Macbeth, so that we might have a fair view of those harlequin aristocrats, those Australian magnificos. We will have them across the stage in all the pomp and circumstance of hereditary titles. First, then, stalked the hoary Wentworth. But he could not believe that to such a head the strawberry leaves would add any honour. Next comes the full-blooded native aristocrat, Mr James Macarthur, who would, he supposed, aspire to an earldom at least; he would therefore call him Earl of Camden, and he would suggest for his coat of arms a field vert, the heraldic term for green, and emblazoned on this field should be the rum keg of a New South Wales order of chivalry. There was also the much-starred Terence Aubrey Murray, with more crosses and orders—not orders of merit—than a state of mandarinhood. . . . He confessed he found extreme difficulty in the effort to classify this mushroom order of nobility. They could not aspire to the miserable and effete dignity of the worn-out grandees of continental Europe. There, even in rags, they had antiquity of birth to point to; here he would defy the most skilled naturalist to assign them a place in the great human family. But perhaps after all it was only a specimen of the remarkable contrariety which existed at the Antipodes. Here they all knew that the common water-mole was transformed into the duck-billed platypus; and in some distant emulation of this degeneracy, he supposed they were to be favoured with a bunyip[1] aristocracy . . .

Let them, with prophetic eye, behold the troops of weary pilgrims from foreign despotism which would ere long be flocking to these shores in search of a more congenial home, and let them now give their most earnest and determined assurance that the domineering clique which made up the Wentworth party were not, and should never be, regarded as the representatives of the manliness, the spirit, and the intelligence of the freemen of New South Wales.

D. H. DENIEHY (1828–1865)
Life and Speeches

THE FATAL END OF THE
BURKE AND WILLS EXPEDITION

This expedition set out from Melbourne in 1860 to explore central Australia for pastoral land and crossed the continent to the Gulf of Carpentaria, but the two leaders died of starvation in Queensland about the end of June 1861. The extract is from the diary kept by Wills.

[1] Mythical monster lurking in waterholes.

Sunday, April 21 . . . Arrived at the depôt this evening, just in time to find it deserted. A note left in the plant by Brahe communicates the pleasing information that they have started to-day for the Darling; their camels and horses all well and in good condition. We and our camels being just done up, and scarcely able to reach the depôt, have very little chance of over-taking them. Brahe has fortunately left us ample provisions to take us to the bounds of civilization, namely: Flour, 50 lb; rice, 20 lb; oatmeal, 60 lb; sugar, 60 lb; and dried meat, 15 lb. These provisions, together with a few horse-shoes and nails and some odds and ends, constitute all the articles left, and place us in a very awkward position in respect of clothing. Our disappointment at finding the depôt deserted may easily be imagined; returning in an exhausted state, after four months of the severest travelling and privation, our legs almost paralyzed, so that each of us found it a most trying task only to walk a few yards. Such a leg-bound feeling I never before experienced, and hope I never shall again. The exertion required to get up a slight piece of rising ground, even without any load, induces an indescribable sensation of pain and helplessness, and the general lassitude makes one unfit for anything. . . .

Wednesday, June 24 . . . Mr Burke and King are preparing to go up the creek in search of the blacks. They will leave me some nardoo,[1] wood and water, with which I must do the best I can until they return. I think this is almost our only chance. I feel myself, if anything, rather better, but I cannot say stronger. The nardoo is beginning to agree better with me; but without some change I see little chance for any of us. They have both shown great hesitation and reluctance with regard to leaving me, and have repeatedly desired my candid opinion in the matter. I could only repeat, however, that I considered it our only chance, for I could not last long on the nardoo, even if a supply could be kept up. . . .

Friday, June 26 . . . I am weaker than ever although I have a good appetite, and relish the nardoo much, but it seems to give us no nutriment, and the birds here are so shy as not to be got at. Even if we got a good supply of fish, I doubt whether we could do much work on them and the nardoo alone. Nothing now but the greatest good luck can now save any of us; and as for myself, I may live four or five days if the weather continues warm. My pulse is at forty-eight, and very weak, and my legs and arms are nearly skin and bone. I can only look out, like Mr Micawber, 'for something to turn up'; but starvation on nardoo is by no means very unpleasant, but

[1] Flour ground from a native plant.

for the weakness one feels, and the utter inability to move oneself, for as far as appetite is concerned, it gives me the greatest satisfaction.

W. J. WILLS (1834–1861)

A PIONEER SETTLER'S JOURNAL

Rose early, according to my custom, and surveyed my new dwelling with a particular sort of satisfaction. 'No rent to pay for you', said I; 'no taxes, that's pleasant; no poor-rates, that's a comfort; and no one can give me warning to quit, and that's another comfort; and it's my own, thank God, and that's the greatest comfort of all'. I cast my eyes on the plain before me, and saw my flock of sheep studding the plain, with my working bullocks at a little distance . . . As we sat at breakfast that morning in my rude cottage, with the bare walls of logs of trees and the shingle roof above us, all rough enough, but spacious, and a little too airy, I began to have a foretaste of that feeling of independence and security of home and subsistence which I have so many years enjoyed.

CHARLES ROWCROFT (1798–1856)
Tales of the Colonies

THE FREE SELECTOR

This folk song of 1861 rejoices at a land act which met the popular agitation for 'unlocking the lands', held by the squatters, for settlement by free selection. Squatters and selectors fought a long and bitter battle over the land. The environment, however, favoured the large pastoralists, and the selectors often lived, as told in the next song, by 'duffing' the squatter's cattle or sheep.

> Come all you Cornstalks the victory's won,
> John Robertson's triumphed, the lean days are gone,
> No more through the bush we'll go humping the drum,
> For the Land Bill has passed and the good times have come.

> *Chorus*
> *Then give me a hut in my own native land,*
> *Or a tent in the bush, near the mountains so grand.*
> *For the scenes of my childhood a joy are to me,*
> *And the dear native girl who will share it with me.*

No more through the bush with our swags need we roam,
For to ask of the squatters to give us a home,
Now the land is unfettered and we may reside,
In a place of our own by the clear waterside.

We will sow our own garden and till our own field,
And eat of the fruits that our labour doth yield,
And be independent, a right long denied,
By those who have ruled us and robbed us beside.

Old Bush Song

THE EUMERALLA SHORE

There's a happy little valley on the Eumeralla shore,
   Where I've lingered many happy hours away,
On my little free selection I have acres by the score,
   Where I unyoke the bullocks from the dray.

Chorus
  To my bullocks then I say
  No matter where you stray,
    You will never be impounded any more;
  For you're running, running, running on the duffer's[1] piece of land,
  Free selected on the Eumeralla shore.

When the moon has climbed the mountains and the stars are shining bright,
   Then we saddle up our horses and away,
And we yard the squatter's cattle in the darkness of the night,
   And we have the calves all branded by the day.

Chorus
  Oh, my pretty little calf,
  At the squatter you may laugh,
    For he'll never be your owner any more;
  For you're running, running, running on the duffer's piece of land,
    Free selected on the Eumeralla shore.

Old Bush Song

[1] Cattle-thief's.

DUNN, GILBERT AND BEN HALL

Come all you wild colonials
And listen to my tale;
A story of bushrangers' deeds
I will to you unveil.
'Tis of those gallant heroes,
Game fighters one and all;
And we'll sit and sing, Long live the King,
Dunn, Gilbert and Ben Hall.

Frank Gardiner was a bushranger
Of terrible renown;
He robbed the Forbes' gold escort,
And eloped with Kitty Brown.
But in the end they lagged him,
Two-and-thirty years in all.
'We must avenge the Darkie',
Says Dunn, Gilbert and Ben Hall. . . .

Ben Hall he was a squatter
Who owned six hundred head;
A peaceful man he was until
Arrested by Sir Fred.
His home burned down, his wife cleared out,
His cattle perished all.
'They'll not take me a second time',
Says valiant Ben Hall.

'Hand over all your watches
And the banknotes in your purses.
All travellers must pay toll to us;
We don't care for your curses.

We are the rulers of the roads,
We've seen the troopers fall,
And we want your gold and money',
Says Dunn, Gilbert and Ben Hall.

'Next week we'll visit Goulburn
And clean the banks out there;
So if you see the peelers,
Just tell them to beware;
Some day to Sydney city
We mean to pay a call,
And we'll take the whole damn country!'
Says Dunn, Gilbert and Ben Hall.

Old Bush Song

SIR HENRY PARKES

First and foremost of course in every eye was the commanding figure of Sir Henry Parkes, than whom no actor ever more carefully posed for effect. His huge figure, slow step, deliberate glance and carefully brushed-out aureole of white hair combined to present the spectator with a picturesque whole which was not detracted from on closer acquaintance. His voice, without being musical and in spite of a slight woolliness of tone and rather affected depth, was pleasant and capable of reaching and controlling a large audience. His studied attitudes expressed either distinguished humility or imperious command. His manner was invariably dignified, his speech slow, and his pronunciation precise, offending only by the occasional omission or misplacing of aspirates. He was fluent but not voluble, his pauses skilfully varied, and in times of excitement he employed a whole gamut of tones ranging from a shrill falsetto to deep resounding chest notes. He had always in his mind's eye his own portrait as that of a great man, and constantly adjusted himself to it. A far-away expression of the eyes, intended to convey his remoteness from the earthly sphere, and often associated with melancholy treble cadences of voice in which he implied a vast and inexpressible weariness, constituted his favourite and at last his almost invariable exterior. Movements, gestures, inflexions, attitudes harmonised, not simply because they were intentionally adopted but because there was in him the substance of the man he dressed himself to appear. The real strength and depth of his capacity were such that it was always a problem with Parkes as with Disraeli where the actor posture-maker and would-be sphinx ended or where the actual man underneath began. He had both by nature and by act the manner of a sage and a statesman.

His abilities were solid though general, as were his reading and his knowledge. Fond of books, a steady reader and a constant writer, his education had been gained in the world and among men. A careful student of all with whom he came in contact, he was amiable, persuasive and friendly by disposition. A life of struggle had found him self-reliant and left him hardened into resolute masterfulness. Apart from his exterior, he was a born leader of men, dwelling by preference of natural choice upon the larger and bolder aspects of things. He had therefore the aptitude of statecraft of a high order, adding to it the tastes of the man of letters, the lover of poetry and the arts, of rare editions and bric-a-brac, of autographs and memorials of the past. His nature, forged on the anvil of necessity, was egotistic though not stern and his career was that of the aspirant who looks to ends and is not too punctilious as to means. He was jealous of equals, bitter with rivals and remorseless with enemies—vain beyond all measure, without strong attachment to colleagues and with strong animal passions —weak in discussion of detail, unfitted for the minor tasks of administration, apt to be stilted in set speeches, and involved in debate, he yet was well qualified for the Premiership by great and genuine oratorical ability. A doughty parliamentary warrior neither giving nor asking quarter, he struck straight home at his adversaries with trenchant power. He was a careful framer of phrases and of insulting epithets which he sought to elaborate so that they would stick and sting. . . .

Very many admired and not a few weaker men loved him; he brooked no rivals near his throne but all found his personality attractive and submitted more or less to his domination. It was not a rich, not a versatile personality, but it was massive, durable and imposing, resting upon elementary qualities of human nature elevated by a strong mind. He was cast in the mould of a great man and though he suffered from numerous pettinesses, spites and failings, he was in himself a full-blooded, large-brained, self-educated Titan whose natural field was found in Parliament and whose resources of character and intellect enabled him in his later years to overshadow all his contemporaries, to exercise an immense influence on his own colony and achieve a great reputation outside it.

ALFRED DEAKIN (1856–1919)
The Federal Story

THE FIRST PRIME MINISTER

Some four years younger than Griffith was Edmund Barton, a striking figure, with finely chiselled features, the delight of sculptors, a noble head, brown hair streaked with one white lock plume-like above his forehead, and an imposing presence. After a brilliant course at the University of Sydney, he had, at the age of forty-two, already made a name for himself at the Bar and in politics, and had been Speaker of the New South Wales Parliament and Attorney-General of New South Wales. But neither law nor party politics had for him the inspiration to rouse his dormant energies: he was reputed a dilettante; and none guessed that thenceforth he would, to the neglect of his profession and all worldly considerations, be the devoted knight-errant of Australian union. . . .

Left for dead by the politicians, federation was brought to life by the people. Parkes had seen one thing that was wrong with the derelict Bill—it had not been founded on a vote of the people; and he had contemplated a new start on a popular basis. But his strength was ebbing. His mantle fell on Barton's shoulders. Now, Barton was reputed to be an indolent man, and in a sense he was. He liked his club, and the amenities of life, and was disinclined to exert himself over things that did not inspire him with passionate interest. But he was capable of intense concentration where that interest was aroused. He had found that interest in the idea of Australian union, and threw himself into the cause with amazing energy.

It is said that in the course of four years he addressed some three hundred meetings in New South Wales; and he gathered about him a body of young disciples, of whom I was one, and Atlee Hunt, afterwards Secretary to the Prime Minister's Department, was another. We used to help him at his meetings, and each of us became a kind of honorary private secretary to him, helping with correspondence and propaganda.

Barton's methods of work would not have commended themselves to a Public Service Board. Hours were irregular, with much overtime. But time lost would always be made up. He was generous with his time to many who had no claim on it. On Sunday evenings he used to keep open house at his home at Kirribilli; and many a time when the last of his other lingering guests had left about midnight we would go into his study, where he would work with amazing concentration and speed for three or four hours, drafting letters and planning an ever-growing campaign.

It was at one of his meetings, at Ashfield, that he coined the memorable impromptu—which would have been unrecorded if I had not happened to jot it down—'For the first time in history, we have a nation for a continent, and a continent for a nation'.

SIR ROBERT RANDOLPH GARRAN (1867–1957)
Prosper the Commonwealth

THE WHITE AUSTRALIA POLICY

The policy of White Australia is the indispensable condition of every other Australian policy. Embodied in the Immigration Restriction Act, 1901–25, its intention and significance are exceedingly easy to understand once they have been freed from the rhetoric and special pleading in which they have been enveloped . . . Chamberlain had requested at the Colonial Conference of 1897, that the colonies should clothe their legislation in 'a form of words which will avoid hurting the feelings of any of Her Majesty's subjects'. He had commended to them the method adopted by Natal, which had dissimulated a resolution to discriminate against Asiatics on the ground of race, by pretending to test their educational attainments. The rhetoricians denounced such diplomacy as 'a hypocritical measure', 'a back-door method', 'a crooked and dishonest evasion'.

Fortunately, the majority of Australians were not rhetoricians, but practical people. The miners who had assailed Chinese fossickers on the diggings in the late fifties and early sixties of the nineteenth century had not pondered deeply over the teachings of God and science. And the responsible leaders of the Parliament of 1901 understood that, in this imperfect world, it is necessary to make concessions to expediency and common sense. By insisting upon the expedient of the dictation test they read their people a lesson in international good manners, and achieved Australia's purpose without recklessly wounding the self-respect of other nations. However, they had sufficient honesty and courage to understand and to confess that their legislation was founded, not on the special nobility of the Australian people, but on the obvious fact of its individuality, which was compounded not only of good qualities, but of bad. 'I contend', declared Deakin, 'that the Japanese need to be excluded because of their high abilities'. Their very virtues would make them dangerous competitors. This is one aspect of the economic argument. But Deakin took his stand on

73

higher ground: 'The unity of Australia means nothing if it does not imply a united race. A united race means not only that its members can intermarry and associate without degradation on either side, but implies . . . a people possessing the same general cast of character, tone of thought, the same constitutional training and traditions'.

Every honest exposition of the White Australia policy must start from this double argument of economic and racial necessity. Every justification of it is hypocrisy and cant if it does not admit that its basis is *salus populi suprema lex*. An influx of the labouring classes of Asia would inevitably disorganise Australia's economic and political life. The experience of Natal, of North America, of the Australian colonies themselves in pre-federation days, proves that labourers of different colours are seldom sufficiently meek to live side by side in human brotherhood. Always there is danger of a threefold demoralisation; demoralisation of the coolie over-driven by white capital, demoralisation of the poor white overwhelmed by coolie competition, demoralisation of the half-breed children of coolie and poor white who can find no firm place in either of the competing civilisations. Reasonable Australians are determined that their country shall not know these evils . . . What they fear is not physical conquest by another race, but rather the internal decomposition and degradation of their own civilisation. They have gloried in their inheritance of free institutions, in their right to govern themselves and freely make their own destiny. But self-government, they know, becomes impossible when the inhabitants of a country do not agree upon essentials. No community can without great danger give a share of political power to aliens unable or unwilling to accept and defend what most it values. Every State must maintain its own *ethos*, and Australians understand that even a successful tyranny over Orientals would destroy the character of their own democracy.

W. K. HANCOCK (1898–   )
Australia

THE HARVESTER JUDGMENT

In 1906 an Act of Commonwealth Parliament imposed certain excise duties from which manufacturers might be exempted provided that the wages they paid were 'fair and reasonable'. The Act was later declared invalid by the High Court, but this judgment made by Mr Justice Higgins, President of the Commonwealth Arbitration Court, in 1907 has remained as the principle behind the basic wage, a distinctive and fundamental part of the Australian way of life.

'I cannot think of any other standard appropriate than the normal needs of the average employee, regarded as a human being living in a civilized community . . . If A lets B have the use of his horses, on the terms that he give them fair and reasonable treatment, I have no doubt that it is B's duty to give them proper food and water, and such shelter and rest as they need; and as wages are the means of obtaining commodities, surely the State, in stipulating for fair and reasonable remuneration for the employees, means that the wages shall be sufficient to provide these things, and clothing, and a condition of frugal comfort estimated by current human standards . . .

. . . I have tried to ascertain the cost of living—the amount which has to be paid for food, shelter, clothing, for an average labourer with normal wants, and under normal conditions. Some very interesting evidence has been given, by working men's wives and others; and the evidence has been absolutely undisputed . . . The usual rent paid by a labourer, as distinguished from an artisan, appears to be 7s; and, taking the rent as 7s, the necessary average weekly expenditure for a labourer's home of about five persons would seem to be about £1 12s 5d . . . I have confined the figures to rent, groceries, bread, meat, milk, fuel, vegetables, and fruit; and the average of the list of nine housekeeping women is £1 12s 5d. This expenditure does not cover light (some of the lists omitted light), clothes, boots, furniture, utensils (being casual, not weekly expenditure), rates, life insurance, savings, accident or benefit societies, loss of employment, union pay, books and newspapers, tram and train fares, sewing machine, mangle, school requisites, amusements and holidays, intoxicating liquors, tobacco, sickness and death, domestic help, or any expenditure for unusual contingencies, religion or charity. If the wages are 36s per week, the amount left to pay for all these things is only 3s 7d; and the area is rather large for 3s 7d to cover. . . . My hesitation (in deciding what is a fair and reasonable daily wage) has been chiefly between 7s and 7s 6d; but I put the minimum at 7s as I do not think I could refuse to declare an employer's remuneration to be fair and reasonable, if I find him paying 7s.'

HENRY BOURNES HIGGINS (1851–1921)

FOR ENGLAND

This poem of the First World War illustrates the romantic sentiment still felt for England as 'home' just as the following poem of the Second World War illustrates, in contrast, a grimly realistic spirit, typically Australian.

The bugles of England were blowing o'er the sea,
As they had called a thousand years, calling now to me;
They woke me from dreaming in the dawning of the day,
The bugles of England—and how could I stay?

The banners of England, unfurled across the sea,
Floating out upon the wind, were beckoning to me;
Storm-rent and battle-torn, smoke-stained and grey,
The banners of England—and how could I stay?

O England, I heard the cry of those that died for thee,
Sounding like an organ-voice across the winter sea;
They lived and died for England and gladly went their way,
England, O England—how could *I* stay?

J. D. BURNS (1895–1915)

ARGUMENT

You can't argue with a dead man.

You can't lift his head from the mud,
Wipe the mud from his eyes
And wrangle with him
Over kings and empires,
Proletarians and popes.

Ask his opinion of a red star
Or a crooked cross
And he'll not tell you.
No stars shine in his black sky.
His only cross, the index to his grave,
And he'll not know of that.

You can look at him helplessly,
You can think,
'Once he chattered

And grew indignant over pots of beer,
Grew red in the face,
Or laughed
And said, "You lovely bastard, you!"'

'Once
He looked at sunsets.
Once
He plucked grass in the dawn
Shook it
And watched the falling, iridescent dew
Flash in the dove-grey light,
"It's cold", he said, "it's clean".
Once
He spoke of Brahms.
Once
He said, "Let's go on a shicker".
Once
He said, "Next time I'm on leave
I'm getting hooked—
She has brown hair and it's curly
And a funny way of glancing over her shoulder
And smiling".'

But now,
Now you want to argue with him.
You want to say, 'You died for something great—
You died for a Cause.
Wasn't it worth while to die for a Cause?
Wasn't it?'

Lay his head in the mud again,
Wipe the blood from your hands.

You can't argue with a dead man.

                          JOHN QUINN (1915–   )

77

THE SECOND A.I.F.

By the end of 1941 the Australian Imperial Force in the Middle East had acquired some of the characteristics of a long-service regular army. The men were all volunteers, and were proud of that fact and of the units and formations to which they belonged; indeed many had developed a far stronger loyalty and affection towards their units than had been inspired by any institutions at home—outside their families. They had been singularly unperturbed by the Japanese onslaught; relatively few seem to have foreseen their transfer to the Far East; and it seems probable that the bitter and misconceived rebukes, which some of them received in letters from Australia for skulking in Palestine and Syria while Japanese threatened their homes, were partly the outcome of their own patent unconcern at the addition of the Japanese to the lengthening list of their opponents. Allied to this was a steadily-increasing pride in their achievements and confidence in their own ability to cope with whatever faced them, a quality no doubt acquired by a force of colonial volunteers. To them war had become a technical accomplishment, its risks calculated, its results predictable.

Moreover they had demonstrated the wisdom of defending Australia by sending an expeditionary force against Germany (and her Italian and French allies). The eastern Mediterranean and the Middle East, which, if held by the Germans, would have enabled them to combine their operations with those of Japan, were still under Allied control, and from that area would soon be sailing east a tried force of some 64,000 men, well-armed, confident and expert, under tested leaders, ranging from those who had handled corps and divisions in the field to youngsters who had fought against Germans, Italians and Frenchmen, in desert and snow, mountain and plain.

GAVIN LONG (1901–1968)
Australia in the War of 1939–45: Greece, Crete and Syria

EFFECT OF THE SECOND WORLD WAR
ON SCIENCE AND INDUSTRY

What, in general terms, was the over-all effect of the war on Australian science and industry?

In science there was a slowing down of fundamental research and a preoccupation with the applications of science. This trend was common to most, if not all, countries at war. Australia continued to train scientists and engineers throughout the war without any serious diminution in numbers, so that it was possible to sustain fairly well the rapid developments of science in the post-war years. The successful application of science to war created a deep impression on the community at large and heightened its appreciation of the part played by science generally in the modern world. Consequently, after the war research received much stronger financial support from governments than it had ever previously enjoyed in this country, and the output of scientific research reached new levels in quality and diversity.

Industry began to contribute its share. While many firms affiliated with overseas organisations continued to rely on their parent bodies for research and developmental work, there were signs that the larger and stronger of them were beginning to assume responsibilities of their own in these matters. A few large, essentially Australian firms also began to establish well-equipped laboratories intended for something more than routine scientific control of manufacturing processes. Firms in both groups also contributed considerable sums of money for the endowment of research fellowships at universities.

Industry met the challenge of war by displaying at all levels—from skilled workmen to engineers and scientists and executives—a resourcefulness and an ability to improvise which enabled it to solve many of the technical problems produced by isolation. For the first time the value of production of secondary industry overtook that of primary industry.

Engineering industry emerged from the war greatly strengthened in its capacity to undertake mass production, and with an appreciation of what was involved in meeting the exacting standards and specifications for making munitions. It was able to make a wider range of structural materials than ever before. Developments that might otherwise have been spread over twenty-five years were compressed into little more than five years. With this background of wartime experience, industry was ready to undertake, after the war, the manufacture of motor-cars, jet aircraft and television equipment.

D. P. MELLOR (1903–   )
Australia in the War of 1939–45: The Role of Science and Industry

PASTORAL

EMUS

My annals have it so;
A thing my mother saw,
Nigh eighty years ago,
With happiness and awe.

Along a level hill—
A clearing in wild space.
And night's last tardy chill
Yet damp on morning's face.

Sight never to forget:
Solemn against the sky
In stately silhouette
Ten emus walking by.

One after one they went
In line, and without haste:
On their unknown intent,
Ten emus grandly paced.

She, used to hedged-in fields
Watched them go filing past
Into the great Bush Wilds
Silent and vast.

Sudden that hour she knew
That this far place was good,
This mighty land and new
For the soul's hardihood.

For hearts that love the strange,
That carry wonder;
The Bush, the hills, the range,
And the dark flats under.

                         'E' (MARY FULLERTON) (1866–1946)

AUSTRAL PAN

Pan is dead? My friends, ah, no! Where the hardy drovers go,
Where the shimmering mirage falsely limns the river's marge,
Where the lone prospector's bones stake the six-foot claim he owns,
Where the thirsty brumbies squeal and thunder off on frantic heel,
Where the moon suspends her lamp above the drowsy cattle camp,
Where the blossom-pink galahs crowd with bloom the coolibars,
Or rise and whirl in sudden flight and scream like devils in the night,
Where the wild men sing and dance, nightlong 'neath the melting glance
Of the magic-making moon, by the lily-flecked lagoon,
Where, in sooth, our works and days still proceed in ancient ways,
And herd and hunter, beast and tree enjoy the old fraternity,
Hither hoary Pan is fled, with His charm and with His dread,
With His honey-fluted stave, with His lore to salve and save,
With His blind, insensate love, joys He filched from Heaven above,
Sharing with His creatures here, whimsical, capricious, queer:
To the very oldest land, product of His prentice hand.
Under tawny Capricorn, cloven hoof and gnarly horn,
Here the living Pan is fled, while the Old World mourns Him dead.

    . . . He seeks again His ancient haunts,
A squatter born, a squatter bred, with horns, Himself, upon His head,
His steps outback with glee are bent. He snuffs the saltbush with content
The deeper for His knowledge sure, His ancient ways and works endure.

                         PETER HOPEGOOD (1891–1967)

THE SCRUBBERS IN CAPTIVITY

Midday had come. Throughout the bush cattle were camped in the shade of the trees away from the heat, but for the scrubbers[1] there was no rest; there was not even any heat as far as their physical consciousness of it was concerned. They gathered together in a forlorn little company on the ground where they had camped the previous night. The sun beat upon their backs; the bush simmered around them; their shadows were like grey blurs beneath them, and their heads were turned always to the ranges, rising blue-veiled and sun-drenched into the sky.

In the middle of the afternoon they resumed their march round the fence, and kept it up, circling the boundary of the paddock again and again. They were creatures of the wild, and an enclosure—a fence—returning ever to its starting point—was as far removed from their power of understanding as the idea of infinity is removed from the human mental grasp. Perhaps they hoped that, somehow the fence would eventually disappear. Perhaps their endless march relieved their longing to be going back to their home in the ranges—a monotony of movement that soothed, though it could not cure.

Late in the afternoon, when the sun had passed behind the ranges, they came to rest again near the sliprails. Here they stood with heads thrown up and their eyes fixed on their home, now fading from their sight.

Black and Splinter, returning from work, halted their horses just outside the fence.

'Hollow, ain't they?' It was Splinter who spoke.

Black nodded. 'Still, they've been in to drink', he said, glancing at the half-dried mud on the cattle's hoofs. 'I expect they'll start feeding soon. They'll settle down as soon as they get properly hungry.' Notwithstanding his assurance of voice, he looked doubtfully at them as he turned away. Their bodies were indeed tucked up and empty.

Black was wrong in thinking the green feed would wean the scrubbers from their longing for their home. During the days that followed they ate nothing. They drank a little. Hour after hour they passed stumbling in weary procession round the fence-line, and hour after hour they stood with heads thrown up and eyes fixed on the distant ranges. The flesh wasted from their frames, their hair grew harsh and stood on end, and their bones were painfully apparent. The light that was the ever-present longing for

[1] Wild cattle from the bush scrub.

84

the wildness of freedom of the hills continued to burn in their eyes. The only physical thing of which they were conscious was the fence that encircled the paddock.

Their ceaseless travelling round and round inside the wire boundaries of their prison had worn away the grass and made a thin dusty track. But now their journeyings had ended. They no longer had the energy to spare. For two days they did not move from their camp near the sliprails. At night, when darkness covered the ranges, they lay down to rest, but at dawn they rose and resumed their watch. All their consciousness of living had passed into a yearning for their hills.

Their condition aroused, at first, speculation, and later, sympathetic profanity.

'Why don't he let the poor devils go!' the men said, speaking of Black.

Conscious of the resentment which his callousness was arousing among the men, Black was frequent in his assurance that the scrubbers, as hunger pressed upon them, would settle down in the paddock. There was good water and grass, and, after all, a beast was only a stomach on four legs. They would soon forget.

He was wrong in that. The scrubbers were dying.

FRANK DALBY DAVISON (1893–1970)
Man-Shy

CLANCY OF THE OVERFLOW

I had written him a letter which I had, for want of better
Knowledge, sent to where I met him down the Lachlan, years ago;
He was shearing when I knew him, so I sent the letter to him,
Just on spec, addressed as follows, 'Clancy, of The Overflow'.

And an answer came directed in a writing unexpected
(And I think the same was written with a thumb-nail dipped in tar);
'Twas his shearing mate who wrote it, and *verbatim* I will quote it:
'Clancy's gone to Queensland droving, and we don't know where he are.'

In my wild erratic fancy visions come to me of Clancy
Gone a-droving 'down the Cooper' where the Western drovers go;
As the stock are slowly stringing, Clancy rides behind them singing,
For the drover's life has pleasures that the townsfolk never know.

And the bush has friends to meet him, and their kindly voices greet him
In the murmur of the breezes and the river on its bars,
And he sees the vision splendid of the sunlit plains extended,
And at night the wondrous glory of the everlasting stars.

      . . . . . .

I am sitting in my dingy little office, where a stingy
Ray of sunlight struggles feebly down between the houses tall,
And the foetid air and gritty of the dusty, dirty city,
Through the open window floating, spreads its foulness over all.

And in place of lowing cattle, I can hear the fiendish rattle
Of the tramways and the buses making hurry down the street;
And the language uninviting of the gutter children fighting
Comes fitfully and faintly through the ceaseless tramp of feet.

And the hurrying people daunt me, and their pallid faces haunt me
As they shoulder one another in their rush and nervous haste,
With their eager eyes and greedy, and their stunted forms and weedy,
For townsfolk have no time to grow, they have no time to waste.

And I somehow rather fancy that I'd like to change with Clancy,
Like to take a turn at droving where the seasons come and go,
While he faced the round eternal of the cash-book and the journal—
But I doubt he'd suit the office, Clancy, of The Overflow.

A. B. ('BANJO') PATERSON (1864–1941)

Now and then the bushwoman lays down her work and watches, and listens, and thinks. She thinks of things in her own life, for there is little else to think about.

The rain will make the grass grow, and this reminds her how she fought a bush-fire once while her husband was away. The grass was long, and very dry, and the fire threatened to burn her out. She put on an old pair of her husband's trousers and beat out the flames with a green bough, till great drops of sooty perspiration stood out on her forehead and ran in streaks down her blackened arms. The sight of his mother in trousers greatly amused Tommy, who worked like a little hero by her side, but the terrified baby howled lustily for his 'mummy'. The fire would have mastered her but for four excited bushmen who arrived in the nick of time. It was a mixed-up affair all round; when she went to take up the baby he screamed and struggled convulsively, thinking it was a 'blackman'; and Alligator, trusting more to the child's sense than his own instinct, charged furiously, and (being old and slightly deaf) did not in his excitement at first recognise his mistress's voice, but continued to hang onto the mole skins until choked off by Tommy with a saddle-strap. The dog's sorrow for his blunder, and his anxiety to let it be known that it was all a mistake, was as evident as his ragged tail and a twelve-inch grin could make it. It was a glorious time for the boys; a day to look back to, and talk about, and laugh over for many years.

She thinks how she fought a flood during her husband's absence. She stood for hours in the drenching downpour, and dug an overflow gutter to save the dam across the creek. But she could not save it. There are things that a bushwoman cannot do. Next morning the dam was broken, and her heart was nearly broken too, for she thought how her husband would feel when he came home and saw the result of years of labour swept away. She cried then.

She also fought the pleuro-pneumonia—dosed and bled the few remaining cattle, and wept again when her two best cows died.

Again, she fought a mad bullock that besieged the house for a day. She made bullets and fired at him through cracks in the slabs with an old shot-gun. He was dead in the morning. She skinned him and got seventeen-and-sixpence for the hide.

88

She also fights the crows and eagles that have designs on her chickens. Her plan of campaign is very original. The children cry 'Crows, mother!' and she rushes out and aims a broomstick at the birds as though it were a gun, and says 'Bung!' The crows leave in a hurry; they are cunning, but a woman's cunning is greater.

Occasionally a bushman in the horrors, or a villainous-looking sundowner, comes and nearly scares the life out of her. She generally tells the suspicious-looking stranger that her husband and two sons are at work below the dam, or over at the yard, for he always cunningly inquires for the boss.

Only last week a gallows-faced swagman—having satisfied himself that there were no men on the place—threw his swag down on the veranda, and demanded tucker. She gave him something to eat; then he expressed his intention of staying for the night. It was sundown then. She got a batten from the sofa, loosened the dog, and confronted the stranger, holding the batten in one hand and the dog's collar with the other. 'Now you go!' she said. He looked at her and at the dog, said 'All right, mum', in a cringing tone, and left. She was a determined-looking woman, and Alligator's yellow eyes glared unpleasantly—besides, the dog's chawing-up apparatus greatly resembled that of the reptile he was named after.

She has few pleasures to think of as she sits here alone by the fire, on guard against a snake. All days are much the same to her; but on Sunday afternoon she dresses herself, tidies the children, smartens up baby, and goes for a lonely walk along the bush-track, pushing an old perambulator in front of her. She does this every Sunday. She takes as much care to make herself and the children look smart as she would if she were going to do the block in the city. There is nothing to see, however, and not a soul to meet. You might walk for twenty miles along this track without being able to fix a point in your mind, unless you are a bushman. This is because of the everlasting, maddening sameness of the stunted trees—that monotony which makes a man long to break away and travel as far as trains can go, and sail as far as ship can sail—and farther.

But this bushwoman is used to the loneliness of it. As a girl-wife she hated it, but now she would feel strange away from it.

She is glad when her husband returns, but she does not gush or make a fuss about it. She gets him something good to eat, and tidies up the children.

She seems contented with her lot. She loves her children, but has no time to show it. She seems harsh to them. Her surroundings are not favourable to the development of the 'womanly' or sentimental side of nature.

HENRY LAWSON (1867–1922)

THE DYING STOCKMAN

A strapping young stockman lay dying,
His saddle supporting his head;
His two mates around him were crying,
As he rose on his elbow and said:

Chorus
'Wrap me up with my stockwhip and blanket,
And bury me deep down below,
Where the dingoes and crows can't molest me,
In the shade where the coolibahs grow.

'Oh! had I the flight of the bronzewing,
Far o'er the plains would I fly,
Straight to the land of my childhood,
And there would I lay down and die.

'Then cut down a couple of saplings,
Place one at my head and my toe,
Carve on them cross, stockwhip, and saddle,
To show there's a stockman below.

'Hark! there's the wail of a dingo,
Watchful and weird—I must go,
For it tolls the death-knell of the stockman
From the gloom of the scrub down below.

'There's tea in the battered old billy;
　　Place the pannikins out in a row,
And we'll drink to the next merry meeting,
　　In the place where all good fellows go.

'And oft in the shades of the twilight,
　　When the soft winds are whispering low,
And the dark'ning shadows are falling,
　　Sometimes think of the stockman below.

'Wrap me up with my stockwhip and blanket,
　　And bury me deep down below,
Where the dingoes and crows can't molest me,
　　In the shade where the coolibahs grow.'

Old Bush Song

HE GOT TOO EFFICIENT

Then he talked about himself and his boyhood. 'When we was kids we used to travel around in a wagon, mostly through the Upper Burnett and the Dawson country—my mother and father and us boys. . . . We had a dog, too, that was a great one for killing a sheep now and then when we wanted meat. We had to shoot him, though, he got too efficient.' Here Jacques grinned and borrowed my tobacco. 'Yes, we sent the dog into the flock to get us some mutton; and before we could ride out and stop him the beggar had killed near a dozen, and had the sheep scampering about, scared right out of their lives. We was just picking out a nice lamb, when my brother sees two men riding over. Then my father, quick as a flash, shoots the dog and whips off his collar; and when the men come up—they were station hands all right—he says to them, "We found this dog playing hell with your sheep, and I shot him". The men, they looked at the dog—it was a speckled sort of pup—and they said, "We've been after that b . . . r for three years; he's the worst cross dingo[1] in the district, and the boss has put twenty quid on his scalp. You'd better take him over to the homestead". Then my father asked them, could we take a mutton, as we was rather short of meat.

[1] Cross between a wild dog and a sheep dog, noted for sheep-killing.

91

And the men said, "Take what you like—they aren't no good to us lying there". So we took a couple of lambs, and I picked up the dog and carried it over my saddle to the wagon; and we took it to the station. We got the twenty quid all right, and the man thanked us; and then we cleared off as fast as we could off their country, in case the real dingo showed up!'

FRANCIS RATCLIFFE (1904–   )
Flying Fox and Drifting Sand

FROM THE GULF

Store cattle from Nelanjie! The mob goes feeding past,
With half-a-mile of sandhill 'twixt the leaders and the last;
The nags that move behind them are the good old Queensland stamp—
Short backs and perfect shoulders that are priceless on a camp;
And these are *Men* that ride them, broad-chested, tanned, and tall,
The bravest hearts amongst us and the lightest hands of all:
Oh, let them wade in Wonga grass and taste the Wonga dew,
And let them spread, those thousand head—for we've been droving too!

Store cattle from Nelanjie! By half-a-hundred towns,
By northern ranges rough and red, by rolling open downs,
By stock-routes brown and burnt and bare, by flood-wrapped river-bends,
They've hunted them from gate to gate—the drover has no friends!
But idly they may ride to-day beneath the scorching sun
And let the hungry bullocks try the grass on Wonga run;
No overseer will dog them here to 'see the cattle through',
But they may spread their thousand head—for we've been droving too!

WILLIAM H. OGILVIE (1869–1963)

THE CHILD LOST IN THE BUSH

However, we had been yarning for hours and the station chaps were about turning-in, when we heard someone coming in a hurry. No less than Webster himself . . . and says he:

'Child lost in the scrub on Goolumbulla, Dan O'Connell's little girl—five or six years old. Anybody know where there's any blackfellows?'[1]

Nobody knew.

'Well, raise horses wherever you can, and clear at once', says he. 'One man, for the next couple of days, will be worth a regiment very shortly.'

Seems that . . . Spanker had called in every man on the station, to muster the ewes. You know how thick the scrub is on Goolumbulla? Dan came in along with the rest, leaving his own place before daylight on the first morning. They swept the paddock the first day for about three parts of the ewes; the second day they got most of what was left; but Spanker wanted every hoof, if possible, and he kept all hands on for the third day.

Seems, the little girl didn't trouble herself the first day, though she hadn't seen Dan in the morning; but the second day there was something peculiar about her . . .

It appears that she was very fond of her father; and this affair of the man perishing in the scrub was working on her mind . . .

Anyway, on the third morning, after breakfast, her mother went out to milk the goats, leaving her in the house. When the woman came back, she found the child gone. She looked round the place, and called, and listened, and prospected everywhere, for an hour; then she went into the house, and examined. She found that the little girl had taken about a pint of milk, in a small billy with a lid, and half a loaf of bread. Then, putting everything together, the mother decided that she had gone into the scrub to look for her father. There was no help to be had nearer than the home-station for the only other boundary man on that part of the run was away at the muster. So she cleared for the station—twelve mile—and got there about three in the afternoon, not able to stand. . . .

. . . We were circling round for miles, without making any headway; and so the time passed till about three in the afternoon. Then up comes Spanker, with his hat lost, and his face cut and bleeding from the scrub, and his horses in a white lather, and a black lubra sitting in the back of the buggy, and the Mulppa stockkeeper tearing along in front, giving him our tracks.

She was an old, grey-haired lubra, blind of one eye; but she knew her business, and she was on the job for life or death. She picked up the track at a glance, and run it like a bloodhound. We found that the little girl hadn't kept the sheep-pads as we expected. Generally she went straight till

---

[1] For tracking the child.

93

something blocked her; then she'd go straight again, at another angle. Very rarely—hardly ever—we could see what signs the lubra was following; but she was all right. Uncivilised, even for an old lubra. Nobody could yabber with her but Bob; and he kept close to her all the time. She began to get uneasy as night came on, but there was no help for it. She went slower and slower, and at last she sat down where she was . . .

Longest night I ever passed, though it was one of the shortest in the year. Eyes burning for want of sleep, and couldn't bear to lie down for a minute. Wandering about for miles; listening; hearing something in the scrub, and finding it was only one of the other chaps, or some sheep. Thunder and lightning, on and off, all night; even two or three drops of rain, towards morning. Once I heard the howl of a dingo,[1] and I thought of the little girl, lying worn-out, half-asleep and half-fainting—far more helpless than a sheep—and I made up my mind that if she came out safe I would lead a better life for the future . . .

The lubra said something to Bob.

'Picaninny[2] tumble down here again', says Bob. 'Getting very weak on her feet.'

By-and-by, 'Picaninny plenty tumble down'. It was pitiful; but we knew that we were close on her at last. By this time, of course, she had been out for seventy-two hours. . . .

We were crossing fresh horse-tracks every few yards; and never two minutes but what somebody turned-up to ask the news. But to show how little use anything was except fair tracking, the lubra herself never saw the child till she went right up to where she was lying between two thick, soft bushes that met over her, and hid her from sight—

'Asleep?' I suggested, with a sinking heart.

No. She had been walking along—less than half-an-hour before—and she had brushed through between these bushes, to avoid some prickly scrub on both sides; but there happened to be a bilby-hole[3] close in front, and she fell in the sort of trough, with her head down the slope; and that was the end of her long journey. It would have taken a child in fair strength to get out of the place she was in; and she was played-out to the last ounce. So her face had sunk down on the loose mould, and she had died without a struggle.

Bob snatched her up the instant he caught sight of her, but we all saw that it was too late. We coo-eed, and the chap with the bell kept it going

[1] Wild dog.   [2] Small child.   [3] Bandicoot-hole.

94

steady. Then all hands reckoned that the search was over, and they were soon collected round the spot.

Now that little girl was only five years old; and she had walked nothing less than twenty-two miles—might be nearer twenty-five. . . .

'How did poor Rory take it?' I asked.

'Dan? Well he took it bad. When he saw her face, he gave one little cry, like a wounded animal; then he sat down on the bilby-heap, with her on his knees, wiping the mould out of her mouth, and talking baby to her.

'Not one of us could find a word to say.'

TOM COLLINS (JOSEPH FURPHY) (1843–1912)

Such is Life

GOLD OF THE WATTLE

The bush was in bloom, the wattles were out. Wattle, or mimosa, is the national flower of Australia. There are said to be thirty-two species. Richard found only seven as they wandered along. The little, pale, sulphur wattle with a reddish stem sends its lovely sprays to aerial out of the sand of the trail, only a foot or two high, but such a delicate, spring-like thing. The thorny wattle with its fuzzy pale balls tangles on the banks. Then beautiful heath-plants with small bells, like white heather, stand in tall, straight tufts, and above them the gold sprays of the intensely gold bush mimosa, with here and there, on long, thin stalks like hairs almost, beautiful blue flowers, with gold grains, three-petalled, like reed-flowers, and blue, blue with a touch of Australian darkness. Then comes a hollow, desolate bare place with empty greyness and a few dead, charred gum-trees, where there has been a bush-fire. At the side of this bare place great flowers, twelve feet high, like sticky dark lilies in bulb-buds at the top of the shaft, blood-red. Then over another stream, and scattered bush once more, and the last queer, gold-red bushes of the bottle-brush tree, like soft-bristly golden bottle-brushes standing stiffly up, and the queer black-boys on one black leg with a tuft of dark-green spears, sending up the high stick of a seed-stalk, much taller than a man. And here and there the gold bushes of wattle with their narrow dark leaves.

Richard turned and they plunged into the wild grass and strange bushes, following the stream. By the stream the mimosa was all gold, great gold bushes full of spring fire rising over your head, and the scent of the Australian spring, and the most ethereal of all golden bloom, the plumy, many-balled wattle, and the utter loneliness, the manlessness, the untouched blue sky overhead, the gaunt, lightless gum-trees rearing a little way off, and sound of strange birds, vivid ones of strange, brilliant birds that flit round. Save for that, and for some weird frog-like sound, indescribable, the age-unbroken silence of the Australian bush.

But it is wonderful, out of the sombreness of gum-trees, that seems the same, hoary for ever, and that are said to begin to wither from the centre the moment they are mature—out of the hollow bush of gum-trees and silent heaths, all at once, in spring, the most delicate feathery yellow of plumes and plumes and plumes and trees and bushes of wattle, as if angels had flown right down out of the softest gold regions of heaven to settle here, in the Australian bush. And the perfume in all the air that might be heaven, and the unutterable stillness, save for strange bright birds and flocks of parrots, and the motionlessness, save for a´stream and butterflies and some small brown bees. Yet a stillness, and a manlessness, and an elation, the bush flowering at the gates of heaven.

D. H. LAWRENCE (1885–1930)
Kangaroo

BOOMERANG

Behold! Wood into bird and bird to wood again.
A brown-winged bird from the hand of a brown man.

Elbow of wood from flexed elbow of bone
to a swift hawk has amazingly grown

that mounts into the sky, sun in its wings,
up, up, over the far tree fluttering

where it turns as if seized with doubt in the air.
Looks back down to the man carved there

and, afraid of the gift of sudden blood,
beats back to his hand and melts once more to wood.

W. HART-SMITH (1911–   )
Poems of Discovery

96

FALCON AND BUDGERIGARS

In Boori Paddock, as over the whole of Western Queensland, the winds whistled from the south-east as they settled down early in May for their winter spell. . . .

A green blanket of birds hurtled through the air. They were a tight-packed mass, several layers deep, over an acre in area. Those budgerigars maintained an incessant chatter as they sliced through the air; they called from flank to flank as the mob swept along; that Babel was an indistinguishable clamour of sounds. Their speed as a mob may have been fifty miles an hour; it might have been more than that.

A black falcon sailed into view high above the mob of parrots. It poised, tilted, gauged its angles and deviations, and dived in a hissing streak straight at the near-centre of the mob.

From a human point of view it was impossible to think any single warning note could have sounded above the clatter and chatter of the mob as they raced through the air. It would be ridiculous to assume all the units of the flock looked up and saw the hawk at the same flash of a second. Perhaps—and it may be accepted for want of a better explanation—a master mind governed them: those tens of thousands of feathered mites carried out intricate manoeuvres as they spun in the air: they swooped as one bird; they spun in a giddy circle; they flashed opalescent streaks of red, green and gold, as the sun slanted from their brilliant bodies.

Their midget wings churned as they bit in hissing strokes; they left a wake of bubbled air behind them; they shot like feathered bullets as they split from the mob; in response to some mental dictator which directed them they came together again in one communal flock as they sped over the ridge of the downs not fifty feet above the ground.

The falcon rose in a grand sweep. It bent its head under its body; it plucked a wing from the victim it had trussed in its claws; it beat heavily with its wings as it struck a line for a distant tree where, perhaps, its young waited their food.

HENRY G. LAMOND (1885–1969)
Big Red

THE CALL OF THE WILD DOG

With mid-evening and the rising of the moon above the tree-tops the dingo bitch was at one with herself, and rose and glided off through the dark. She trotted on soundless paws through the aloof and tranquil bush. Her passage among the leafy places was wholly secret and she was discernible by little more than her flitting shadow as she crossed moonlit ground.

She was making along the foot of the range, through the timber edging the grasslands of the valley. From time to time—at a distance of a mile or so—she paused and sat with nose pointed to the moon and gave voice to herself. Her deep cry resounded distinctly through the still night, rebounding in the dark gullies, floating eerily across the valley. It was the voice of the untamed dog, and might have come echoing out of ages long past; a long-drawn yodelling howl that rose and fell and seemed to double upon itself, so that in places it might have been that one or two ghostly companions had come to join in her plaint. It had notes of mournfulness and dark mirth, of drollery and love and hate and longing, of the joy and the sorrow of life and of the will to live, notes of ribaldry and despair, and died away in a low sobbing in which the ghostly voices seemed to join.

To hear it at close quarters would have been to feel the skin turn cold, for there was a quality in it not of the earth and the rocks and the trees, but of a prescience that might have haunted the first stirrings of sentient life. When it ended, the trees and the sky seemed more aloof and tranquil than ever, and the silence deeper than before.

After each call she remained quiet a while, her ears pricked at the night, waiting for some answering voice; and when she heard nothing she resumed her way. Her quest might have been long—even unavailing, unless it were taken up again and again—for dingoes mate for life.

FRANK DALBY DAVISON (1893–1970)
Dusty

KANGAROO

Delicate mother Kangaroo
Sitting up there rabbit-wise, but huge, plumb-weighted,
And lifting her beautiful slender face, oh! so much more gently and finely
  lined than a rabbit's, or than a hare's,
Lifting her face to nibble at a round white peppermint drop, which she
  loves, sensitive mother Kangaroo.

Her sensitive, long, pure-bred face.
Her full antipodal eyes, so dark,
So big and quiet and remote, having watched so many empty dawns in
    silent Australia.

Her little loose hands, and drooping Victorian shoulders,
And then her great weight below the waist, her vast pale belly
With a thin young yellow little paw hanging out, and straggle of a long thin
    ear, like ribbon,
Like a funny trimming to the middle of her belly, thin little dangle of an
    immature paw, and one thin ear.

Her belly, her big haunches
And, in addition, the great muscular python-stretch of her tail

There, she shan't have any more peppermint drops.
So she wistfully, sensitively sniffs the air, and then turns,
    goes off in slow sad leaps

On the long flat skis of her legs,
Steered and propelled by that steel-strong snake of a tail.
Stops again, half turns, inquisitive to look back.
While something stirs quickly in her belly, and a lean little face comes out,
    as from a window,

Peaked and a bit dismayed,
Only to disappear again quickly away from the sight of the world,
    to snuggle down in the warmth,
Leaving the trail of a different paw hanging out.

Still she watches with eternal, cocked wistfulness!
How full her eyes are, like the full, fathomless, shining eyes of an
    Australian black-boy
Who has been lost so many centuries on the margins of existence!

She watches with insatiable wistfulness.
Untold centuries of watching for something to come,
For a new signal from life, in that silent lost land of the South.

D. H. LAWRENCE (1885–1930)

QUEENSLAND LYRE-BIRD

The lyre-bird is renowned not only for its unusual tail feathers but as a wonderful mimic of other bird songs or forest sounds.

When the repertory has been completed, the performer signs it with the 'natural' call of his species, a penetrating and ringing but very sweet whistle. The lyre-bird's hallmark is quite unmistakable and at once brings to mind an exuberant errand boy putting his fingers to his mouth and emitting the shrill clear whistle which only errand boys seem able to blow. It is a sound which could only come from the resonant throat of a large bird.

Having thus written 'finis' to his act, the lyre-bird immediately starts an encore; and so far as I can discover, he is quite happy to repeat himself for fourteen hours out of the twenty-four.

The various imitations have to be acquired, one presumes. I once had the luck to hear an unseen performer practising the call of the stockwhip bird. Now this is such an incredible noise that even the vocal cords of a lyre-bird require some drilling to get round it. This one started off with an attempt that was definitely poor, a mere clumsy caricature of the long clear whistle and the echoing crack. (He got the whistle easily enough; it was the crack that beat him.) There followed an obviously dissatisfied silence. Then he tried again. This time it was better. Again a thoughtful silence and again a new attempt. Now he had succeeded in capturing some of the mechanical venom which marks the stockwhip's crack. He repeated his attempt some dozen times, each essay being quite noticeably more nearly perfect than the one before. At last he was satisfied. The miracle had been achieved: it would have taken an expert to spot the fake. He signified his pleasure (it was his only way of throwing his hat in the air) by letting rip the lyre-bird larrikin whistle as loudly as his well-trained lungs could blow it. It was nothing less than a wild proud paean of triumph, and I somehow felt disappointed in the absence of applause from the forest shadows. I know I instinctively raised my hands to clap.

FRANCIS RATCLIFFE (1904–   )
Flying Fox and Drifting Sand

100

CEDAR CUTTING IN THE 1820s AND 1830s

... the fall of timber that *The Liar* (it is quite a common and inoffensive abbreviation, dear reader, among ourselves) showed us, turned out a capital one. Numbers of the trees were sixty feet in the barrel without a limb, and so thick that as they lay on the hill side after they were down, I could barely lay my hand on the top of them at ten and fifteen feet from the butt. They were very generally sound, and many of them as round as stone pillars, and lay for the most part on the hill sides, so that rolling them to the pit was effected by merely slackening chocks away from them in front, instead of heaving them along by handspikes and levers as is done on level ground; though, be it observed, letting logs down hill in this way is much the most dangerous work; lastly, they lay so grouped that numbers of logs came to the same pit. There was one drawback, however, which to civilised ears may seem a serious one; we had to make most of the pits in creeks, and if it came on to rain ever so little, the brush ground already saturated turned off the whole of the falling water into the creeks; thus my mate often had to work up to his knees in water for several days together. We kept to one hut all the time, having fixed ourselves deep down the descent of one of the hill points in a sort of basin, where five creeks met, so as to be near the water and the work. It was a lonely place, where you heard nothing but the perpetual plashing of the creeks, and once or twice a day the thunder of a falling tree, or sometimes in the still warm noon the startling note of the coachman-bird, or the no less wonderful mimicry of the mocking-bird imitating the shrill grating of our files in sharpening the saw so exactly, that we often could not believe but that some other pair had come and set in close to us. Countless, and motionless, and gigantic stood the forest army, up and down all the hill sides around us; in strong contrast to this, stood the great red piles of plank, squared with mathematical exactness, which spoke of *man and labour.* How simple the lesson that contrast read, and yet how grave! This toil-bearer must have a motive; he must want something that he has not; he must be unhappy.

In this wilderness we passed more than twelve months, and before this time my mate too had become a great reader; so between the work, and the obstacles to be overcome in getting the plank dragged out of such a hole (which had to be done) by spare-chaining it along the ground, a plank at a time), and the books, we got through the twelve months pretty well.

ALEXANDER HARRIS (1805–1874)
Settlers and Convicts

PIONEER PANNIKINS

One day in the summer of 1847, Mr Murray and the Author were returning homewards from Goulburn, and at the old crossing place over the Wollondilly, at Kenmore, we met the late Francis McArthur, then owner of Norwood. Mr McArthur, as old hands will remember, was of a very genial disposition, and as we had some spirits with us, we asked 'Black Francis', as McArthur was called, to have a 'nip'. But neither of us at the moment could find a pannikin handy. Mr Murray, however, taking the Author's bullock-bell, rinsed it in the river, and, handing it to Mr McArthur, he said, 'We've lost the run of the pannikins; but, never mind, here's the bullock-bell—try a drop out of that'.

'Well', said McArthur, 'that's a better tumbler than the one I had the other day. I was out on the plains with one of my men looking for horses, and we had a bottle of rum with us, but no tumbler or pannikin. But there was a blackfellow's skull handy—so we drank out of that. Here's luck', he said, 'and I hope when you want a drink, if you cannot find a blackfellow's skull, you'll never go short of a bullock-bell'.

CHARLES MacALISTER (1830–1908)
Old Pioneering Days in the Sunny South

BUSH-FIRE

At night
The winds were up, and then with fourfold speed,
A harsh gigantic growth of smoke and fire
Would roar along the bottoms, in the wake
Of fainting flocks of parrots, wallaroos,
And 'wildered wild things, scattering right and left
For safety vague, throughout the general gloom.

Anon, the nearer hill-side growing trees
Would take the surges; thus, from bough to bough,
Was borne the flaming terror! Bole and spire,
Rank after rank, now pillared, ringed, and rolled
In blinding blaze, stood out against the dead
Down-smothered dark, for fifty leagues away.

HENRY KENDALL (1839–1882)

THE BUSHMAN

The one powerful and unique national type yet produced in Australia is, I have asserted, that of the Bushman.

The smaller resident or squatter or manager almost always shows signs of him: sometimes is merely a slightly refined or outwardly polished form of him.

The selector comes nearer to him still, so near as often to seem almost identic, yet a fine but unmistakable shade of difference severs him from the true Bushman, the Bushman pure and simple, the man of the nation.

It is, then, in the ranks of the shearers, boundary riders, and general station hands, that the perfected sample must be sought, and it is the rapid thoroughness of the new social system . . . which has chiefly 'differentiated' him already into this new species.

FRANCIS ADAMS (1862–1893)
The Australians

CLEARING THE BUSH

The first act in clearing was to go through the bush and ringbark the larger trees—anything over a foot in diameter; trees so treated were said to be 'rung'. The following year all the smaller trees, saplings and undergrowth were cut down with an axe and billhook. This was called 'scrubbing'; and in the bush 'scrubbing' has nothing to do with brushes and floors. Scrub was felled outwards and lay in a tangled mass behind the axeman as he advanced. Sometimes the undergrowth was linked together by vines and creepers—mainly the tough far-reaching ropes of the Macquarie Vine, which, incidentally bears sweet edible little grapes. Scrub thus tied would be partly cut in the front to weaken it and a small tree felled across it to bring down the whole lot together. On small holdings twenty or thirty acres of virgin forest would usually be scrubbed each year.

Scrubbing was done in late winter or early spring so that by late summer the leaves were like tinder and the smaller branches dry enough to burn readily. Then, when a favourable day came, a match was put to it, and the whole lot went up in a huge bonfire. The choice of the day was important. Obviously the scrub must not be wet after rain; but neither must the weather be too windy, nor conditions too dry, lest the fire spread where it was not wanted, endangering neighbouring properties or spoiling the undergrowth for the next year's burning.

If the burn was good there was often no more left on the ground than the larger ends of the saplings, the bigger trees that had already fallen and the standing stumps. The next job of the settlers was 'picking up', the pieces not consumed by the fire being carried into heaps or piled against a fallen tree, and there burnt. Then grass and clover seed was broadcast over the loose ashes of the burn, and the settler prayed and hoped for rain. If there was a good strike of seed, a lush growth of pasture was assured for next year. Apart from any natural fertility of the soil, the ashes and the accumulated humus of the centuries ensured such a stimulus that no artificial manure was ever necessary in those first sowings.

If, however, the settler wanted to grow a crop of roots or cereals, the burnt ground was left till the spring, when the hoe was put to work and the seeds chipped in, again without artificial manure. This time the smaller stumps would be grubbed and the smaller logs put into heaps, or rolled off the patch to form a fence, which was completed with more saplings and spars from the nearby bush. This might only be a 'dog-leg' fence but if more permanence was required a 'chock and log' fence was built. For stock-yards and permanent paddocks, such fences were afterwards replaced by post and rail fencing or palings. Wire fences came in much later—in the 1900s.

JOHN ROWLAND SKEMP (1900–c.1970)
Memories of Myrtle Bank

FARRER'S WORK IN WHEAT-BREEDING

By his devoted scientific experiments in wheat-breeding William James Farrer created varieties of wheat that were used throughout the world and that transformed the Australian wheat industry. Here he himself describes some of the work he carried out at Lambrigg Station from 1886 to his death in 1906.

These trials and errors and disappointments were not lost on Farrer. He was already critical of his efforts and results: now he tightened up, with the co-operation of Guthrie and his assistant, every aspect of his work. On 19 November 1893, in the middle of his hybridisation season, he tells Lowrie that:

'I have been working like the very devil this year . . . I have now made 275 distinct crosses, and whereas last year I made 260 crosses, I only operated on one side of an ear. This year I have mostly operated on both sides. In order to do my work more effectively this year, when I planted the seed I entered in my field book a description of the grain—the size, colour, length, plumpness, depth of crease, etc. I also sent to a milling expert samples of about 180 sorts that I thought of using for parents, to be submitted to the chewing test. . . .'

In a subsequent passage headed Sunday evening, Farrer related how:

'I hurried down to the farm (Lambrigg) this morning in order to cross King's Jubilee on Improved Fife, if I could find a head of the former in flower, but I could get no satisfactory pollen. I did, however, find some ears of King's Jubilee x Indian G (Y) in flower and I used the pollen on Improved Fife. I think it will do just as well, if not better, for I do not like King's Jubilee, so rust-liable is it here.'

Although this has no special bearing on the matter, being merely the story of a multitude of such experiments, yet it does serve to indicate Farrer's growing feeling for the Fife-Indian-Purple Straw combination. It was this feeling, as we know now, that became such a vital force in the ultimate production of the most successful wheats that Farrer was to make—the wheats, indeed, that re-created an industry.

. . . Indeed, it was in 1894 that Federation, perhaps the greatest of his wheats, had its original beginning—a Fife-Indian variety crossed with Purple Straw.

ARCHER RUSSELL (1881–1960)
William James Farrer

THE FRUIT CANNERY

There was in the town and on all the farms around a feeling that the cannery 'belonged' to Boswell. The townspeople loved it, they were proud of it, they took visitors to see it; and the cannery basked in this affection and was reasonably kind to the eight hundred women who assembled beneath its great roof, with its three hundred men, to add their quota to the two-hundred-and-fifty thousand cans of fruit that issued daily from its maw. The very children in the town knew that the cannery had turned out nine-and-a-half million cans last season; and could talk about 'local ripe' and 'export ripe' and 'local green' and 'export green'; just as the children of a wheat farmer can tell you the rainfall in inches and points for the district.

The cannery hissed and steamed with the great, green vats, like ten tame railway engines rearing up to the glass roof, where lattice shutters screened off the worst of the heat. Though, as the Stray and her mates found, with a temperature of over a hundred outside, it was much more inside, and the provision of beds for those who fainted was a desperate necessity. The cannery had to work when the fruit was ripe: and this was at the hottest time of the year, the apricots just before Christmas, then, after a break of three weeks, the peaches and nectarines.

More and more the place seemed like Hell, as the weeks wore on, and the temperature rose; nerves were frayed; tempers developed blisters of hate. A simmering haze rose up over sorters, packers, canners, pitters, speckers on the belt cutting out specks from the fruit; they worked with a maniac energy, ready to drop from exhaustion, too busy to talk. As soon as the whistle went, the women would run to their corners and begin work as though their lives depended on it. Soon the sweat would be pouring off them. The barrow-men on the pitting-floor rushed up with fruit; the men pulling down boxes, bringing cans and taking them away were cursed or bribed by the women to work faster. Minor grievances developed, as a woman felt that her neighbour was given cans and she neglected; complaints and squabbles arose over someone taking a place that was close to the supply but belonging to another woman.

The closers soldering down can-lids, the men taking off fruit as it came through the cooker, the tappers out, the stackers—they all felt that they were being simmered in this cannery, as though it were a great, red vat; their very life-blood running away and trickling from them in a syrupy sweat.

KYLIE TENNANT (1912–   )
The Battlers

CLICK GO THE SHEARS

Down by the pen the old shearer stands,
Grasping the shears in his thin bony hands,
Fixed is his gaze on a bare-bellied joe,
If he gets another one, oh Lord, won't he blow!

106

Chorus
Click go the shears, boys, Click! Click! Click!
Wide is his blow, and his hands move quick.
The ringer looks around and is beaten by a blow,
And curses the old codger with the bare-bellied joe.

In the middle of the floor in his cane bottom chair
Sits the boss of the board with his eyes everywhere.
Notes well each fleece as it comes to the screen,
Paying strict attention that it's taken off clean.

The tar boy is there, waiting in demand,
With his blacken'd tar pot and his tarry hands.
See one old sheep with a cut upon its back,
Here's what he's waiting for, it's 'Tar here, Jack!'

Shearing is all over and we've all got our cheques,
So it's roll up your swags, boys, we're off to the next,
The first pub we come to we'll all have a spree,
And everyone who comes along, it's come and drink with me.

Down by the bar the old shearer stands,
Grasping his glass in his thin bony hands,
Fixed is his gaze on a green painted keg,
Glory, he'll get down on it, ere he stirs a leg.

Old Bush Song

WINDY GAP

As I was going through Windy Gap
A hawk and a cloud hung over the map.

The land lay bare and the wind blew loud
And the hawk cried out from the heart of the cloud,

'Before I fold my wings to sleep
I'll pick the bones of your travelling sheep,

For the leaves blow black and the wintry sun
Shows the tree's white skeleton'.

A magpie sat in the tree's high top
Singing a song on Windy Gap

That streamed far down to the plain below
Like a shaft of light from a high window.

From the bending tree he sang aloud,
And the sun shone out of the heart of the cloud

And it seemed to me as we travelled through
That my sheep were the notes that trumpet blew.

And so I sing this song of praise
For travelling sheep and blowing days.

DAVID CAMPBELL (1915–1979)

THE CHAMPION BULLOCK-DRIVER

The boss jumped down off the fence.

'Look here', he said, 'It's no good you telling me you can drive a team of bullocks if you can't'.

And pointing to a little graveyard he added:

'Do you see that little cemetery over there?'

The young man pulled his hat down over his eye, looked across, and said: 'Yes'.

'Well', continued the boss, 'there are sixteen bullock-drivers lying there. They came here to drive this team of mine'.

I watched the young man's face when the boss said that to see if he would flinch: but a little smile broke away from the corner of his mouth, curled around his cheek and disappeared in his earhole, and as the effect died away he said:

'They won't put me there.'

'I don't know so much about that', said the boss.

'I'll give you a trial', the young man suggested.

'It would take too long to muster the bullocks', said the boss. 'But take that bullock-whip there'—it was standing near the big ironbark—'and, say, for instance, eight panels of that fence are sixteen bullocks, show me how you would start up the team'.

'Right', said the young man.

Walking over he picked up the big bullock-whip and very carefully examined it to see how it was fastened to the handle. Then he ran his hand down along the whip, examining it as though he were searching for a broken link in a chain. Then he looked closely to see how the fall was fastened to the whip. After that he stood back and swung it around and gave a cheer.

First he threw the whip up to the leaders, and then threw it back to the polers. He stepped in as though to dig the near-side pin-bullock under the arm with the handle of the whip, then stepped back and swung the big bullock-whip around. He kept on talking, and the whip kept on cracking, until a little flame ran right along the top of the fence. And he kept on talking and the whip kept on cracking until the phantom forms of sixteen bullocks appeared along the fence—blues, blacks and brindles. And he kept on talking and the whip kept on cracking till the phantom forms of sixteen bullock-drivers appeared on the scene. And they kept on talking and their whips kept on cracking till the fence started to walk on, and pulled the big ironbark-tree down.

'That will do', said the boss.

'Not a bit of it', said the young man, 'Where's your woodheap?'

We all pointed to the woodheap near the old bark kitchen.

And they kept on talking and their whips kept on cracking till they made the fence pull the tree right up to the woodheap.

We were all sitting round on the limbs of the tree, and the young man was talking to the boss, and we felt sure he would get the job, when the boss called out:

'Get the fencing-gear, lads, and put that fence up again.'

'Excuse me for interrupting, boss', said the young man, 'but would you like to see how I back a team of bullocks?'

'Yes, I would', said the boss.

So the young man walked over and picked up the big bullock-whip again. He swung it around and called out:

'Now then, boys, all together!'

110

And the phantom forms of the sixteen bullock-drivers appeared on the scene again; and they kept on talking and their whips kept on cracking, till every post and rail burst out into flame, and when the flame cleared away each post and rail backed into its place, and the phantom forms of the sixteen bullock-drivers saluted the young man, then bowed and backed, and bowed and backed right into their graves, recognising him as the champion bullock-driver.

LANCE SKUTHORPE (1871–1958)

FIVE MILES FROM GUNDAGAI

This legend is celebrated by a statue of a dog seated on a tucker-box beside the road to the town of Gundagai, New South Wales.

As I was coming down Conroy's Gap
  I heard a maiden cry,
There goes Bill the Bullocky,
  He's bound for Gundagai.
A better poor old _____
  Never cracked an honest crust:
A tougher poor old _____
  Never drug a whip through dust.

His team got bogged at the Five-Mile Creek,
  Bill lashed and swore and cried:
'If Nobby don't get me out of this,
  I'll tattoo his _____ hide'.

But Nobby strained and broke the yoke
  And poked out the leader's eye,
Then the dog sat on the tucker-box
  Five miles from Gundagai.

Old Bush Song

BULLOCKY

Beside his heavy-shouldered team,
thirsty with drought and chilled with rain,
he weathered all the striding years
till they ran widdershins in his brain:

Till the long solitary tracks
etched deeper with each lurching load
were populous before his eyes,
and fiends and angels used his road.

All the long straining journey grew
a mad apocalyptic dream,
and he old Moses, and the slaves
his suffering and stubborn team.

Then in his evening camp beneath
the half-light pillars of the trees
he filled the steepled cone of night
with shouted prayers and prophecies

While past the camp-fire's crimson ring
the star-struck darkness cupped him round,
and centuries of cattlebells
rang with their sweet uneasy sound.

Grass is across the waggon-tracks,
and plough strikes bone beneath the grass,
and vineyards cover all the slopes
where the dead teams were used to pass.

O vine, grow close upon that bone
and hold it with your rooted hand.
The prophet Moses feeds the grape,
and fruitful is the Promised Land.

JUDITH WRIGHT (1915–   )

PEOPLE, GREAT AND SMALL

QUEENSLAND ABORIGINES

Coontajanderrah, his skin glistening with oil of goanna fat, was a statue burnished by the strong sunlight. He stood motionless upon a boulder of granite which out-cropped from a spur of the Manumbar Range.

. . . For a hundred thousand years Coontajanderrah's race had roamed the rugged country, which, from the Bunya Range in the west, ran to the south and to the east to that point where the Great Divide sent a mighty rampart off towards the sea. A hunting people, the men of the Wakka were as keen in sight as the wedge-tailed eagle, the mightiest of his kind; as the subtle dingo in scent and endurance; as the native cat in bushcraft and the swift pounce of attack. All the Wakka country was replete with food. In the forests were the wallabies and wombats, the possums, bandicoots and goannas. Spears and fishtraps never failed the blacks in the rivers and creeks. River flats and the timber country yielded them the large grey kangaroo and the swift-running but flightless emu. No billabong, but in its cool shallows the gins could find the succulent water-lily roots. Fat grubs of delicate flavour lived in the holes of the swamp oaks. Scarcely a blue gum hollow branch which did not hold the delicious honeycomb of the tiny native bees. Once upon a time—yet it was less than a decade ago—there had been other tribes as numerous as the Wakkas that came from distant territories to feast at the season of the bonyi. Their numbers were fewer now at each successive season. Yet until the great calamity of the white man these tribes, with the merest variations in dialect, ceremonial and craftsman-fashioning, had survived, unchanging and unchanged, from the stone age of their remote ancestry.

The Wakkas did not till the soil, for growing about them was the bread-grass which the gins crushed in stone mills. They built no enduring homes, for what need have hunters of homes when their range is the far horizon. Their food was to be had for the getting, running over forest floor, leaping on meadow flats, rustling warily in the branches overhead, swirling in the creeks, growing, burrowing or boring in the thick vine scrubs. As their forefathers had lived, they too lived, their shelters built of bark, casual, sufficient, before they wandered elsewhere. So hunting and feasting, initiating into tribal maturity their youths, observing their strict ceremony and law, keeping inviolate the secrets of their primitive freemasonry, each generation of Wakkas completed its span upon the earth and went in the dusk of its passing back to the dawn men of their ancestry, awaiting in the hunting ground beyond the skies.

ROY CONNOLLY (1896–1966)
Southern Saga

ADAM LINDSAY GORDON

Gordon's character is best learned by considering him not as an Australian, not as an Englishman, but as a Scottish Highlander; that is to say, as a Celt, whatever the circumstantial difference. Born without full physical health and steady balance of mind, his Celtic qualities and defects seemed excessive. Typically he was a chieftain of Celts: he had power of leadership and everywhere strove to lead. In the current of existence he was prevented from realising his ideal of himself; living thwarted, he died baffled. His poetry shows his rare passages of success, his abiding sense of failure.

. . . His poetry is intellectually obvious. Often crossed with a personal warp, commonplace wisdom is its typical woof. Everybody's wisdom makes Everyman's prophet. The world and the Bush hold many defeated people; Gordon preserves the reflective sorrow of his own defeat in Everyman's verses. . . . Of free utterance, large harmony, he has little; but for melody we can say that he became a good pupil of Swinburne.

Then we reckon with Gordon himself, with his dash and his pluck, his sincerity, simplicity, his pride and modesty, his manliness and gentle-manliness, his sympathy with nature. These, past the grave, have built his memorial in literature. He wrote, as he rode, 'straight'. Mind and body he was a steeplechaser, reaching through obstacles the lofty image aspiring, the white post seen afar.

His small harvest of verses was gathered in three years preceding his death. Fitly enough, he wrote little during his period of Australian prosperity. Instead of rhyming, he hunts; instead of brooding, he enters Parliament. Only when ill fortune clouds his blue sky does he take his black pen. As his troubles increase, so his verses; and just when his talent seems developing to a rich fruitage he feels himself driven to suicide.

In the end we love him for transfusing life: his poetry is a man's heart beating.

A. G. STEPHENS (1865–1933)
Preface to Gordon's Poems

THE SICK STOCKRIDER

'Twas merry in the glowing morn, among the gleaming grass,
To wander as we've wandered many a mile,
And blow the cool tobacco cloud, and watch the white wreaths pass,
Sitting loosely in the saddle all the while.

'Twas merry 'mid the blackwoods, when we spied the station roofs,
To wheel the wild scrub cattle at the yard,
With a running fire of stockwhips and a fiery run of hoofs;
Oh! the hardest day was never then too hard!

Ay! we had a glorious gallop after 'Starlight' and his gang,
When they bolted from Sylvester's on the flat;
How the sun-dried reed-beds crackled, how the flint-strewn ranges rang,
To the strokes of 'Mountaineer' and 'Acrobat'.

Hard behind them in the timber, harder still across the heath,
Close beside them through the tea-tree scrub we dash'd;
And the golden-tinted fern leaves, how they rustled underneath;
And the honeysuckle osiers how they crash'd!

We led the hunt throughout, Ned, on the chestnut and the grey,
And the troopers were three hundred yards behind,
While we emptied our six-shooters on the bushrangers at bay
In the creek with stunted box-trees for a blind!

There you grappled with the leader, man to man, and horse to horse,
And you roll'd together when the chestnut rear'd;
He blazed away and missed you in that shallow watercourse—
A narrow shave—his powder singed your beard!

ADAM LINDSAY GORDON (1833–1870)

THE BUSHRANGERS

The coach was to pass half-an-hour after midnight. An awful long time to wait, it seemed. We finished the bottle of brandy, I know. I thought they would never come, when all of a sudden we saw the lamp.

Up the hill they came slow enough. About half-way up they stopped, and most of the passengers got out and walked up after her. As they came closer to us we could hear them laughing and talking and skylarking, like a lot of boys. They didn't think who was listening. 'You won't be so jolly in a minute or two', I thinks to myself.

They were near the top when Starlight sings out, 'Stand! Bail up!' and the three of us, all masked, showed ourselves. You never saw a man look so scared as the passenger on the box-seat, a stout, jolly commercial, who'd been giving the coachman Havana cigars, and yarning and nipping with him at every house they passed. Bill Webster, the driver, pulls up all standing when he sees what was in Starlight's hand, and holds the reins so loose for a minute I thought they'd drop out of his hands. I went up to the coach. There was no one inside—only an old woman and a young one. They seemed struck all of a heap, and couldn't hardly speak for fright.

The best of the joke was that the passengers started running up full split to warm themselves, and came bump against the coach before they found out what was up. One of them had just opened out for a bit of blowing. 'Billy, old man' he says, 'I'll report you to the Company if you crawl along this way', when he catches sight of me and Starlight, standing still and silent, with our revolvers pointing his way. By George! I could hardly help laughing. His jaw dropped, and he couldn't get a word out. His throat seemed quite dry.

'Now, gentlemen', says Starlight, quite cool and cheerful-like, 'you understand her Majesty's mail is stuck up, to use a vulgar expression, and there's no resisting. I must ask you to stand in a row there by the fence, and hand out all the loose cash, watches, or rings you may have about you. Don't move; don't, I say, sir, or I must fire'. (This was to a fidgety, nervous man who couldn't keep quiet.) 'Now, Number One, fetch down the mail bags; Number Two, close up here.'

Here Jim walked up, revolver in hand, and Starlight begins at the first man, very stern—

'Hand out your cash; keep back nothing, if you value your life.'

ROLF BOLDREWOOD (T. A. BROWNE) (1826–1915)
Robbery Under Arms

118

MARCUS CLARKE

My father's most irresponsible friend, Marcus Andrew Hislop Clarke, was a kind of hop-o'-my-thumb, or adult fairy. A little man, he could magically lose himself whenever he wished, then reappear like a sparkle of light, passing between shadow and shine, on a holiday morning. His companions loved him, and he deserved their love. He was generous; he was gay; he had seen the world; and the world was his oyster—and the world knew it.

George, who admired him, often pointed out to me a green metal lion half-way up the steps leading to the Melbourne Public Library. It was into the mouth of this lion that Marcus used to commit his unfinished cigar, before being manacled to the desk at his office. The lion, smoking the cigar, became a signal to his friends that Marcus was within . . .

Marcus could never be found when he was wanted. Sir Ferdinand Jakob Heinrich von Mueller once said that he might go to the Botanic Gardens and be certain of seeing there an example of the native fuschia, tied to a stake from Monday to Monday—but that Clarke was no native fuschia; and that he carried his household with him wherever he went. At the beginning of the week he might be in Coburg; at the middle of it in Essendon; and, at the end of it, in Brighton—or Moonee Ponds.

HUGH McCRAE (1876–1958)
My Father and My Father's Friends

THE RAMBLE-EER

The earth rolls on through empty space, its journey's never done,
It's entered for a starry race throughout the Kingdom Come.
And, as I am a bit of earth, I follow it because—
And I prove I am a rolling stone and never gather moss.

Chorus
For I am a ramble-eer, a rollicking ramble-eer,
I'm a roving rake of poverty and son of a gun for beer.

I've done a bit of fossicking for tucker and for gold;
I've been a menial rouseabout and a rollicking shearer bold,
I've 'shanked' across the Old Man Plain, after busting up a cheque,
And 'whipped the cat' once more again, though I haven't met it yet.

119

I've done a bit of droving of cattle and of sheep.
And I've done a bit of moving with 'Matilda' for a mate;
Of fencing I have done my share, wool-scouring on the green;
Axeman, navvy—Old Nick can bear me out in what I haven't been.

I've worked the treadmill thresher, the scythe and reaping-hook,
Been wood-and-water fetcher for Mary Jane the cook;
I've done a few 'cronk' things too, when I have struck a town,
There's few things I wouldn't do—but I never did lambing-down.

Old Bush Song

A CHRISTIAN SQUATTER

Of course, we use the term 'squatter' indifferently to denote a station-owner, a managing partner, or a salaried manager. Lacking generations of development, there is no typical squatter. Or, if you like, there are a thousand types. Hungry M'Intyre is one type; Smythe—petty, genteel, and parsimonious—is another; patriarchal Royce is another; Montgomery—kind, yet haughty and imperious—is another; Stewart is another. My diary might, just as likely as not, have compelled me to introduce, instead of these, a few of the remaining nine-hundred and ninety-five types—any type conceivable, in fact, except the slender-witted, virgin-souled, over-grown schoolboys who filled Henry Kingsley's exceedingly trashy and misleading novel[1] with their insufferable twaddle . . .

Stewart, it must be admitted, was no gentleman. Starting with a generous handicap, as the younger son of a wealthy and aristocratic Scottish laird, he had, during a Colonial race of forty years, daily committed himself by actions which shut him out from the fine old title. He was in the gall of altruism, and in the bond of democracy. Amiable demeanour, unmeasured magnanimity, and spotless integrity, could never carry off the unpardonable sin in which this lost sheep-owner wallowed—the taint, namely, of isocratic principle. When a member of the classes takes to his bosom that unclean thing, in its naked reality, he thereby forfeits the title of 'gentleman', and becomes a mere man. For there is no such thing as a democratic gentleman; the adjective and noun are hyphenated by a drawn sword . . . Taking the

[1] *The Recollections of Geoffrey Hamlyn.*

120

shifty, insidious title in its go-to-meeting sense, every Christian is *prima facie* a gentleman; taking it in its every-day sense, no 'gentleman' can be a Christian; for Christianity postulates initial equality, and recognises no gradation except in usefulness.

So Stewart was never, even by inadvertence, spoken of as a gentleman— always as a Christian. Three-score years of wise choice in the perpetually-recurring alternatives of life, had made the Golden Rule his spontaneous impulse; and now, though according to the shapen-in-iniquity theory, he must have had faults, no one in Riverina, below the degree of squatter, had proved sharp enough to detect them. It was considered bad form to express approval of anything he did. 'Stewart! Oh, he's a (adj.) Christian!' That was all. He had reached a certain standard, and was expected to live up to it. Such is life.

TOM COLLINS (JOSEPH FURPHY) (1843–1912)
Such is Life

THE DEATH OF RICHARD MAHONY

For three days he lay in coma. On the third, the doctor gave it as his opinion that he would not outlive the night.

Beside the low trestle-bed in which, for greater convenience, they had laid him, and on which his motionless body formed a long, straight hummock under the blankets, Mary sat and looked her last on the familiar face, now so soon to be hidden from her . . .

How long she sat thus she did not know: she had lost count of time. But, of a sudden, something . . . a something felt not heard, and felt only by a quickening of her pulses . . . made her catch her breath, pause in her crying, strain her ears, look up. And as she did so her heart gave a great bound, then seemed to leave off beating. *He had come back.* His lids were raised, his eyes half open. And in the breathless silence that followed, when each tick of the little clock on the chest of drawers was separately audible, she saw his lips, too, move. He was trying to speak. She bent over him, hardly daring to breathe, and caught, or thought she caught the words: 'Not grieve . . . for me. I'm going . . . into Eternity'.

Whether they were actually meant for her, or whether a mere instinctive response to the sound of her weeping, she could not tell. But dropping on her knees by the bedside, she took his half-cold hand in her warm, live one, and kissed and fondled it. And his lids, which had fallen to again, made one last supreme effort to rise, and this time there was no mistaking the whisper that came over his lips.

'Dear wife!'

He was gone again, even as he said it, but it was enough . . . more than enough! Laying her head down beside his, she pressed her face against the linen of the pillow, paying back to this inanimate object the burning thankfulness with which she no longer dared to trouble him. Eternity was something vast, cold, impersonal. But this little phrase, from the long past days of love and comradeship, these homely, familiar words, fell like balsam on her heart. All his love for her, his gratitude to her, was in them: they were her reward, and a full and ample one, for a lifetime of unwearied sacrifice.

Dear wife! . . . dear wife.

He died at dawn, his faint breaths fluttering to rest.

HENRY HANDEL RICHARDSON (MRS E. F. L. ROBERTSON) (1870–1946)
The Fortunes of Richard Mahony

THE MAN FROM SNOWY RIVER

There was movement at the station, for the word had passed around
That the colt from old Regret had got away,
And had joined the wild bush horses—he was worth a thousand pound,
So all the cracks had gathered to the fray.
All the tried and noted riders from the stations near and far
Had mustered at the homestead overnight,
For the bushmen love hard riding where the wild bush horses are,
And the stock-horse snuffs the battle with delight.

There was Harrison, who made his pile when Pardon won the cup,
The old man with his hair as white as snow;
But few could ride beside him when his blood was fairly up—
He would go wherever horse and man could go.
And Clancy of the Overflow came down to lend a hand,
No better horseman ever held the reins;
For never horse could throw him while the saddle-girths would stand—
He learnt to ride while droving on the plains.

And one was there, a stripling on a small and weedy beast;
He was something like a racehorse undersized,
With a touch of Timor pony—three parts thoroughbred at least—
And such as are by mountain horsemen prized.
He was hard and tough and wiry—just the sort that won't say die—
There was courage in his quick impatient tread:
And he bore the badge of gameness in his bright and fiery eye.
And the proud and lofty carriage of his head.

But still so slight and weedy, one would doubt his power to stay,
And the old man said, 'That horse will never do
For a long and tiring gallop—lad, you'd better stop away,
Those hills are far too rough for such as you'.
So he waited, sad and wistful—only Clancy stood his friend—
'I think we ought to let him come', he said;
'I warrant he'll be with us when he's wanted at the end,
For both his horse and he are mountain bred.

'He hails from Snowy River, up by Kosciusko's side,
Where the hills are twice as steep and twice as rough;
Where a horse's hoofs strike firelight from the flint-stones every stride,
The man that holds his own is good enough.
And the Snowy River riders on the mountains make their home,
Where the river runs those giant hills between;
I have seen full many a horseman since I first commenced to roam,
But nowhere yet such horsemen have I seen'.

So he went; they found the horses by the big mimosa clump,
They raced away towards the mountain's brow,
And the old man gave his orders, 'Boys, go at them from the jump,
No use to try for fancy riding now.
And, Clancy, you must wheel them, try and wheel them to the right.
Ride boldly, lad, and never fear the spills,
For never yet was rider that could keep the mob in sight,
If once they gain the shelter of those hills'.

So Clancy rode to wheel them—he was racing on the wing
Where the best and boldest riders take their place,
And he raced his stock-horse past them, and he made the ranges ring
With the stockwhip, as he met them face to face.
Then they halted for a moment, while he swung the dreaded lash,
But they saw their well-loved mountain full in view,
And they charged beneath the stockwhip with a sharp and sudden dash,
And off into the mountain scrub they flew.

Then fast the horsemen followed, where the gorges deep and black
Resounded to the thunder of their tread,
And the stockwhips woke the echoes, and they fiercely answered back
From cliffs and crags that beetled overhead.
And upward, ever upward, the wild horses held their way,
Where mountain ash and kurrajong grew wide;
And the old man muttered fiercely, 'We may bid the mob good-day,
No man can hold them down the other side'.

When they reached the mountain's summit, even Clancy took a pull—
It well might make the boldest hold their breath;
The wild hop scrub grew thickly, and the hidden ground was full
Of wombat holes, and any slip was death.
But the man from Snowy River let the pony have his head,
And he swung his stockwhip round and gave a cheer,
And he raced him down the mountain like a torrent down its bed,
While the others stood and watched in very fear.

He sent the flint-stones flying, but the pony kept his feet,
He cleared the fallen timber in his stride,
And the man from Snowy River never shifted in his seat—
It was grand to see that mountain horseman ride.
Through the stringy-barks and saplings, on the rough and broken ground,
Down the hillside at a racing pace he went;
And he never drew the bridle till he landed safe and sound
At the bottom of that terrible descent.

124

He was right among the horses as they climbed the farther hill,
And the watchers on the mountain, standing mute,
Saw him ply the stockwhip fiercely; he was right among them still,
As he raced across the clearing in pursuit.
Then they lost him for a moment, where two mountain gullies met
In the ranges—but a final glimpse reveals
On a dim and distant hillside the wild horses racing yet,
With the man from Snowy River at their heels.

And he ran them single-handed till their sides were white with foam;
He followed like a bloodhound on their track,
Till they halted, cowed and beaten; then he turned their heads for home,
And alone and unassisted brought them back.
But his hardy mountain pony he could scarcely raise a trot,
He was blood from hip to shoulder from the spur;
But his pluck was still undaunted, and his courage fiery hot,
For never yet was mountain horse a cur.

And down by Kosciusko, where the pine-clad ridges raise
Their torn and rugged battlements on high,
Where the air is clear as crystal, and the white stars fairly blaze
At midnight in the cold and frosty sky,
And where around the Overflow the reed-beds sweep and sway
To the breezes, and the rolling plains are wide,
The Man from Snowy River is a household word to-day,
And the stockmen tell the story of his ride.

A. B. ('BANJO') PATERSON (1864–1941)

THE EXPLORER VOSS

'Ah', smiled the aged, gummy man. 'Voss.'
    He looked at the ground, but presently spoke again.
    'Voss left his mark on the country', he said.
    'How?' asked Miss Trevelyan, cautiously.
    'Well, the trees, of course. He was cutting his initials in the trees. He
was a queer beggar, Voss. The blacks talk about him to this day. He is still

there—that is the honest opinion of many of them—he is there in the country, and always will be.'

'How?' repeated Miss Trevelyan. Her voice was that of a man. She dared anyone.

Judd was feeling his way with his hands.

'Well, you see, if you live and suffer long enough in a place you do not leave it altogether. Your spirit is still there.'

'Like a god, in fact', said Colonel Hebden, but laughed to show his scepticism.

Judd looked up, out of the distance.

'Voss? No. He was never God, though he liked to think that he was. Sometimes, when he forgot, he was a man.'

He hesitated, and fumbled.

'He was more than a man', Judd continued, with the gratified air of one who had found that for which he had been looking. 'He was a Christian, such as I understand it.'

Miss Trevelyan was holding a handkerchief to her lips, as though her life-blood might gush out.

'Not according to my interpretation of the word', the Colonel interrupted, remorselessly, 'not by what I have heard'.

'Poor fellow', sighed old Sanderson, again unhappy. 'He was somewhat twisted. But is dead and gone.'

Now that he was launched, Judd was determined to pursue his wavering way.

'He would wash the sores of the men. He would sit all night with them when they were sick, and clean up their filth with his own hands. I cried, I tell you, after he was dead.'

PATRICK WHITE (1912–   )
Voss

GEORGE HIGINBOTHAM, A DEMOCRATIC JUDGE

These two sides of him, the modest but lively human being and the austere office-holder, were just as marked when he left politics and sat on the Bench. He was rigid about procedure in court, sternly rebuking a witness who stood with his hands in his pockets, and insisted on respect being paid to his high office. And, though he refused a knighthood, he stayed away from a public dinner because the Speaker of the House was to take precedence of the Chief Justice. But, deep within him, was the democrat who lived in hopes of social justice: who revelled, as he confessed to an English visitor, in the growing solidarity of Labour, and believed in its future. When, in 1890, the great maritime strike took place, and the Employers' Union refused the Trades Hall Council's request for a conference, he forsook the traditional aloofness of the Bench and wrote:

'The Chief Justice presents his compliments to the President of the Trades Hall Council, and requests that he will be so good as to place the amount of the enclosed cheque of £50 to the credit of the strike fund. While the United Trades are awaiting compliance with their reasonable request for a conference with the employers, the Chief Justice will continue for the present to forward a weekly contribution of £10 to the same object.'

VANCE PALMER (1885–1959)
National Portraits

MRS YABSLEY

Mrs Yabsley was a widow; for Ada's father, scorning old age, had preferred to die of drink in his prime. The publicans lost a good customer, but his widow found life easier.

'Talk about payin' ter see men swaller knives an' swords', she exclaimed. 'My old man could swaller tables an' chairs faster than I could buy 'em.'

So she opened a laundry, and washed and ironed for the neighbourhood. Cardigan Street was proud of her. Her eyes twinkled in a big, humorous face; her arm was like a leg of mutton; the floors creaked beneath her as she walked. She laughed as a bull roars; her face turned purple; she fought for air; the veins rose like cords on her forehead. She was pointed out to strangers like a public building as she sat on her verandah, gossiping with the neighbours in a voice that shook windows. There was no tongue like hers within a mile. Her sayings were quoted like the newspaper. Draymen laughed at her jokes.

Yet the women took their secret troubles to her. For this unwieldy jester, with the jolly, red face and rough tongue, could touch the heart with a word when she was in the humour. Then she spoke so wisely and kindly that the tears gathered in stubborn eyes, and the poor fools went home comforted. . . .

128

... 'Well', said Mrs Yabsley, reflectively, 'an 'usband is like the weather, or a wart on yer nose. It's no use quarrelling with it. If yer don't like it, yer've got ter lump it. An' if yer believe all yer 'ear, everybody else 'as got a worse.'

LOUIS STONE (1871–1935)
Jonah

THE WOMEN OF THE WEST

They left the vine-wreathed cottage and the mansion on the hill,
The houses in the busy streets where life is never still,
The pleasures of the city, and the friends they cherished best:
For love they faced the wilderness—the Women of the West.

The roar, and rush, and fever of the city died away,
And the old-time joys and faces—they were gone for many a day;
In their place the lurching coach-wheel, or the creaking bullock-chains,
O'er the everlasting sameness of the never-ending plains.

In the slab-built, zinc-roofed homestead of some lately taken run,
In the tent beside the bankment of a railway just begun,
In the huts on new selections, in the camps of man's unrest,
On the frontiers of the Nation, live the Women of the West.

The red sun robs their beauty and, in weariness and pain,
The slow years steal the nameless grace that never comes again;
And there are hours men cannot soothe, and words men cannot say—
The nearest woman's face may be a hundred miles away. . . .

GEORGE ESSEX EVANS (1863–1909)

SIR GEORGE REID

The most conspicuous figure of the Federal Convention of 1897–98, its official author and in matters of moment its leader, was the Premier of New South Wales, G. H. Reid, physically as remarkable as his predecessor,

Parkes, but without his dignity, and even more formidable in discussion because less self-respecting. Even caricature has been unable to travesty his extraordinary appearance, his immense, unwieldy, jelly-like stomach always threatening to break his waist-band, his little legs apparently bowed under its weight to the verge of their endurance, his thick neck rising behind his ears rounding to his many-folded chin. His protuberant blue eyes were expressionless until roused or half hidden in cunning, and a blonde complexion and infantile breadth of baldness gave him an air of insolent juvenility. He walked with a staggering roll like that of a sailor, helping himself as he went by resting on the backs of chairs as if he were reminiscent of some far-off arboreal ancestor. To a superficial eye his obesity was either repellant or else amusing. A heavy German moustache concealed a mouth of considerable size from which there emanated a high-pitched voice rising to a shriek or sinking to a fawning, purring, persuasive orotund with a nasal tinge. To a more careful inspection he disclosed a splendid dome-like head, high and broad and indicative of intellectual power, a gleaming eye which betokened a natural gift of humour and an alertness that not even his habit of dropping asleep at all times and places in the most ungraceful attitudes and in the most impolite manner could defeat. He never slept in a public gathering more than a moment or two, being quickly awakened by his own snore.

. . . As a platform orator he was unsurpassed. His voice could reach a great crowd and his deliberate drawl enabled the densest among them to follow him. At his best his arguments were well shaped and perspicuously expressed with admirable directness and in the plainest words, often in slang, but always so as to be understood. . . . Reid was not merely a humourist but a great actor assisting his low comedy parts with irresistible gesture and expression. He cared nothing for the heights of outlook or depths of insight, discarding all decorum of deliverance, finish of style or grace of expression, aiming always at the level of the man of the street and reaching it by jest, logic, appeal, rant or ruthless abuse as appeared most effective. He always was effective for he possessed a really marvellous political instinct, a readiness and adaptability, a quickness of repartee and a rolling surge of *ad captandum* arguments which were simply irresistible.

ALFRED DEAKIN (1856–1919)
The Federal Story

LITERARY MEMORIES

My gallery of memory has many pictures.

Brunton Stephens in his Brisbane attic, a little elderly man in an old coat, the soft eyes under his fine forehead shining with benignity as he poured out Bulimba beer and praises of Tennyson, the master.

Henry Lawson, tramping to and fro in his room at the *Boomerang* office, tramping hour after hour as he pounded local news into rhymes, set up as prose and called 'Country Crumbs', tramping and muttering 'four horses in the pound—bound—round—owner found—owner drowned', interminably.

Victor Daley with his Saturday morning verses—three stanzas written overnight, three before breakfast, and three on the office counter. Daley's mind matched my own; we judged and valued by the standard of a similar taste; and the marketing was keen. So poetry was bought and sold subtly, weighed in the balance against silver, rarely gold, with seldom a difference in our scales. And still I can hear Daley muttering: 'I had to finish it here—didn't get a cup of tea when I woke up—I am no good in the morning without a cup of tea'. I say to myself, 'You poor creature! Did Hannibal have a cup of tea? Did Napoleon have a cup of tea? No use!'

A. G. STEPHENS (1865–1933)
The Bookfellow

A.G.S. AND THE BULLETIN

Stephens' position on the *Bulletin* was that of junior sub-editor, but before long he began to extend the range of his work. Near the end of 1894, the paper began to utilise the inside page of its front cover for notes on books. These were informal and sporadic; anyone might do them, though they were usually left to Stephens. On August 8, 1896, however, an article by J. F. Millington appeared, headed 'For the Red Page', and three weeks later the Red Page proper was launched as a feature, under Stephens' editorship.

Appropriately enough, he began with an article on Lawson, who had just published 'While the Billy Boils'.

'His quaint, simple style', wrote Stephens, 'suits his themes and modes of thought. And his manner is strengthening. The happy word and phrase come to him easily: the incidents fall without effort into place: his picture is made before he knows. Lawson is beginning to find himself'.

So was Stephens. Literature had become his chief passion, and the new position gave him a chance to concentrate upon it as he never had done before. The *Bulletin* had by then won a considerable place in the community; it was read from Cape York to the Leeuwin, and it was the paper to which everyone with a talent for writing inevitably turned. Founded by Archibald and Haynes in 1880, it had had stormy times to weather, but it had gradually grown from a bright, waspish little journal into the main organ of national opinion.

And without Stephens the paper would have had no literary centre; the stream of creative writing that was beginning to flow through it would have lacked direction. Archibald had an uncanny gift for unearthing the man who had something to say, but he had not the trained critical faculty of Stephens, nor had he a fundamental interest in literature. First and last, he was an editor. His concern was to fill the paper with matter that was bright, provocative, redolent of the dry Australian soil. He looked upon his contributors as colleagues who were working with him in a patriotic enterprise, the establishment of the *Bulletin* as a dominating force in national affairs, a healthy native voice in a community that was still provincial and colonial. . . .

The creation of the Red Page by Stephens provided a centre and a stimulus for all these diverse talents. His literary tastes were catholic, his natural interests wide. He knew the life of the country, revelled in its idiom, enjoyed any story that had an authentic Australian character stamped on it. But he had also been quickened by the contemporary writing of Europe. His policy on the Red Page was to stimulate Australian writing, to assess its value, and to connect it with the main stream of European culture. . . .

It was a more penetrating criticism than any that had been known in Australia; it broke down walls and let in air and light. Stephens' writing was never literary. The colloquial phrase or the vernacular saying was always at the tip of his pen, ready to be inverted with a twirl. (If that doesn't bang Bannagher, then Bannagher never was bung.) In his approach to literature he did not treat it as a special compartment of life; an attic near the roof; and the criticism on the Red Page did not differ greatly in tone from that in the rest of the paper. Undoubtedly it stimulated the writers of the day and gave them a feeling that they had an audience, that they were not talking into the void. There was the lively, challenging presence of the

132

Grand Inquisitor himself, who had begun to take shape behind the initials, A.G.S., and there was the community of readers he had gathered around him. Writing took on a new excitement now that this definite attention was concentrated on the work appearing, though Archibald had always been quick to send a friendly line to the author of any story or set of verses that particularly appealed to him.

After a space of forty years his judgments remain valid. The writers he singled out really were significant. And no important work has emerged from the files of those days to accuse him of neglect.

VANCE PALMER (1885–1959)

A. G. Stephens

A SKETCH OF LAWSON

There are still among us people who knew Lawson—who ate and drank with him, worked with him, loafed with him, and who cannot readily forget the forcible pressure of a hand that gripped hard and slowly relinquished its grasp of fingers affectionately crushed. As we pass out, one by one, the survivors realise more and more the value of such memories, not merely as cherished personal possessions, but as details of the composite portrait which Lawson's mates must paint for posterity. I myself seem, in this connection, to have published here and there every one of my recollections that was really worth recording, and yet, as I think of Henry, small facts keep recurring. His deafness and its consequences in his work and conduct come to mind. Because he could not hear very well he was the more dependent upon other senses for his impressions. Those wonderful dark eloquent eyes saw all the more because his hearing was dull. He was extraordinarily observant; no significant movement escaped his watchfulness. Slight gestures, which most people would pass unnoticed, spoke to him more clearly than words, they interpreted subtly the unspoken secrets of heart and mind. A bushman would tilt his hat or scratch the nape of his neck, and in some simple prose sketch Lawson would describe the action so that the reader would not only have it brought vividly before him, but would divine a human meaning in it. And possibly it was because he could not readily catch what was said, that Lawson so often gave a reply in communicative nods and glances.

J. LE GAY BRERETON (1871–1933)

Henry Lawson, By His Mates

133

CHRISTOPHER BRENNAN

His face was bulky, like his body; with the *morbidezza* that an Irishman's whiteness sometimes has (both his parents were from Ireland). But this whiteness was permantly flushed a little, and a little weatherbeaten; flushed partly from drink perhaps, but partly also from sheer vitality. For Brennan was in those days extraordinarily robust, and had one of the strongest stomachs imaginable. He could eat huge meals, sit down immediately in front of his books, and never feel a twinge of indigestion; swallow great quantities of alcohol, and never turn a hair. . . .

Brennan was not a mere scholar-poet, though some of the pieces in the earlier section of *Poems 1913* smell a little too strongly of midnight oil. The fact is that he was a great scholar *and* a great poet. . . .

Brennan was a man of genius, with a naturally deep insight into reality and an innate desire to increase this depth. Such a desire made him an indefatigable and insatiate scholar; but his native insight led him further than scholarship alone could have taken him; into a Reality that lies beyond realities. Yet it was an uncomfortable and even a desolate reality; a place where bitter winds were blowing, and life seemed a poor, intermittent flame; where he could not find the comforting finality that he had known as a boy; where the God of his fathers was visible no more, and nothing remained but to replace Him by a dream, knowing that the dream was imposed by a sense of metaphysical misery; that it was inescapable and unsatisfying.

A. R. CHISHOLM (1888–1981)
Men Were My Milestones

THE WOMAN AT THE WASHTUB

The Woman at the Washtub,
    She works till fall of night;
With soap, and suds and soda
    Her hands are wrinkled white.
Her diamonds are the sparkles
    The copper-fire supplies;
Her opals are the bubbles
    That from the suds arise.

O Woman at the Washtub,
    And do you ever dream
Of all your days gone by in
    Your aureole of steam?
From birth till we are dying
    You wash our sordid duds,
O Woman of the Washtub!
    O Sister of the Suds!

One night I saw a vision
    That filled my soul with dread,
I saw a Woman washing
    The grave-clothes of the dead;
The dead were all the living,
    And dry were lakes and meres,
The Woman at the Washtub
    She washed them with her tears.

I saw a line with banners
    Hung forth in proud array—
The banners of all battles
    From Cain to Judgment Day.
And they were stiff with slaughter
    And blood, from hem to hem,
And they were red with glory,
    And she was washing them.

'Who comes forth to the Judgment,
    And who will doubt my plan?'
'I come forth to the Judgment
    And for the Race of Man.
I rocked him in his cradle,
    I washed him for his tomb,
I claim his soul and body,
    And I will share his doom.'

                    VICTOR DALEY (1858–1905)

Mace was leaning against the wall taking his breath in strangled gasps.

. . . Feeling as I was, I sort of jumped back from old Mace. Like you would from a leper. But, of course, there was nothing that infectious about him. He was just the result of thirty years underground. A nice, cheerful sight for a chap that can taste the Twelve-hundred-foot Level on his tongue every morning and can't shake off winter colds! With five years underground behind me, and feeling the way I was, old Mace made my stomach turn.

'Heavy goin', heavy goin' up the dumps', said old Mace. 'I thought it was one o' me good days, too.'

Even five years back, when I'd come to the Extended, he'd been a big man, the old fellow. Six feet of him, but not just tall; arms as thick as your thigh, hair all over him, and a neck like a lump of tree. I'd been his bogger when I started, and he was the chap to show you how to load trucks and unload them, too. He used to get sick of the machine and take a bit of exercise now and again. Never knew there was anything wrong with him. When he went up to the Health Laboratory for the usual examination and they gave him his 'First Ticket' he laughed like hell.

'Bin underground thirty years', he said. 'Bin examined ten times in the last ten years, an' now them fellers reckon there's a spot on me lung! Git out o' the mines be damned! I'll still be handlin' the old Holman on the Extended when that doctor bloke's dead of overstuffin' hisself'.

But it got him. Fast. The very next examination they wiped him out for good. No more work on the mines! Out on a pension or a lump sum. He blustered a bit, but he didn't laugh. He disappeared out of the Extended. His boy Dick started bogging on the Twelve a few weeks later.

After that I didn't see Mace often. Just sometimes I'd spot him down at the pub. Moving a bit slower, looking a bit more sallow, dropping a pound or two of weight.

But now he was done for. He wouldn't see Christmas. When they talk about a man being all skin and bone they just mean thin. They ought to see someone in the last stages of miner's complaint. Old Mace was pretty near transparent in places. You couldn't help noticing the back of his hands. They still had black hair on them, but they were so bleached underneath that you could see the white flesh through the fur. His fingers were thin, delicate, with brittle-looking nails. His eyes were bright. Too bright. And his breath hooked up in his throat and whistled and wheezed. When he moved about, getting the parcel of clothes his boy had left in the change-room, he put each foot on the floor as if it hurt, and he automatically held on to things. You could smell his breath. Death in it. We didn't stay to yarn to him.

'Dirty times, them early days', said Tom. 'No ventilation worth having. No regulations and inspections. No anything but dust when Mace did his first twenty years down below. We're luckier. Poor old cow!'

Tom didn't sound quite natural. I reckoned he was trying to convince himself, as well as me, that nothing like old Mace could possibly happen nowadays. I'd shoot myself, I thought, if it happened to me. I thought it the way you think things, not the way you talk them. I thought of Annie and young Bill, and of myself like that. I thought more of how I'd feel than how they would, but I felt bad again.

'The mines!' I said. 'They're better, but still not so good.'

GAVIN CASEY (1907–1964)
Short Shift Saturday and Other Stories

MRS WHITE

Dave's wife died of a chill complicated by the arrival of her thirteenth child. She had formed the habit of driving into town with Dave and sitting all day in the sulky in the hotel yard watching the people and the motor-cars go by. It was a nice change, she said, from Dwyer's Bend. Long after closing time she could be seen, sitting like a graven image in the dark, waiting patiently for the rattle of the side door opening, the laughter and voices and the uncertain footsteps which announced Dave's coming. As soon as she heard these sounds she would climb down, light the lamps, cluck to the horse and move over to make room, while a couple of friends heaved Dave into his seat. Then Blasted, the horse, would go clopping slowly down the road, the sulky creaking and protesting under the weight and the lamps blinking uncertainly until they vanished round the corner by the Chinamen's gardens.

Mrs White was a woman contented with very little, otherwise she would never have stood Dave, although when she married him he was a good-looking enough chap. She did not mind the perpetual clutter of children, because she hardly noticed them. They had to look after themselves while she stumbled round in her slow way, pottering with a bit of cooking or just sitting in the sun. She couldn't be bothered cleaning anything, because it only got dirty again. She couldn't even be bothered talking to the women in the near-by camps, although when she did start she could be quite blood-curdling in an obstetric style. Winter or summer, she wore the same black hat of straw lace with faded red roses under the brim. In summer a torn, very tight black silk dress, with short sleeves that showed her big red arms, kept the roses company, and in winter the black silk dress was covered by a brown woollen coat. If there is a ghost haunting the pepper-trees outside O'Brien's Hotel, it haunts after closing-time and wears a black lace hat with faded red roses.

When Mrs White caught a chill waiting for Dave one wet night, the town was divided between the opinion that she ought to have more sense and surprise that anything could kill a White.

KYLIE TENNANT (1912–   )
Tiburon

SIR SAMUEL GRIFFITH

A notable senior member (of the Federal Convention of 1891) was Queensland's Premier, Sir Samuel Griffith. A brilliant scholar and jurist, keenly intellectual, he had made a close study of federal institutions, and was the chief draftsman of the Constitution, the text of which owes more to him than to any other man, though his elevation soon afterwards to the Chief Justiceship of Queensland prevented his taking a prominent part in its later revision. He and Inglis Clark, another fine jurist from Tasmania, were said to have brought with them complete drafts of a Constitution, whilst Sir Richard Baker from South Australia circulated a Manual of Federal Constitutions. One of Griffith's hobbies was the translation into English of Dante's *Divina Commedia*, of which one critic, while praising its literal accuracy, complained that it left out all the poetry. He had a fault fatal to translators—a theory of translation—his particular theory being that every word of the original ought to be represented in the translation. A glance at the work shows, to anyone who has even the slightest acquaintance with the original, that Griffith, with his legalistic, logical bent of mind, was not the man to convey into another tongue the beauties of the greatest work of Italy's greatest poet. Later, when Griffith was Chief

Justice of the High Court, I asked him whether it was true that he had worked on the *Inferno* in Brisbane, the *Purgatorio* in Melbourne, and the *Paradiso* in Sydney. He replied with a smile that, whilst he was not prepared to give a categoric no to the question, he did not admit the innuendo.

When Griffith later, as a member of the Privy Council, took his seat on the Judicial Committee, his British colleagues were astonished at his learning. Sir John Simon, at a dinner in London, said to me, 'Garran, I am not surprised at the excellence of Australia's raw produce—we expect your wool and wheat and butter to be good. But I am sometimes surprised at the excellence of your finished articles'. I asked what he had in mind. He ticked off on his fingers: 'Nellie Melba, Sam Griffith, Victor Trumper'.

SIR ROBERT RANDOLPH GARRAN (1867–1957)
Prosper the Commonwealth

MELBA

Melba was in her late forties when I first heard her sing, but her voice was still a remarkable instrument, with only a few worn places in the highest reaches of her two-and-a-half octave span. In her most brilliant *fioritura* every note was as clear as a bell, and as individual as a star; she tossed off a high B flat with the ease of a great tennis-player lobbing a ball over the net. It is doubtful whether there has ever been a woman singer whose vocalism was so easily controlled. It seemed just as natural with her as talking. To this day, the connoisseurs talk about the beauty of Melba's long shake at her exit after 'Caro Nome' in *Rigoletto*.

In 1894, Bernard Shaw, who was then a musical critic, writing of Melba's performance of Juliette, expressed the following, for him, ecstatic opinion: 'You never realise how wide the gap between the ordinary singer who simply avoids the fault of singing obviously out of tune and the singer who sings really and truly in tune, except when Melba is singing'.

Melba's perfect command of intonation remained with her to the end; I heard her in her last performance in opera at Covent Garden, when she was sixty-three years of age, and in Mimi's death scene in *Boheme* every note was of such perfect pitch that you could almost see the printed score...

Melba did incalculable service for music in Australia. In fact, she placed Australia musically on the map. It can be said, to use the phrase of our own period, that she sang before all the crowned heads of Europe, and that at a time when the majority of people in Europe did not even know where Australia was. She became an empress in all the great courts of the world.

SIR NEVILLE CARDUS (1889–1975)
Music for Pleasure

BERT SCHULTZ

Bert Schultz on his West Coast farm
Eases backwards through the doorway of his truck,
And the cabin grows around him, the wheel
Finds comfort in a padded stomach rut.
Bert Schultz in motion is a monstrous forward shoot
Because he crushes the accelerator like a toadstool
Under his six-pound boot.

Bert Schultz on his West Coast farm
Wears braces like railway tracks
That start from button boulders,
Junction in the middle of his back
And climb over the mountains of his shoulders.

Bert Schultz in his West Coast town
Has a fence-post arm to buttress up the bar,
Spins a thimble schooner in the stale-smelling ebb,
Talks about sheep and the way prices are.

The glass hidden in his ham-bone fist,
An hour later he still talks farm,
While the flies tip and veer
In the tangle of the wire sprouting on his arm.

Bert Schultz down a West Coast street
Makes me certain Eyre Peninsula
Has taken to its legs,

And is walking round the place on tree-stump feet;
Makes me feel the steel of yaccas,
And the supple punch of mallee,
And the thirsty tug of eighteen-gallon kegs.

Bert Schultz knows something of tractor oils and sumps,
Sheep dogs and petrol pumps
And an occasional punch to the chin.
But when he laughs like a shaking mountain,
And gullies his face badly with a grin,
He opens suddenly and lets you in.

COLIN THIELE (1920–   )

THE ANZACS AT GALLIPOLI

The Australian and New Zealand Army Corps and the Royal Naval Division, who together made up more than half the army, were almost all men who had enlisted since the declaration of war, and had had not more than six months' active training. They were, however, the finest body of young men ever brought together in modern times. For physical beauty and nobility of bearing they surpassed any men I have ever seen; they walked and looked like the kings in old poems, and reminded me of the line in Shakespeare:
   'Baited like eagles having lately bathed.'
As their officers put it, 'they were in the pink of condition and didn't care a damn for anybody'. Most of these new and irregular formations were going into action for the first time, to receive their baptism of fire in 'a feat of arms only possible to the flower of a very fine army'.

JOHN MASEFIELD (1878–1967)
Gallipoli

141

DIGGERS OF THE FIRST A.I.F.

The First A.I.F. (Australian Imperial Force) was the army raised by voluntary enlistment in 1914 for overseas service during the First World War. The similar volunteer army for the Second World War became 'The Second A.I.F.' In both armies the soldiers were usually known as the 'diggers'.

Some who had been officers in the militia entered the force as privates. Many a youngster, who could have had a commission, enlisted in the ranks and remained there in order to serve beside a friend. There were in the Australian force no special corps in which University or 'public school' men enlisted apart from others. One light horse regiment indeed there was, the 10th, to which the sons of almost every well-known pastoralist or farmer in Western Australia came bringing their own horses and their own saddles. Just a year later half of the regiment was wiped out within a few seconds in one of the bravest charges ever made. Similarly the great public schools of Victoria formed a company in the 5th Battalion. But for the most part the wealthy, the educated, the rough and the case-hardened, poor Australians, rich Australians, went into the ranks together unconscious of any distinction. When they came into an atmosphere of class difference later in the war, they stoutly and rebelliously resented it.

It might seem that in the creation of a new army—half from men trained as militia and the rest from men completely untrained—the instruction of the rank and file in the technique of modern fighting would prove the heaviest task. Such, indeed, was the expectation of many commanding officers in this new force . . .

In practice it was found that the rank and file of the Australian Imperial Force could be trained in a few months, provided that the officers knew their work and were men capable of handling men. But the man who commanded them must needs be a man in every sense of the word. Most Australian soldiers had never in their lives known what it was to be given a direct order undisguised by 'you might' or 'would you mind?' Since the discipline of the much-harassed bush school-teacher, they had never known any restraint that was not self-imposed. In this fact lay potentialities both for good and for evil not to be found in the men of those nations which bring up their young in leading-strings. If an Australian soldier wanted to do a thing, he possessed the capacity for acting on his own initiative. He seldom hesitated on the brink of action. To paint him as a being of lamb-like nature and the gentle virtues would be entirely to miss his character. 'Colourless' is the last adjective that could be applied to him. He was full of

142

colour, entirely positive, constantly surprising those who knew him by some fresh display of qualities which even his own officers (who in most cases had been his mates) had never suspected.

If the Australian soldier were ever in need of a plea, it would be upon his positive qualities, not upon the negative quality of docility, that his advocate must rely. The British 'Tommies' among whom he afterwards mixed, best-natured of men, extraordinarily guileless, humble-minded to a degree, never boastful, and seldom the cause of any serious trouble, instinctively looked up to the Australian private as a leader. If he was a good Australian he led them into good things, and if he was a bad Australian he led them into evil, but he always led. He was more a child of nature even than the New Zealanders. When the Americans foregathered with him at the end of the war, he led them also.

Such men could not easily be controlled by the traditional methods of the British Army. The fact that a man had received a good education, dressed well, spoke English faultlessly and belonged to the 'officer' class, would merely incline them, at first sight, to laugh at him, or at least to suspect that he was guilty of affectation—in their own language, 'putting on dog'. But they were seriously intent upon learning, and were readily controlled by anyone really competent to teach them. They were hero-worshippers to the backbone. There was a difficulty in reconciling them to any sort of irksome rule; the putting of any precinct 'out of bounds' they regarded as an attempt to treat them as children. At first there undoubtedly existed among them a sort of suppressed resentfulness, never very serious, but yet noticeable, of the whole system of 'officers'.

C. E. W. BEAN (1879–1968)
The Official History of Australia in the War of 1914–1918

NORMAN LINDSAY

No other Australian artist has appealed to Australian writers in this way, that poems should be written about him and his work. From the very beginning, from the days when Hugh McCrae saw him as a beacon blazing in the mountains 'Up Springwood way, across the skies' to the week when this article is written and a novel about Tobruk by Lawson Glassop with a Lindsay foreword is on display in the bookshop, Norman Lindsay had been sought out by the writers.

His friendship with McCrae, the interchange of images and ideas that resulted in some of the finest of McCrae's lyrics and the finest of the artist's pen drawings, is a matter of history. He rode with 'Banjo' Paterson. Kenneth Slessor and Kenneth Mackenzie both acknowledged his services by dedicating poems and books to him. He decorated Leon Gellert's *Songs of a Campaign*.

In his foreword to Lawson Glassop's novel he mentions how the author came to him with the manuscript of his first novel; scores of beginners— some who have failed, some who have made big names—have come to him over the years in the same way. He was largely responsible for the establishment of the Endeavor Press by the *Bulletin*, and was associated with the whole group of novelists brought out by it. I know of several of Australia's best short-story writers who have put themselves under his tutelage before embarking on the long and difficult voyage of the novel.

Not all Australian writers, of course, have come to him. And some who have come have come to quarrel. That is inevitable. But it is beyond question that the majority of Australian writers—and especially the poets—have accepted him from the beginning not only as an artist but as the fountain-head of the Australian culture in our time. In that fact lies the clue to the meaning and significance of his work. . . .

His skill as an illustrator, his name, his place as a novelist, his authority as a critic, his enthusiasm for anything that helps the movement of culture in Australia, these are some of the reasons why the writers seek his company. But the real, the basic reason lies deeper. Beyond anything else Norman Lindsay is a painter; and surely it is his paintings that have drawn the writers to him.

There is some quality in his work—not to be found in the same measure in the work of any other Australian painter—that calls to the novelists and the poets.

DOUGLAS STEWART (1913–   )
The Flesh and the Spirit

ELEGY FOR MY SAD-FACED UNCLE

My sad-faced uncle, who went through life melancholy
with a loud voice and the story he was always telling,
did not anticipate death as a real alternative,

never contemplated the certainty of cut string
or squashed mosquitoes:
                                    met death
as a thirty-six model Chev: died suddenly
crossing the street under a futile umbrella that he always   '
said—I-never-use: shut eyes
in some affectation of amazement; found the lids heavy
and without time to push them, died.
Was buried on a Monday by mourners with black cars and hankies
indecently white who thought of his childhood and six-o'clock closing,
the ironing at home and the chops to be got.
No, he had not tangled the meaning of dirt-thud on the wood,
nor the emptiness of speech-golden tombstones, nor thought of the wonder
of star-eyes at night. He had not thought of it at all.
Which was fitting and better.
Surely death was kind to my uncle with the sad-puppy face
and better not delayed till thinking.

RAY MATHEW (1929–   )

A MIGRANT STARTS AS A BUILDER'S LABOURER

Joe said, 'Had ter pick up yer new mate, mate. 'Ow yer goin' mate orright?'
  'Yeah mate. 'Ow yer goin' orright?'
  'Orright mate. Nino, this is Pat. Pat—Nino.'
  Pat extended a hand, and said, 'Please ter meet yer'.
  I shook hands with him and said, 'How do you do?'
  He said, 'Orright mate'.
  Joe said, 'I gotta go an' see about that metal an' stuff, an' tee up the
mixer. How long yer reckon, Pat? Coupla days?'
  'You gunna help?'
  'No matey, gotta finish up that other job.'
  Pat said, 'Three days'.
  'Orright. Ter-day's Friday. We'll pour on Wensdy. Okay?'
  'Okay mate.'
  'Come an' get the gear outa the truck. Where's yer togs, Nino?'
  I said, 'Togs?'

145

'Yer workin' clothes? Like me an' Pat?'

'Oh. I do not have any.'

They both looked at me, so I said, 'I could take off my coat'.

Joe said, 'That might be an idea. Wodda yer reckon, Pat?'

'N-o-o . . . No can't 'ave 'im taking orf 'is tie. The neighbours'd think yer was a lot o' common workmen.'

'Could 'e take orf 'is hat?'

'Yeah. Yeah 'e could take orf 'is 'at. Look matey, I gotta go. See if there's some old togs in that bag o' Dennis's next door. I'll leave ut ter you. I'll try an' drop back this arvo an' see how yer goin'.'

'Yer better.'

'Why?'

'Don' we get paid this week?'

'Gees, that's right mate. Orright, I'll be back at lunchtime. D'yer bring yer lunch, Nino?'

'I am sorry, Joe, no. I did not know . . .'

'Orright. Give us a few bob an' I'll bring some sandwiches when I come back.'

'You want some money, Joe?'

'Yeah, give us a coupla bob.'

I held out some money, and he took three shillings. Pat said, 'Wot a bastard you turned out ter be'.

Joe said, 'Give 'im a go, mate. 'E 'asn't done any before, but 'e'll be orright. Give 'im a go'.

'Why didn't yer get me Mr Menzies?'

''E was too buy, mate. See yer later.'

NINO CULOTTA (JOHN O'GRADY) (1908–1981)
They're a Weird Mob

BILL HARNEY

The following week-end, two or three of us sailed across the wide green waters of Darwin Harbour, making for Darramunkamuni Beach. Bill Harney keeps open house there, with a bushman's welcome for those who can contribute to the common pool of reminiscence and debate. If you feel like it, you can stay a week, or a month. Nature will provide. The north is lavish with its resources on the shores of the Timor Sea. There are turtle eggs, dugong and barramundi to be found along the beach, and fish, duck and geese in the broad lily lagoon behind his bungalow. If you like to go bush there are wild rice, yams, fruits, honey, and always a few blacks roaming about to help you find them. There is everything for the contentment of body and soul. . . .

'The secret of living', he is fond of saying, 'is not to make money. It is to live without money'. Unlike most old bushmen, he neither drinks nor smokes.

'If you want to keep up those habits', he says, 'you've got to work for a master. I don't work for a master'.

I have never met a man so completely free, to whom independence is so sacred. . . .

Bushman born and bred, knowing more about the natives than most men living—including professional anthropologists, many of whom have learnt much of what they know from Harney—he has been a considerable force in the life of the Territory. Stockman, drover, prospector, trepang-fisher, tin-miner, beachcomber, he came to know intimately every corner of the Far North long before he began as a patrol officer. . . .

He is a man of many talents; perhaps even of many characters. A beachcomber who lives like a nomad, a writer of books and poems who prefers a life of action, a battler who has made a livelihood from most callings open to white men in the North and yet prefers to do no work at all, he has the gift of turning his whole existence into an adventure. . . .

As it happened, when I sailed across the bay to visit him, he was just back from a holiday with a mate of his. 'What do beachcombers want with holidays?' I asked.

'Well', he said in his great bushman's voice, 'we reckoned we needed a change. We took the launch down the coast to Indian Island. Only thirty miles, y'know. Might have done more, only things were too good down there. We lay off for ten days, spearing fish and digging up turtles' eggs'. He grinned happily. 'Well, mate, a man's got to make the most of life, ain't he? Think of the slaves toiling away down South. Somebody's got to make use of the world.'. . .

It was the kind of atmosphere to stimulate good talk. Or at least to set Bill Harney talking, for his quick and vivid imagination is apt to corner every conversation he enters. One might listen to him uninterrupted for an

147

hour or more, both with profit and entertainment. Those who know him only by the written word know merely the shadow of Harney. As a raconteur I have yet to meet his equal. . . .

Long years among them, living with tribal nomads and the detribalized, has given him the ability to think almost with a native mind. Therein lay his success as a patrol officer. Blacks would open up to him where they would have withheld their confidences from an alien. Many times he has been called in to settle some tribal dispute, some moral injury or bargaining point with the whites of the North. Half the natives in the Territory know and respect him, greeting him with unaffected ease as 'Billarnee'.

GEORGE FARWELL (1911–1976)
The Outside Track

THE FRIEND OF THE PAPUANS

Sir Hubert Murray, the elder brother of Sir Gilbert Murray, born in Sydney of an Australian pioneering family, won a world reputation as a native administrator in governing the Territory of Papua, formerly British New Guinea, from 1909 until his death in 1940. The native population then performed a rare tribal death-feast in his honour.

For forty days and nights the watch fires burned in the villages, on their outskirts, and in the surrounding hills, carefully tended by privileged members of the Motu tribe. This was the period of mourning, during which all dances and organised games were prohibited by tribal tradition. On the forty-first day a vast gathering of natives from the surrounding districts assembled at Tanobada.

The Motu people have a genius for ceremonial, and the present occasion was spectacular, dignified, and impressive. There was none of the noise usually associated with an assemblage of primitive people. The heaps of food inseparable from native ceremonies were stacked neatly in two long lines down the middle of the village, and between the lines the few white officials invited to the ceremony were escorted in a silence broken only by the soft tapping of a thousand drums; an insistent beat that expressed in its relentless rhythm the sorrow of the speechless thousands who stood, reverent and attentive, until the guests had taken their seats.

The soft tapping of drums died down to a murmur of sound, and, above the soft throbbing, his words punctuated by its rise and fall, the voice of the Senior Councillor spoke the following epitaph.

148

Governor Murray is dead. He worked until he died. He was our Governor for more than thirty years.

During all that time we saw his work and his laws. And we have seen his good deeds also.

When our people were in trouble they went to him and he did not turn them away. In our trouble he gave us help and made us happy again. There was no man like him in this way.

Wherever he went in Papua he spoke friendly words. He was never harsh towards men, or women, or children.

He brought great happiness into our lives. Therefore we say that he was good.

But in February this year he died. We, his people, remember him and weep.

He treated us always as friends. His way towards us was the way of a friend.

We think of him still, and we shall think of him always, for he guided us well. Now we make for him this feast according to the customs of our people.

The ways of his people were not our ways. But he understood us and made our lives happy.

We, too, understood him, and we loved him. Therefore we now make this *Masi-Ariana*.

But who is like him in Papua? There is none. There will never be one like him . . .

He promised us all 'I will not leave you. I will die in Papua'. His words were the words of a true man, for his body now lies in our ground.

LEWIS LETT (1878–1966)
Sir Hubert Murray of Papua

150

HUMOUR AND SENTIMENT

A WARNING AGAINST WOMEN

In this feminine air of comfort, warmth, plenty and security, Mr McCree recognised the enemy of his sex. In this cloying, this enervating atmosphere, this 'monstrous regiment of women', the rector saw his grandson's undoing. He would become 'soft'. His manly character would be ruined.

Since the poor child had no father, his grandfather had determined to warn him, to point out to him the dangers lurking in the society of females, and he took him by the hand and led him out through the orchard to the fallen pear-tree, their usual trysting-place, Donalbain's ducklings following.

Every woman looked out of a window to watch them. Eight faces, appearing at the toy-like, white-curtained apertures in the red-brick rectory walls, which were like those in a doll's house, or a building in a harlequinade, registered the same fear, the same knowledge; 'he is going to set the child against us'. Intuitively, the women realised this; rightly. . . .

'Donalbain, you are five years old', Mr McCree began in his quavering, hesitant voice; he had been made speechless by a stroke a year back, and was only just regaining the power of clear articulation; 'I am your grandfather, eighty-four years old. Soon you will be alone with no father and no brother, and only three women to look after you'.

'It is too sad', Donalbain said, tears filling his eyes.

'No, it is not a bit sad', Mr McCree said testily; 'it is merely inconvenient. Well, now, listen well! If a man has land or a house, he can leave his land or his house to his sons, or his grandsons. But I have no land and no house'.

'Can't I have this land? Or this house?' Donalbain asked, looking round him with a wondering air.

'No. These belong to the Church. They are not mine. When I die they will go to the new rector of Mallow's Marsh. Well, now, if a man has tools, he can leave them to his children or his grandchildren. But I have no tools to give you. The only tools I have had with which to earn a living have been an old book and a quill pen, and a halting tongue. And it cost my father a lot of money to have me taught to read the old book, and write with the scratchy quill and speak with the halting tongue.'

'Mr Noakes, the gardener, has got a pick, a shovel, a bill-hook, a pruning-hook, a scythe and a wheel-barrow', Donalbain volunteered. . . .

'Yes, so he has, and he can teach his sons to use them. But I can't teach you to use my tools, because you are too young and I am too old. However, there is one thing I can tell you, and that is this! You are too big a boy to hang round the house with the women all day long!'. . . .

'Mr Noakes says I am to avoid women as I would the devil', said Donalbain.

Hearing this, Mr McCree felt a slight lightening of the burden on his conscience; it was, apparently, to be shared; his grandson was, it appeared, to be accepted into the garnered wealth, the experience of the world of men; he was to be Everyman's son. Each bit of wisdom each man had gathered for himself he would in all kindness be ready to hand on to those who followed him. Of course, so it had always been, so it would always be.

The old man smiled, the sweet smile of age, of one helpless, yet unaware of his helplessness, and his whole face brightened with that same look of doting fondness which he had so reprobated in the women of his household.

'Yes', the boy continued, 'Mr Noakes says, if you meet a girl and a death-adder, kill the girl and cuddle the adder. He says it's safer'.

Sitting in his threadbare black cassock on the grey bole of the fallen pear-tree, Mr McCree, who had served his God devotedly for over sixty years, felt that none of his experience had brought him any knowledge so salty. He considered, half-astonished, the implications of such an attitude. He was himself warning his grandson against the deleterious effects of a woman's love; of any woman's affection. But need one go so far?

ETHEL ANDERSON (1886–1958)
Tales of Parramatta and India

THE MAGIC PUDDING

As he was indulging in these melancholy reflections Bunyip Bluegum, the koala, came round a bend in the road, and discovered two people in the very act of having lunch. These people were none other than Bill Barnacle, the sailor, and his friend, Sam Sawnoff, the penguin bold.

Bill was a small man with a large hat, a beard half as large as his hat, and feet half as large as his beard. Sam Sawnoff's feet were sitting down and his body was standing up, because his feet were so short and his body so long that he had to do both together. They had a pudding in a basin, and the smell that arose from it was so delightful that Bunyip Bluegum was quite unable to pass on.

152

'Pardon me', he said, raising his hat, 'but am I right in supposing that this is a steak-and-kidney pudding?'

'At present it is', said Bill Barnacle.

'It smells delightful', said Bunyip Bluegum.

'It is delightful', said Bill, eating a large mouthful. Bunyip Bluegum was too much of a gentleman to invite himself to lunch, but he said carelessly, 'Am I right in supposing that there are onions in this pudding?'

Before Bill could reply, a thick, angry voice came out of the pudding, saying—

'Onions, bunions, corns and crabs,
Whiskers, wheels and hamsom cabs,
Beef and bottles, beer and bones,
Give him a feed and end his groans.'

'Albert, Albert', said Bill to the Puddin', 'where's your manners?'

'Where's yours?' said the Puddin' rudely, 'guzzling away there, and never so much as offering this stranger a slice'.

'There you are', said Bill. 'There's nothing this Puddin' enjoys more than offering slices of himself to strangers.'

'How very polite of him', said Bunyip, but the Puddin' replied loudly—

'Politeness be sugared, politeness be hanged,
Politeness be jumbled and tumbled and banged.
It's simply a matter of putting on pace,
Politeness has nothing to do with the case.'

'Always anxious to be eaten', said Bill, 'that's this Puddin's mania. Well, to oblige him, I ask you to join us at lunch'.

NORMAN LINDSAY (1879–1969)
The Magic Pudding

THE BANKS OF THE CONDAMINE

MAN

O hark the dogs are barking, love, I can no longer stay;
The men are all gone mustering and it is nearly day.
And I must be off by the morning light, before the sun does shine
To meet the Sydney shearers on the Banks of the Condamine.

O Willy, dearest Willy, O let me go with you!
I'll cut off all my auburn fringe and be a shearer too;
I'll cook and count your tally, love, while ringer-o[1] you shine,
And I'll wash your greasy moleskins on the Banks of the Condamine.

MAN

O Nancy, dearest Nancy, with me you cannot go;
The squatters have given orders, love, no woman should do so.
And your delicate constitution is not equal unto mine,
To withstand the constant tigering[2] on the Banks of the Condamine.

GIRL

O Willy, dearest Willy, then stay at home with me;
We'll take up a selection, and a farmer's wife I'll be.
I'll help you husk the corn, love, and cook your meals so fine,
You'll forget the rem-stag[3] mutton on the Banks of the Condamine.

MAN

O Nancy, dearest Nancy, pray do not hold me back!
Down there the boys are mustering, and I must be on the track.
So here's a good-bye kiss, love; back home I will incline
When we've shore the last of the jumbucks[4] on the Banks of the Condamine.

Old Bush Song

STIR THE WALLABY STEW

Poor Dad he got five years or more as everybody knows,
And now he lives in Maitland Jail with broad arrows on his clothes,
He branded all of Brown's clean-skins and never left a tail,
So I'll relate the family's woes since Dad got put in jail.

[1] Fastest shearer.   [2] Hard working.   [3] Tough.   [4] Sheep.

154

Chorus
So stir the wallaby stew,
Make soup of the kangaroo tail,
I tell you things is pretty tough
Since Dad got put in jail.

Our sheep were dead a month ago, not rot but blooming fluke,
Our cow was boozed last Christmas Day by my big brother Luke,
And Mother has a shearer cove for ever within hail,
The family will have grown a bit since Dad got put in jail.

Our Bess got shook upon a bloke, he's gone we don't know where,
He used to act about the shed, but he ain't acted square;
I've sold the buggy on my own, the place is up for sale,
That won't be all that isn't junked when Dad comes out of jail.

They let Dad out before his time, to give us a surprise.
He came and slowly looked around, and gently blessed our eyes,
He shook hands with the shearer cove and said he thought things stale,
So left him here to shepherd us and battled back to jail.

Old Bush Song

CHAMPAGNE AND BRIDGE

The waiter coasted down to our table and pulled up with the silence of a
Rolls-Royce hearse.
  'Yessir?'
  'A bottle of champagne, waiter', ordered Stanley.
  'Two bottles', I put in.
  The waiter's eyes glistened.
  'Three bottles!' declared Stanley.
  'Four no-trumps!' cried the waiter.
  We stared at him.
  'Sorry, sir', he stammered. 'Pardon—forgot myself. Three bottles.
Yessir.'
  Stanley tapped his forehead as the man hurried away.

'Bridged', he muttered pityingly; 'probably from birth'.

I nodded. I had seen too much of that sort of thing to pity the man. In the early days of my married life Agatha had threatened to divorce me for failing to lead the ten of diamonds. By some outrageous whim of malicious fate we subsequently won the rubber and she stayed with me. I have never played the game since.

The champagne enlivened me. It thrilled and uplifted me like the fangs of a bull-ant. Champagne is another symbol of achievement. It puts a laurel wreath back among the rest of the shrubs. If headaches were created for any practical purpose, it was to show the glory of champagne. To emphasise the beauty of the rose by the magnitude of its thorns. And we had five bottles, altogether.

It was with great difficulty that the waiter and I managed to carry Stanley out to a taxi, some time later. It would have been easy, only the fool waiter, muddling round with his end of Stanley, made me lose my balance and fall to the floor several times before reaching the footpath. The man was obliging enough and I gave him a handful of pound notes as some slight recompense for his trouble, urging him at the same time to bank some. He offered to go in the taxi with us and wanted to brush me down. I couldn't stand for the brushing down. Positively couldn't stand for it.

We left the restaurant, with the waiter standing in the doorway gazing sadly after us, as though he had missed an opportunity to relieve his fellow-men.

L. W. LOWER (1904–1947)
Here's Luck

A MELBOURNE LARRIKIN ON SHAKESPEARE

Doreen an' me, we bin to see a show—
The swell two-dollar touch. Bong tong, yeh know.
A chair apiece wiv velvit on the seat;
A slap-up treat.
The drarmer's writ be Shakespeare, years ago,
About a barmy goat called Romeo.

156

'Lady, be yonder moon I swear!' sez 'e.
An' then 'e climbs up on the balkiney;
An' there they smooge a treat, wiv pretty words
Like two love-birds.
I nudge Doreen. She whispers, 'Ain't it grand!'
'Er eyes is shining'; an' I squeeze 'er 'and.

This Romeo 'e's lurkin' wiv a crew—
A dead tough crowd o' crooks—called Montague.
'Is cliner's¹ push—wot's nicknamed Capulet—
They 'as 'em set.
Fair narks they are, jist like them back-street clicks,²
Ixcep' they fights wiv skewers 'stid o' bricks.

Nex' day 'e words a gorspil cove about
A secrit weddin'; an' they plan it out.
'E spouts a piece about 'ow 'e's bewitched:
Then they git 'itched . . .
Now, 'ere's the place where I fair git the pip!
She's 'is for keeps, an' yet 'e lets 'er slip!

Ar! but 'e makes me sick! A fair gazob!³
'E's jist the glarsey⁴ on the soulful sob,
'E'll sigh and spruik, an' 'owl a love-sick vow—
(The silly cow!)
But when 'e's got 'er, spliced an' on the straight,
'E crools the pitch,⁵ an' tries to kid it's Fate.

Aw! Fate me foot! Instid of slopin' soon
As 'e was wed, off on 'is 'oneymoon,
'Im an' 'is cobber, called Mick Curio,
They 'ave to go
An' mix it wiv that push o' Capulets.
They look fer trouble; an' it's wot they gets.

<hr />

¹ Girl's.   ² Cliques.   ³ Fool.   ⁴ Glass eye.   ⁵ Spoils it.

A tug[6] named Tyball (cousin to the skirt)
Sprags[7] 'em an' makes a start to sling off dirt.
Nex' minnit there's a reel ole ding-dong go—
'Arf round or so.
Mick Curio, 'e gets it in the neck,
'Ar rats!' 'e sez, an' passes in 'is check.

Quite natchril, Romeo gits wet as 'ell.
'It's me or you!' 'e 'owls, an' wiv a yell,
Plunks Tyball through the gizzard wiv 'is sword,
'Ow I ongcored!
'Put in the boot!' I sez. 'Put in the boot!'
'Ush!' sez Doreen . . . 'Shame!' sez some silly coot.

      · · · · · ·

Then things gits mixed a treat an' starts to whirl.
'Ere's Romeo comes back an' finds 'is girl
Tucked in 'er little coffing, cold an' stiff,
An' in a jiff,
'E swallers lysol, throws a fancy fit,
'Ead over turkey, an' 'is soul 'as flit.

Then Juli-et wakes up an' sees 'im there,
Turns on the water-works an' tears 'er 'air,
'Dear love', she sez, 'I cannot live alone!'
An' wif a moan,
She grabs 'is pockit knife, an' ends 'er cares . . .
'*Peanuts or lollies!*' sez a boy upstairs.

C. J. DENNIS (1876–1938)
The Sentimental Bloke

A MYSTERIOUS BUSH-FIRE

Few men, I think, have a healthier hatred of incendiarism than I have. This
hatred dates from my eleventh year, or thereabout; when I was strongly
impressed by a bush-fire which cleaned the grass off half the county. The

---

[6] Rough fellow.   [7] Accosts truculently.

origin of that fire still remains a mystery, though all manner of investigation was made at the time; one of the most diligent inquirers being a boy of ten or twelve, who used to lie awake half the night, wondering what could be done to a person for trying to smoke a bandicoot out of a hollow log, without thinking of the dead grass.

TOM COLLINS (JOSEPH FURPHY) (1843–1912)
Such is Life

THE DROVERS

Briglow Bill the drover, fatally injured in a cattle stampede, is left to die attended by Pidgeon, a black boy.

Boss: How's it now, Briglow?

Briglow: Easier. The pain's gone.

Boss: That's something. Why should it end like this? (*He looks across the plains.*) The cattle are uneasy and bellowing with thirst.

Briglow: What are you going to do, Alec?

Boss: We can't stay here, and we can't take you, Briglow. It's the devil's own luck—but there—what's the use of nagging like an old crow?

Briglow: Who's grumbling? We know the bush, me and you. We're old at the game.

Boss: We've got to get on. I'm in charge, and I'd push them through if every blanky man in camp snuffed his candle.

Briglow: You don't have to tell me that, mate.

Boss: I've got to deliver the cattle.

Briglow: I'd like to be going with you . . . but . . . there's no chance.

Boss: There's no bones broken. Let's see.

Briglow: It's inside . . . something's crushed in the fall.

Boss: I've seen such cases.

Briglow: Haemorrhage.

Boss: You might get better yet.

Briglow: It's no use pretending. I'm settled, Alec!

Boss: Curse the Jackeroo!

Briglow: Let the lad off light if you can. He didn't know what he was doing when he fired that shot. He's new to the bush.

159

Boss: And it's all a damned accident . . .

Briglow: It don't matter. It had to come sooner or later. I've lived my life, careless and free, looking after my work when I was at it, and splashing my cheque up like a good one when I struck civilisation. I've lived hard, droving and horse-breaking, station work, and overlanding, the hard life of the bush, but there's nothing better, and death's come quick, before I'm played out—it's the way I wanted.

Boss: Maybe I'll finish like you, Briglow, out in the bush. I hope so, anyway.

Briglow: I've got no family to leave behind. Maybe the bush'll miss me a bit . . . the tracks I've travelled, and a star or two, and the old mulga.

Boss: And I'll miss you. I've never travelled with a better man.

Briglow: I hope you get the mob through safe. I'm real sorry I ain't no use, but it ain't my fault.

Boss: Don't I know it! You've always done your share, Briglow, and a lot extra. I'll never find another mate like you. The others are good lads, but they're young yet.

Briglow: They'll soon get over it, and forget all about me.

Boss: But I'll never forget, Briglow. It's part of my life.

Briglow: Well, it's been a good life. I'm satisfied. . . .

Boss: . . . I'll come back myself when we get the cattle to water.

Briglow: I'll be gone then. (*They shake hands.*)

Boss: So long, old mate.

Briglow: So long, Alec.

Boss: (*to Pidgeon*):   You good-fellow watch.

   (*Exit* Boss.)

   (*A pause.*)

   (*The sun rises. From the edge of the Barklay Tableland, the great plains stretch away, unbroken by timber, except the few gydgea trees that fringe the muddy water-hole. The drovers have disappeared on their journey across the long, dry stage.*)

LOUIS ESSON (1879–1943)
The Drovers

160

ME AND MY DOG

Me and my dog
    have tramped together
in cold weather
    and hot.

Me and my dog
    don't care whether
    we get any work
      or not.

ANONYMOUS

GIOVANNI RINALDO, P.O.W.

He had heard in a wind cooling his wounds of fire,
in the whisper of the mango to the moon that climbed the wire,

Maria, his wife, and Nino, the son of their tears,
calling more sweetly than Death, all through the years.

Nearer now and surer they sound, so he ploughs
the frosty fallow singing and, fetching our cows

home through the yaccas that burn on the misty flats,
he sings as the sundown dislodges the owls and the bats.

At school my youngster, Billy, boasts of the size
of the stones by our swamp that his friend, the prisoner, shies;

so Giovanni is coaxed into feats of strength and tussles
by little boys brought home to admire his bulging muscles.

And my wife and daughters go humming unawares,
I, too, the saddest of Sicilian airs.

161

Last night his laughter surrendered the outposts of pride,
and, moaning, he rushed from the table to his room outside;

and the crumpled paper told us our troops were bombarding
the town his sleepless prayers had long been guarding.

'*Dio buono!*' he moaned—and his wife's name—
sending his heart to an orchard dissolved in flame;

while the little photos he had often shown us streamed
blood down our minds as we listened and then as we dreamed.

Cutting chaff this morning, I heard the birds,
the sheep, and the engine itself, dinning the words,
'*Dio buono!*'

And they told me that Billy, staring wide-eyed
while the rest of the class were writing, suddenly sighed,
'*Dio buono!*'

FLEXMORE HUDSON (1913 –   )

MARRI'D

It's singin' in an' out,
    An' feelin' full of grace;
Here 'n' there, up an' down,
    An' round about th' place.

It's rollin' up your sleeves,
    An' whit'nin' up the hearths,
An' scrubbin' out th' floors,
    An' sweepin' down th' path;

It's bakin' tarts an' pies,
    An' shinin' up th' knives;
An' feelin' 's if some days
    Was worth a thousand lives.

163

It's watchin' out th' door,
　An' watchin' by th' gate;
An' watchin' down th' road,
　An' wonderin' why he's late';

An' feelin' anxious-like,
　For fear there's something wrong;
An' wonderin' why he's kep',
　An' why he takes so long.

It's comin' back inside
　An' sittin' down a spell,
To sort o' make believe
　You're thinkin' things is well.

It's gettin' up again
　An' wand'rin' in an' out;
An' feelin' wistful-like,
　Not knowin' what about;

An' flushin' all at once,
　An' smilin' just so sweet,
An' feelin' real proud
　The place is fresh an' neat.

An' feelin' awful glad
　Like them that watch'd Silo'm;
An' everything because
　A man is comin' Home!

MARY GILMORE (1865–1962)

SOUTH OF MY DAYS

South of my day's circle, part of my blood's country,
rises that tableland,[1] high delicate outline
of bony slopes wincing under the winter,
low trees blue-leaved and olive, outcropping granite—
clean, lean, hungry country. The creek's leaf-silenced,
willow-choked, the slope a tangle of medlar and crabapple
branching over and under, blotched with a green lichen;
and the old cottage lurches in for shelter.

O cold the black-frost night. The walls draw in to the warmth
and the old roof cracks its joints; the slung kettle
hisses a leak on the fire. Hardly to be believed that summer
will turn up again some day in a wave of rambler roses,
thrust its hot face in here to tell another yarn—
a story old Dan can spin into a blanket against the winter.
Seventy years of stories he clutches round his bones.
Seventy summers are hived in him like old honey.

Droving that year, Charleville to the Hunter,
nineteen-one it was, and the drought beginning;
sixty head left at the McIntyre, the mud round them
hardened like iron; and the yellow boy died
in the sulky ahead with the gear, but the horse went on,
stopped at the Sandy Camp and waited in the evening.
It was the flies we seen first, swarming like bees.
Came to the Hunter, three hundred head of a thousand—
cruel to keep them alive—and the river was dust.

Or mustering up in the Bogongs in the Autumn
when the blizzards came early. Brought them down; we brought them
down, what aren't there yet. Or driving for Cobb's on the run
up from Tamworth—Thunderbolt[2] at the top of Hungry Hill,
and I give him a wink. I wouldn't wait long, Fred,
not if I was you; the troopers are just behind,
coming for that job at the Hillgrove. He went like a luny,
him on his big black horse.

[1] New England tableland in northern N.S.W.
[2] A local bushranger.

Oh, they slide and they vanish
as he shuffles the years like a pack of conjuror's cards.
True or not, it's all the same; and the frost on the roof
cracks like a whip, and the back-log breaks into ash.
Wake, old man. This is winter, and the yarns are over.
No-one is listening.
                    South of my days' circle
I know it dark against the stars, the high lean country
full of old stories that still go walking in my sleep.

JUDITH WRIGHT (1915–   )

A CHILD IN CONVULSIONS

Did you ever see a child in convulsions? You wouldn't want to see it again: it plays the devil with a man's nerves. I'd got the beds fixed up on the floor and the billies on the fire—I was going to make some tea, and put a piece of corned beef on to boil overnight—when Jim (he'd been queer all day, and his mother was trying to hush him to sleep)—Jim, he screamed out twice. He'd been crying a good deal, and I was dog-tired and worried (over some money a man owed me) or I'd have noticed at once that there was something unusual in the way the child cried out: as it was I didn't turn round till Mary screamed 'Joe! Joe!' You know how a woman cries out when her child is in danger or dying—short, and sharp, and terrible. 'Joe! Look! look! Oh, my God, our child! Get the bath, quick! quick! it's convulsions!'

Jim was bent back like a bow, stiff as a bullock-yoke, in his mother's arms, and his eyeballs were turned up and fixed—a thing I saw twice afterwards and don't want ever to see again.

I was falling over things getting the tub and the hot water, when the woman who lived next door rushed in. She called to her husband to run for the doctor, and before the doctor came she and Mary had got Jim into a hot bath and pulled him through.

The neighbour woman made me up a shake-down in another room, and stayed with Mary that night; but it was a long while before I got Jim and Mary's screams out of my head and fell asleep.

166

You may depend I kept the fire in, and a bucket of water hot over it for a good many nights after that; but (it always happens like this) there came a night, when the fright had worn off, when I was too tired to bother about the fire, and that night Jim took us by surprise. Our wood-heap was done, and I broke up a new chair to get a fire, and had to run a quarter of a mile for water; but this turn wasn't so bad as the first, and we pulled him through.

You never saw a child in convulsions? Well, you don't want to. It must be only a matter of seconds, but it seems long minutes; and half an hour afterwards the child might be laughing and playing with you, or stretched out dead. It shook me up a lot. I was always pretty high-strung and sensitive. After Jim took the first fit, every time he cried, or turned over, or stretched out in the night, I'd jump: I was always feeling his forehead in the dark to see if he was feverish, or feeling his limbs to see if he was 'limp' yet. Mary and I often laughed about it—afterwards. I tried sleeping in another room, but for nights after Jim's first attack I'd just be dozing off into a sound sleep, when I'd hear him scream as plain as could be, and I'd hear Mary cry, 'Joe!—Joe!'—short, sharp, and terrible—and I'd be up and into their room like a shot, only to find them sleeping peacefully. Then I'd feel Jim's head and his breathing for signs of convulsions, see to the fire and water, and go back to bed and try to sleep. For the first few nights I was like that all night, and I'd feel relieved when daylight came. I'd be in first thing to see if they were all right; then I'd sleep till dinner-time if it was Sunday or I had no work. But then I was run down about that time: I was worried about some money for a wool-shed I put up and I never got paid for; and besides, I'd been pretty wild before I met Mary.

HENRY LAWSON (1867–1922)
Brighten's Sister-in-Law

ELEGY

Here, awaiting what hereafter,
Lie lissom love and lyric laughter.

She was born for earth's delight,
Not to couch in earthy night.
Crime against mankind to slay her!
Double crime to rot and clay her!

Let the lord of heaven taste
Bitterly this tragic waste,
See the beauty here destroyed,
View that breast and head left void
Of all that gave their piercing charm,
And weep irreparable harm.

Here, expecting no hereafter,
Lie murdered love and stifled laughter.

R. G. HOWARTH (1906–1973)
Spright and Geist

SONG FOR LOVERS

Love needs no pondered words,
   No high philosophy;
Enough the singing birds
   In the green tree.

Enough the touch of hand,
   Whose trembling worship tells
Faiths deeper than command
   Cathedral bells.

Blood sings fresh truths that wise
   Old Plato never knew;
Dimmed are thought's evening eyes
   By sun on dew.

Come rainbow or the rose,
   Vision shall find new birth:
With love more lovely grows
   Beauty on earth.

Darkly death waits, yet we
   In a wild hour shall know
Bright immortality,
   Before we go.

T. INGLIS MOORE (1901–1978)

TOBRUK EPISODE

Sam told me all about it. 'We tried to get his body', he said, 'but they pinned us down with M.G.s and mortars. We weren't in the race. But we'll get to him all right. We'll go back to-morrow night. . . .'

Sam led his section mates out the next night, and when they came back one of them was being carried. He had a bullet through the thigh.

'Fixed lines', said Sam. 'We'll try again to-morrow.'

They went out again the next night, and this time another was carried in. A bullet had gone right through him, probably through his lung, but it was not as bad as it sounded. We knew now that those 'sucking wounds'— the air was sucked in and out as the wounded man breathed—were not nearly as serious as a hole in the stomach. They lived with sucking wounds, they even came back to Tobruk.

'Fixed lines', said Sam. 'Those Jerry bastards.'

I heard the voice of Captain Herbertson, the company commander, and Old Gutsache's peevish voice in reply. Somebody said, 'Christ, the trump', and then we were all being called together.

'The C.O.', said Captain Herbertson, 'would like to have a word with you all'.

Old Gutsache cleared his throat, put his finger along the side of his nose in his characteristic way, and said,

'Er—it has come to my notice that patrols have been going out from this post the last two nights to bring in the body of a dead comrade, Private Carter. I understand, too, that two men have been wounded in this futile but heroic—er—gesture. Well—er—all I want to say is this; I deplore this as a soldier—it's reprehensible to have men wounded in a fruitless venture like this—I deplore it as a soldier, I say, but, by God, I admire it as a man. For truly it has been said "Greater love hath no man than this—that he give up his life for his friend". Er—that's all, men. Carry on'.

'Can I say something, sir?' asked Sam.

'Yes, corporal. Speak up, man.'

'Well sir, it's not much. It's just this: You've got most of the story right, but there's one part that's skew-whiff. We didn't go out to get Blue Carter's body. What's the use of bodies anyhow once they're dead? We didn't go out for his body. We went out to get thirty-five pounds he won at two-up. We wanted to send it home to his wife.'

LAWSON GLASSOP (1913–1966)
We Were the Rats

FREEMAN

The parson died to-day—you didn't hear?
Well, he and my old woman kept me straight,
And she's dead, too—so have another beer;
They're safe enough behind the pearly gate.

ERNEST G. MOLL (1900–   )

EVE-SONG

I span and Eve span
A thread to bind the heart of man;
But the heart of man was a wandering thing
That came and went with little to bring:
Nothing he minded what we made,
As here he loitered, and there he stayed.

I span and Eve span
A thread to bind the heart of man;
But the more we span the more we found
It wasn't his heart but ours we bound.
For children gathered about our knees:
The thread was a chain that stole our ease.
And one of us learned in our children's eyes
That more than man was love and prize.
But deep in the heart of one of us lay
A root of loss and hidden dismay.

He said he was strong. He had no strength
But that which comes of breadth and length.
He said he was fond. But his fondness proved
The flame of an hour when he was moved.
He said he was true. His truth was but
A door that winds could open and shut.

170

And yet, and yet, as he came back,
Wandering in from the outward track,
We held our arms, and gave him our breast,
As a pillowing place for his head to rest.
I span and Eve span,
A thread to bind the heart of man!

MARY GILMORE (1865–1962)

LOVE'S COMING

Quietly as rosebuds
    Talk to the thin air,
Love came so lightly
    I knew not he was there.

Quietly as lovers
    Creep at the middle moon,
Softly as players tremble
    In the tears of a tune;

Quietly as lilies
    Their faint vows declare
Came the shy pilgrim
    I knew not he was there.

Quietly as tears fall
    On a wild sin,
Softly as griefs call
    In a violin;

Without hail or tempest,
    Blue sword or flame,
Love came so lightly
    I knew not that he came.

SHAW NEILSON (1872–1942)

A BIRTH IN THE FLOOD

That's how it was for pioneer women up the country not so long ago, and Mrs Mazere had her first unaided undertaking in midwifery in which she was highly skilled by the time she took the boat across the Yarrabongo in the cloudburst flood of '52 . . .

Every evening, rain or shine, for the last fortnight Mrs Mazere had walked on the ridge back of the homestead and gazed across the river. To the right of the household rescued by the blacks was the hut of a shiftless settler whose wife had borne seven children in about six years. When husbands and maidens were out of hearing matrons discussed the case with heat and threats of what they should like to do to Porter. The victim of this satyr had had a terrifying time with the two last, and a month since had pilgrimaged to Mrs Mazere, imploring aid in her approaching trouble. Mrs Mazere had readily promised, instructing Porter that should his wife's hour come suddenly he was, any evening up till nine o'clock—at which hour the good lady and her daughters normally went to bed—to signal from the high point across the river, and she would immediately set out.

Walking in the appointed place on the Sunday of the flood she saw Porter's signal, a fire and a whirled brand. She sped into the kitchen and seizing a newspaper sent up an answering flare. It was nearing eight o'clock, a lowering night without a moon and already dark. The Yarrabongo could be faintly discerned foaming around the bend by the township. Its unusual roar filled the sullen evening, and told that it was still in wild flood. Punt and boats were gone. No horse could yet breast that stream and be sure of coming out alive, for its banks at that time were a glory of trees and shrubs, which in their remnants make the reach still one of the world's gems.

Nevertheless, Porter signalled as arranged. Rachel Mazere responded according to pledge. . . .

When the three in the boat reached the river proper it took prodigious strength and coolness to avert wreck. Impact with the current shipped a good deal of water and put the lantern out, but with determination and skill they made slight progress, and presently had as good a chance to reach the far bank as to return to the near. Mrs Mazere bailed some of the water out. The men pulled up-stream furiously, but it scarcely acted as a brake on their rapid rush. As Bert got his night eyes he saw they were below the punt crossing, at which point they had hoped to be across.

When Mrs Mazere learned how far they were down and how swiftly they

were going she first felt the full danger, and that she had been foolhardy to risk the lives of her neighbours' sons . . .

Rachel Mazere prayed from her soul, 'Spare the lives of these brave young men whom I have brought into danger, and may I too be spared for a life of usefulness in Thy service, for Christ our dear Saviour's sake. Amen'.

The prayer was answered. They were swirled by the inrushing Bulgoa right out into calm water, the only effort being to maintain equilibrium. At hand was a little pinch of high ground and while Tim held the boat, Bert picked Mrs Mazere out and carried her to safety. . . .

Then they saw the blacks' signals and Bert took Tim's place, as these were his friends. By lusty coo-ees he speedily got into touch with them and procured a horse. Seated on this with a wet coat as saddle, Tim leading, Bert walking beside her, the blacks picking the way across the inundated flats, they were not long in reaching the Porter hovel.

Mrs Mazere was soaked, but the patient's need was so urgent and terrifying that she started to the rescue without preliminaries. The case inclined her to think that God had no practical knowledge of birth as experienced by women; she further reflected that had God given birth to his son Himself, instead of imposing the task upon a woman, it might have resulted in fundamental reforms, but this she suppressed as blasphemy instigated by the Devil.

BRENT OF BIN BIN (MILES FRANKLIN) (1879–1954)
Up The Country

MOKIE'S MADRIGAL

Some little boys get shushed all day,
Can't make noises when they play;
All they do is just annoy—
I want to be a paper-boy;
Paper-boys can ride and ride
Free on all the trams outside,
No one shushes when they sing,
They can shout like anything:

Sunamirra, murdafiar!
Pyar, pyar! Wannapyar?
Tirra lirra, tirra lirra!
Murdafiar, Sunamirra!

Some little boys can never go
Everywhere they're wanting to;
Paper-boys can choose their track,
Hop on their bikes, and not come back—
Poppa, Poppa, can't you see
How you can get rid of me?
No more Mokie, no more noise,
Only other paper-boys.

Sunamirra, murdafiar!
Pyar, Pyar! Wannapyar?
Tirra lirra, tirra lirra!
Murdafiar, Sunamirra!

RONALD McCUAIG (1908–   )

JOE WILSON'S COURTSHIP

And, oh, but wasn't I happy walking home with Mary that night! She was too little for me to put my arm round her waist, so I put it round her shoulder, and that felt just as good. I remember I asked her who'd cleaned up my room and washed my things, but she wouldn't tell.

She wouldn't go back to the dance yet; she said she'd go into her room and rest a while. There was no one near the old veranda; and when she stood on the end of the floor she was just on a level with my shoulder.

'Mary', I whispered, 'put your arms round my neck and kiss me'.

She put her arms round my neck, but she didn't kiss me; she only hid her face.

'Kiss me, Mary!' I said.

'I—I don't like to', she whispered.

'Why not, Mary?'

Then I felt her crying or laughing, or half-crying and half-laughing. I'm not sure to this day which it was.

'Why won't you kiss me, Mary? Don't you love me?'

'Because', she said, 'because—because I—I don't—I don't think it's right for—for a girl to—to kiss a man unless she's going to be his wife'.

Then it dawned on me! I'd forgot all about proposing.

'Mary', I said, 'would you marry a chap like me?'

And that was all right.

HENRY LAWSON (1867–1922)
Joe Wilson and His Mates

A DOUBLE BUGGY AT LAHEY'S CREEK

Mary went and perched on the wood-heap, and shaded her eyes—though the sun had gone—and peered through between the eternal grey trunks of the stunted trees on the flat across the creek. Presently she jumped down and came running in.

'There's someone coming in a buggy, Joe!' she cried, excitedly. 'And both my white table-cloths are rough dry. Harry! put two flat-irons down to the fire, quick, and put on some more wood. It's lucky I kept those new sheets packed away. Get up out of that, Joe! What are you sitting grinning like that for? Go and get on another shirt. Hurry— Why, it's only James—by himself.'

She stared at me, and I sat there, grinning like a fool.

'Joe!' she said. 'Whose buggy is that?'

'Well, I suppose it's yours', I said.

She caught her breath, and stared at the buggy, and then at me again. James drove down out of sight into the crossing, and came up close to the house.

'Oh, Joe! what have you done?' cried Mary. 'Why, it's a new double buggy.' Then she rushed at me and hugged my head. 'Why didn't you tell me, Joe? You poor old boy!—and I've been nagging at you all day!' And she hugged me again.

James got down and started taking the horses out—as if it was an every-day occurrence. I saw the double-barrel gun sticking out from under the seat. He'd stopped to wash the buggy, and I suppose that's what made him grumpy. Mary stood on the veranda, with her eyes twice as big as usual, and breathing hard—taking the buggy in. . . .

When we were alone Mary climbed into the buggy to the seat, and made me get up alongside her. We hadn't had such a comfortable seat for years; but we soon got down, in case anyone came by, for we began to feel like a pair of fools up there.

Then we sat, side by side, on the edge of the veranda, and talked more than we'd done for years—and there was a good deal of 'Do you remember?' in it—and I think we got to understand each other better that night.

And at last Mary said, 'Do you know, Joe, why, I feel to-night just—just like I did the day we were married'.

And somehow I had that strange, shy sort of feeling too.

HENRY LAWSON (1867–1922)
Joe Wilson and His Mates

CUSTOMS AND SPORTS

CORROBOREE

The sun was near to setting—the traditional time for corroboree to begin. Down along the creek the *corps de ballet* was quieter now. The dancers were listening intently for the first booming note of the didjeridoo. Beside the fires Bun-bun had taken up his long wooden pipe. Buntuck the song-man sat next to him. Bun-bun lifted the unwieldy instrument to his lips. His right leg was extended so that the toes of the right foot took the weight of the didjeridoo. For a while his abdominal muscles worked convulsively as he built up a supply of breath. Then, as the shining rim of the sun slipped below the horizon he blew, and upon our ears broke the first note of the ancient music of the Wargaitj.

Buntuck waited until the rhythm was firmly established. Then he lifted two small sticks and beat them in rapid accompaniment. At the same moment he began to sing—a thin, piping song on a high-pitched note. If the didjeridoo was like the throb of the heart of the earth, Buntuck's song had the quality of the air. It was a wraith of a song, without body.

As the music gathered intensity, the dancers answered its ancient call.

They streamed towards us in a long, thin line, their bodies decorated with straight lines and cross-hatchings of pipe-clay. Several times they halted in their advance and, gathering together, with heads bowed to the ground, uttered a long 'Wah!' Then they flung their heads back and with arms uplifted shouted 'Hee!'

With this alternating 'Wah!' and 'Hee!', stamping as they came and flourishing their spears, they massed before the smoking fires and, crowding close, began to dance. . . .

The first dance was a piece of modern choreography composed by the leading dancer, Mosik. It was a Hunting Dance and the men, carrying spears and wommeras, stepped lightly in search of their quarry. Hooded eyes peered this way and that. There was a pretence of spear-throwing and shouts of exultation at a kill. . . .

In the Mewauk Dance the male ballet gave an impersonation of lubras at work and at play. . . .

The third piece showed how the Australian Aborigine enriches his dancing repertoire from current events. During the second world war these Wargaitj were employed on patrols sent out into their tribal country to discover crashed aeroplanes and succour their crews. In charge of a white man they travelled by launch up and down the coast or combed the bush in land parties. From this experience came the Dance of the Aeroplane Patrol. A lost aeroplane was indicated by arm and body attitudes and the dancers set out on their search. They scanned the landscape for signs of wreckage, they groped through dense undergrowth, they crossed mangrove creeks. When an advance scout reported the discovery, they crowded round him and the dance gathered fervour and intensity. Their joy at the success of the patrol was expressed in characteristic Wargaitj fashion—a group formation with heads bent to the earth and a concerted cry of 'Wah!' followed by the lifting of heads and arms to the sky and a high-pitched 'Hee!'. . . .

The fourth item was a traditional Turtle-hunting Dance.

JOHN K. EWERS (1904–1978)
With the Sun on My Back

A SYDNEY DRINKING SHOP, ABOUT 1825

After our cursory look at the market—if look it could be called which was performed in the dark—we went into 'The Market-house'. I really forget whether this was its name by licence or whether it was merely so called on account of being the principal rendezvous of the market-people. It, however, was a regular licensed public-house; but I should suppose at this time there were nearly twice as many unlicensed grog-shops as licensed public-houses in the town of Sydney, in despite of the constables and a heavy fine. In the large tap-room of the Market-house (which we entered more for the purposes of curiosity than anything else) we found a strange assemblage; and stranger still were their dialect and their notions. Most had been convicts: there were a good many Englishmen and Irishmen, an odd Scotchman, and several foreigners, besides some youngish men, natives of the colony. Amongst them was present here and there a woman, apparently the wife of a settler. The few women were all sober and quiet, but many of the men were either quite intoxicated or much elevated by liquor. The chief conversation consisted of vaunts of the goodness of their bullocks, the productiveness of their farms, or the quantity of work they could

180

perform. Almost everybody was drinking rum in drams, or very slightly qualified with water; nor were they niggard of it, for we had several invitations from those around us to drink. I could not however, even at this early period of my acquaintance with this class of people, help observing one remarkable peculiarity common to them all—there was no offensive intrusiveness about their civility; every man seemed to consider himself just on a level with all the rest, and so quite content either to be sociable or not, as the circumstance of the moment indicated as most proper. The whole company was divided into minor groups of twos, threes, and fours, and the *dudeen* (a pipe with stem reduced to three, two, one, or half an inch) was in everybody's mouth. I think there was not an individual in the room, but one female, who did not smoke more or less, during the brief time we sat there. Their dresses were of all sorts: the blue jacket and trousers of the English lagger, the short blue cotton smock-frock and trousers, the short woollen frock and trousers, fustian jacket and trousers, and so forth, beyond my utmost power of recollection. Some wore neck-handkerchiefs; some none. Some wore straw hats, some beavers, some caps of untanned kangaroo-skin. And not a shin in the room that displayed itself to my eyes had on either stocking or sock. Of course I speak here only of the very lowest class; such as were derived from the lowest rank at home, and who, whatever advantages they had had in the colony, still continued unexalted by improved opportunities, unstimulated by hope, and making no efforts beyond what were necessary to supply their mere animal wants. To the same mart came down others in various degrees superior; many, particularly among the young natives, of plain but solid worth: but this was not the place to meet with them.

ALEXANDER HARRIS (1805–1874)
Settlers and Convicts

ON THE ROAD TO GUNDAGAI

Oh, we started down from Roto when the sheds had all cut out,
We'd whips and whips of rhino[1] as we meant to push about,
So we humped our blues[2] serenely and made for Sydney town,
With a three-spot cheque between us as wanted knocking down.

[1] Money.   [2] Carried our swags.

Chorus
But we camped at Lazy Harry's on the road to Gundagai,
The road to Gundagai! Five miles from Gundagai!
Yes, we camped at Lazy Harry's on the road to Gundagai.

Oh, I've seen a lot of girls, my boys, and drunk a lot of beer,
And I've met with some of both, my boys, as left me mighty queer,
But for beer to knock you sideways and girls to make you sigh,
You must camp at Lazy Harry's on the road to Gundagai.

In a week the spree was over and the cheque was all knocked down,
And we shouldered our Matildas[3] and we turned our backs on town,
The girls they stood a nobbler as we sadly said good-bye,
And we tramped from Lazy Harry's on the road to Gundagai.

Old Bush Song

YOUR TURN TO SHOUT

I stopped outside a hotel called 'The Mansions'. The bar doors were partly open, and there were a lot of men drinking beer. I was a little thirsty from my walk, so I went in. A woman approached me, and said, 'Wot'll ut be?'
   'If you please, I would like to drink some beer.'
   She said, 'Schooner or middy?'
   After a while, I said, 'If you please, I would like to drink some beer'.
   She said much louder, 'Schooner or middy?'
   There was a man alongside me who had no coat on. He said to me, 'How long have you been in Australia, mate?'
   'I have arrived in Australia to-day.'
   'That explains ut. Those big glasses are called schooners and those small ones are called middies.'
   'Now I understand', I said. 'Thank you.'
   The woman said, 'Schooner or middy?'
   'If you please, I will have a middy.'
   The man with no coat said, 'Have one with me'.
   I said, 'Thank you sir, I would be delighted'.

   [3] Swags.

182

He said, 'Two middies, Jean'. Then to me, 'Where do you come from?'

'I am an Italian.'

'Are you? You don't look ut.'

'In Italy', I said, 'there are two kinds of people. Those who live in the north, and those who live in the south. I am of the north'.

'Are they all big blokes like you?'

'What, please, is a bloke?'

'Eh? Oh, everybody's a bloke. You're a bloke. I'm a bloke. We're all blokes.'

'Oh, I see. Like what the Americans call guys?'

'Yeah, something.' He handed me the beer, and raised his own to his lips. 'Cheers.'

I replied, 'Cheers', and drank some of my beer. It was very good.

He said, 'Tasted Australian beer before?'

'No. This is the first time.'

'Best beer in the world. Puts a gut on yer, though. Wodda yer do for a crust?'

'I am sorry. I do not understand the Australian patois. Could you please use English words?'

'Sure, you'll get used to our slang if yer live long enough. How do you earn your living?'

'I am a writer.'

'In Italian?'

'Yes. In Italian.'

'They tell me it's an easy language to learn?'

'It is not as difficult as English.'

'Yeah, English is a bastard of a language.'

'I think Australian is a bastard of a language.'

He laughed, 'You're learning already. Your turn'.

'What is my turn?'

'Your turn to shout.'

'Why should I shout?'

'Because I shouted you.'

'I did not hear you shout at me.'

He thought for a while and said, 'I get ut. When you buy a bloke a beer, it's called a shout, see?'

'Why is that?'

'Haven't a clue, but that's what it's called. I shouted for you, now it's your turn to shout for me.'

'I was only a little thirsty. I do not think I wish another drink.'

He looked quite stern. 'In this country, if you want to keep out of trouble, you always return a shout, see?'

'It is the custom?'

'Bloody oath it's the custom. Your turn.'

'Would it be all right if I bought a drink for you, and did not have one myself?'

'No, it wouldn't be all right. That's the worst insult you can offer a man.'

'Why?'

'Means you don't think he's good enough to drink with.'

'Oh. Then I will shout.'

'You better.' He called to the woman, 'Jean . . . two more'.

She approached us, and said, 'Something similar?'

I said, 'Yes. I wish to shout'.

She looked at me as though I had said something wrong, but got two more beers. I raised mine, and said, 'Cheers'.

NINO CULOTTA (JOHN O'GRADY) (1908–1981)

They're a Weird Mob

INTEGRATED ADJECTIVE

I was down on Riverina,[1] knockin' round the towns a bit,
An' occasionally restin', with a schooner[2] in me mitt;
An' on one o' these occasions, when the bar was pretty full
An' the local blokes were arguin' assorted kind o' bull,[3]
I heard a conversation, most peculiar in its way,
Because only in Australia would you hear a joker say
'Where yer bloody been yer drongo?[4] 'Aven't seen yer fer a week;
An' yer mate was lookin' for yer when 'e come in from the Creek;
'E was lookin' up at Ryan's, an' around at bloody Joe's,
An' even at the Royal where 'e bloody never goes'.
An' the other bloke said 'Seen 'im. Owed 'im 'alf a bloody quid.
Forgot ter give ut back to 'im; but now I bloody did.
Coulda used the thing me-bloody-self; been orf the bloody booze,
Up at Tumba-bloody-rumba[5] shootin' kanga-bloody-roos'.

---

[1] Southern district in New South Wales.   [2] Large glass of beer.
[3] Nonsense.   [4] Nitwit, used facetiously here.   [5] Tumbarumba, a N.S.W. town.

Now their voices were a little loud, an' everybody heard
The peculiar integration of this adjectival word,
But no one there was laughin', an' me I wasn't game,
So I stood around an' let 'em think I spoke the bloody same.
An' one of 'em was interested to ask 'im what he'd got—
How many kanga-bloody-roos he bloody went an' shot—
An' the shootin' bloke said 'Things are crook; the drought's too bloody tough;
I got forty-bloody-seven, an' that's good e-bloody-nough'.
An' this polite rejoinder seemed to satisfy the mob,
An' everyone stopped listenin' an' got on with the job,
Which was drinkin' beer an' arguin' an' talkin' of the heat,
An' boggin' in the bitumen in the middle of the street;
But as for me I'm here to say the interestin' news
Was 'Tumba-bloody-rumba shootin' kanga-bloody-roos'.

JOHN O'GRADY (NINO CULOTTA) (1908–1981)

KATE'S WEDDING

It was when Kate was married to Sandy Taylor that we realised what a blessing it is to be able to dance. How we looked forward to that wedding! We were always talking about it, and were very pleased it would be held in our own house, because all of us could go then. . . .

Each of us had his own work to do. Sandy knocked the partition down and decorated the place with boughs; Mother and the girls cooked and covered the walls with newspapers, and Dad gathered cow-dung and did the ground floor. . . .

The wedding was on a Wednesday, and at three o'clock in the afternoon. Most of the people came before dinner; the Hamiltons arrived just after breakfast. Talk of drays!—the little paddock couldn't hold them.

Jim Mullins was the only one who came in to dinner; the others mostly sat on their heels in a row and waited in the shade of the wire-fence. The parson was the last to come, and as he passed in he knocked his head against the kangaroo-leg hanging under the veranda. Dad saw it swinging, and said angrily to Joe: 'Didn't I tell you to take that down this morning?'

Joe unhooked it and said: 'But if I hang it anywhere else the dog'll get it'.

185

Dad tried to laugh at Joe, and said, loudly: 'And what else is it for?' Then he bustled Joe off before he could answer him again.

Joe didn't understand.

Then Dad said (putting the leg in a bag): 'Do you want everyone to know we eat it, ———— you?'

Joe understood.

The ceremony commenced. Those who could squeeze inside did so—the others looked in at the window and through the cracks in the chimney.

Mrs M'Doolan led Kate out of the back-room; then Sandy rose from the fire-place and stood beside her. Everyone thought Kate looked very nice—and orange blossoms! You'd think she was an orange-tree with a new bed-curtain thrown over it. Sandy looked well, too, in his snake-belt and new tweeds; but he seemed uncomfortable when the pin that Dave put in the back of his collar came out.

The parson didn't take long; and how they scrambled and tumbled over each other at the finish! Charley Mace said that he got the first kiss; Big George said *he* did; and Mrs M'Doolan was certain she would have got it only for the baby.

Fun! there *was* fun! The room was cleared and they promenaded for a dance—Sandy and Kate in the lead. They continued promenading until one of the well-sinkers called for the concertina—ours had been repaired till you could only get three notes out of it; but Jim Burke jumped on his horse and went home for his accordion.

Dance! they did dance!—until sun-rise. But unless you were dancing you couldn't stay inside, because the floor broke up, and talk about dust!—before morning the room was like a drafting-yard.

It was a great wedding; and though years have since passed, all the neighbours say still it was the best they were ever at.

STEELE RUDD (A. H. DAVIS) (1868–1935)
On Our Selection

HOW BILLY HUGHES WON THE BALLOT

William Morris Hughes, most colourful and dynamic of Australia's political leaders, who became an international figure as Australian Prime Minister during the First World War, here describes how he won his first selection ballot as a Labour candidate in Sydney. He won the election and thereafter sat in Parliament without a break for fifty-eight years, six years in New South Wales and fifty-two years in the Commonwealth Parliament.

186

When the tocsin sounded in 1894 and a dissolution called the newly formed legions of Labour to the assault of the citadel of privilege, I was summoned to Sydney, and, leaving my horse at Molong, came down without loss of time to discuss with the leaders of the movement the arrangements for conducting the campaign. The selection of candidates first claimed our attention. In some electorates men had been already chosen, and amongst these my name appeared twice, for I had been selected by the Leagues in two different constituencies. My friends warmly congratulated me . . .

'My friends', I said, 'those seats are no good to me. I must have one within the radius of a penny tram section'.

My friends looked at me in stupefied amazement. 'Within a penny tram section?' They could not have been more surprised had I declared in favour of a light blue electorate with mauve trimmings! They thought I was not quite right in my head. But when I explained that poverty and not my will fettered my eager soul, they reluctantly accepted the position.

We ran through the lists of electorates within the penny tram radius for which candidates had not yet been selected. There was only one that filled the bill—that was the Lang Division of West Sydney. I had the haziest notions of its boundaries; of its people I knew nothing; but without more ado I plumped for it. Then my troubles began. I found, on inquiry, that there were already five Richmonds in the field, every one of whom bitterly resented my intrusion. One of these aspirants was a publican, and all were sinners . . .

And then the votings began. I shall not forget that night in a hurry. I have never found life dull; I like life, bustle, movement, and I thrive on excitement; but, after all, one can have too much of a good thing. From the word go the electors of the Lang Division made it willing—they poured into the Little Mission Church like flood waters rushing down a mountain gorge. They wanted not the spur of compulsory voting. The trouble was not to get them to vote, but to induce them to leave off. They were so desperately in earnest that it was only by unwearying vigilance backed by *force majeure* that they were prevented from voting again and again. They would go out, refresh themselves with beer, rearrange their hats, turn up the collars of their coats, and jauntily re-enter and once more endeavour to record their vote. Baulked in one direction, they tried another. Since they could not vote twice on the same 'electric right'— or vote at all unless they had one—they immediately set out in search of loose or unattended rights.

Some sneaked furtively into their homes and lifted the old man's right while he was at tea. The tedium of those stretched on beds of sickness was relieved by numerous callers, who, oozing sympathy at ever pore, sought to coax from the invalid 'the loan of your electric right'. And many a man dead these six months and more put in his little vote that night through the hand of one who had not forgotten him, or where his elector's right was to be found.

At nine o'clock MacDermott announced in thunderous tones that the ballot had closed, and that the result would be declared as soon as possible. The narrow street was crowded, an air of suppressed excitement prevailed. . . . Then, suddenly, the end came! The crowd, which had been unnaturally quiet, sprang into life. A roar burst upon my ears. 'What is it?' I asked. 'Run for your life', said one of my friends, 'you have been selected'.

W. M. HUGHES (1864–1952)
Crusts and Crusades

STANDING BY HIS MATE

The typical Australian had no respect whatever for the possessor of money as such. The whole tendency of his individualism had been to protect the weaker member. While the sympathy of the American was usually for the strong, that of the Australian was for those who lacked advantage. He was seldom religious in the sense in which the word is generally used. So far as he held a prevailing creed, it was a romantic one inherited from the gold-miner and the bushman, of which the chief article was that a man should at all times and at any cost stand by his mate. This was and is the one law which the good Australian must never break. It is bred in the child and stays with him through life. In the last few moments before the bloody attack upon Lone Pine in Gallipoli, when the 3rd Australian Infantry Battalion was crowded on the fire-steps of each bay of its old front-line trench waiting for the final signal to scramble over the sand-bags above, a man with rifle in hand, bayonet fixed, came peering along the trench below. 'Jim here?' he asked. A voice on the fire-step answered 'Right, Bill; here'. 'Do you chaps mind shiftin' up a piece?' said the man in the trench. 'Him and me are mates, an' we're goin' over together.' The same thing must have happened many thousands of times in the Australian divisions. The strongest bond in the Australian Imperial Force was that between a man and his mate. No matter how hardened a sinner against camp rules, how often in trouble at the *estaminet,* an Australian seemed never to fail in the purely self-imposed duty of standing by his wounded friend whenever his task in the battle permitted him to do so. In the foulest French winter, or at Cape Helles when bullets seemed to be raining in sheets, on every occasion when an Australian force went into action there were to be found men who, come what might, regardless of death or wounds, stayed by their fallen friends until they had seen them into safety.

C. E. W. BEAN (1879–1968)
The Official History of Australia in the War of 1914–1918

THE UNION BURIES ITS DEAD

Next day a funeral gathered at a corner pub and asked each other in to have a drink while waiting for the hearse. They passed away some of the time dancing jigs to a piano in the bar parlour. They passed away the rest of the time skylarking and fighting.

The defunct was a young Union labourer, about twenty-five, who had been drowned the previous day while trying to swim some horses across a billabong of the Darling.

He was almost a stranger in town, and the fact of his having been a Union man accounted for the funeral. The police found some Union papers in his swag, and called at the General Labourers' Union Office for information about him. That's how we knew. The secretary had very little information to give. The departed was a 'Roman', and the majority of the town were otherwise—but Unionism is stronger than creed. Liquor, however, is stronger than Unionism; and when the hearse presently arrived, more than two-thirds of the funeral were unable to follow.

The procession numbered fifteen, fourteen souls following the broken shell of a soul. Perhaps not one of the fourteen possessed a soul any more than the corpse did—but that doesn't matter.

Four or five of the funeral, who were boarders at the pub, borrowed a trap which the landlord used to carry passengers to and from the railway station. They were strangers to us who were on foot, and we to them. We were all strangers to the corpse.

A horseman, who looked like a drover just returned from a big trip, dropped into our dusty wake and followed us a few hundred yards, dragging his packhorse behind him, but a friend made wild and demonstrative signals from a hotel veranda—hooking at the air in front with his right hand and jobbing his left thumb over his shoulder in the direction of the bar—so the drover hauled off and didn't catch up to us any more. He was a stranger to the entire show.

We walked in twos. There were three twos. It was very hot and dusty; the heat rushed in fierce dazzling rays across every iron roof and light-coloured wall that was turned to the sun. One or two pubs closed respectfully until we got past. They closed their bar doors and the patrons went in and out through some side or back entrance for a few minutes. Bushmen seldom grumble at an inconvenience of this sort, when it is caused by a funeral. They have too much respect for the dead.

HENRY LAWSON (1867–1922)

JOINING THE UNION

In this case, we're all good fellows—or supposed to be. Three hundred of us, all in our Sunday best, crowded into the narrow lane alongside the Hall on a bright afternoon in mid-winter. Three hundred Second Preference men all agog at the prospect of becoming Federation[1] men in the next few blessed hours, of walking the Dock Road next week with the magical little blue button in our lapels, of standing up for work in the sacred inner precincts of the Compound, of getting good ships and being in on the big money. It's been a long road for most of us, a road measured in years, in workless weeks, in bitter struggles 'on the outer' for all the wretched scraps of jobs that were turned down inside: sulphur, superphosphates, soda ash, freezer, double-dump wool. We've cursed the Federation from Hell to Booligal for all the muck they've tossed out at us, but there isn't one of us here who isn't licking his lips over what's going to happen next week. It'll be worth it all, if only for the joy of presenting our insolent backs to the first foreman who picks up for wool on Monday morning—'Take it out to the bloody Seconds!'. . .

The recruit immediately preceding me turns to give me a happy smile, and both of us spontaneously salute. We feel suddenly rich. And not because of bigger pay envelopes to come. We've got ourselves three

[1] Waterside Workers' Federation.

thousand mates. We've come through. We're Federation men. We can wear the little blue button with the clasped hands on it . . .

My palms tingle. How much more is it than the simple design of a badge!

JOHN MORRISON (1904–   )
Going Through

THE FLYING DOCTOR

In May 1928 Dr K. St Vincent Welch and pilot Arthur Affleck set out without any fuss on the first flight that inaugurated the Aerial Medical Service, one of the most important flights in the history of aviation in Australia. And a world flight historically, for it inaugurated the world's first flying-ambulance service. The doctor's first case (calling immediately he reached Cloncurry) was to save the life of a man who had cut his throat!. . . .

The A.M.S. was firmly established. The first flying doctor had increased the ordinary 'radius' of the A.M.S. to four hundred miles, saved valuable lives, alleviated untold suffering, and brought a feeling of security to that particular portion of the Inland which the people had never experienced before. The area actually flown over by the Red Cross machine during the experimental stage was larger than New South Wales. . . .

The apparently insuperable difficulty of landing grounds had been overcome in the good old bush way. Stations prepared their own landing grounds by knocking down a tree or two and bowling over a few ant beds. Others when they radio for help describe the 'cleared paddock' or bare patch that must serve for the aerodrome. Then, the doctor far away asks a few terse questions:

'Have you four hundred yards clear run against winds?'

'Yes.'

'Are there any trees close?'

'A few.'

'Well, could you drive a car straight over that ground at thirty miles an hour? — You think you could? H'm. Well, then, expect us in an hour!' And the machine roars up and away.

ION L. IDRIESS (1890–1979)
Flynn of the Inland

A GAME OF TWO-UP

They stopped at the outer edge of the crowd for a while, Ransome having a look at how the pennies were falling and searching for the tail-bettors and faces he knew. Some of the players drifted away, and before long they had edged right on to the side of the ring.

Ransome had stood on the edge of a ring like that more times than he could remember, and in some funny spots; especially while he was in the Army, but the curious drama of a two-up ring at night was never lost to him. Perhaps it was just the light that palely gilded the two circles of dis-embodied faces, of the men kneeling at the ringside and of those standing behind. Perhaps it was the faces themselves, all naked expression without a visible body to water it down—he found himself thinking, as he had done a thousand times before, *If I make a killing-to-night, I'll be damn careful getting away from the ring and back to camp!* . . .

Staring straight ahead of him he became aware of a small, skinny man in a grimy singlet who squatted on the opposite side of the ring, his hands red with the red dust of the hillside, his eyes black and button-bright with inquiry in the light of the lamp. A wet, foul butt drooped from one end of this thin mouth and he spoke around it, looking straight at Kernow.

'Ten-bob he tails 'em!' he said, the butt wagging raffishly as he spoke. 'I got ten-bob to say he tails 'em—ten-bob the micks!' He raised his brow and shook the notes in his hand.

Kernow, as though he had been doing it for years, slowly peeled a note off the roll he had in his hand and tossed it across to the other side of the ring.

'Set', he said, as he had heard the other say, and Ransome, standing alongside him, grinned. The pennies flickered in the air, the ringkeeper's mate stooped over them where they lay on the ground and sang out, 'Heads—heads 're right!' . . .

Kernow stood in the middle of the bare patch of red dirt, still as a rock while the ringkeeper's mate put the pennies on the kip. A couple of later bettors called their bets, and were set; silence settled over the ring except for the hissing of the lamps. . . .

'You ain't kiddin'!' the ringkeeper's mate muttered, and stepped back from him. 'You right, mate? All set on the side, gents? All right, come in, spinner!'

The two rows of faces around the ring, Ransome's among them, lifted and dropped again. Kernow headed them, and no mistake; two lovely pictures of Victoria looking up at them from the red dust.

T. A. G. HUNGERFORD (1915–   )
Riverslake

CARBINE WINS THE MELBOURNE CUP

Many hearty ovations have in the past awaited popular winners at Flemington, but never in the history of the Australian turf has there been such a demonstration as that which marked Carbine's phenomenal victory. Even before the race started it was made manifest that the famous son of Musket and Mersey was 'the people's favourite', as he was heartily cheered as he emerged from the saddling paddock and walked slowly down to do his preliminary. Carbine was the first to appear on the course, and on his arrival at the post such a rush of admirers took place that the assistance of the police was necessary before the course could be cleared. Long before the No. 1 was hoisted by the judge, in fact before the champion had reached the winning post, the spectators burst into wild expressions of delight and admiration, as it could be seen some distance from the post that Carbine would have to fall down to lose. As the clerk of the course escorted him back to the weighing yard, winner of the most valuable handicap race ever run in the world (10,000 sovs.), the scene was one to be remembered. Inside the enclosure his popular owner was receiving the hearty congratulations of his friends, and acknowledging the cheers of the assembled thousands. . . .

By his great triumph in the Melbourne Cup, Carbine has broken more than one record in connection with that famous event. He carried 10 st 5 lbs, a weight never previously borne to victory in a Melbourne Cup, and beat the best time previously recorded for that race (3 min. 28½ secs.) by a quarter of a second.

The *Age* (5 November 1890)

WHEN KING RABBIT WON
THE GRANTHAM STAKES

The frantic clamour of the bookmakers roared around us as we entered the ring. Men and women surged about the stands hurling money away with both hands. Punters pleaded to be allowed to lay odds on the favourite and elbowed each other out of the way in their earnest desire to be robbed. Tip-slingers, urgers and whisperers slunk like jackals through the crowd, and grave and massive policemen placed their furtive bets. I shrunk from the ordeal, but how can man die better than by facing fearful odds? The rest of the gang came up and with a parting glance at Steak, I plunged into the riot.

Pausing at a stand, I addressed the open mouth of a bawling bookmaker.

'What price King Rabbit?'

''Oo? King Rabbit? Never 'eard of it. King Rabbit?—Ar, yes, four to one, King Rabbit.'

I turned away.

'Well, eight to one', he bawled. 'Tens!'

I continued on my way.

'Fifteens!' he yelled. 'Twenties! Well, go to blazes!'

I emerged at long last with my head throbbing under Temple's hat and the dust of conflict clinging to my boots.

Steak was waiting for me, with Eggs. I handed her a ticket.

'Sixty-eight pounds!' she shrieked. 'He must have been thirty-three to one!'

'You went to a good school', I said.

'Gimme half if it wins', pleaded Eggs.

Steak impaled her with a glance.

'This is my ticket', she said coldly. 'Stanley will get yours.'

'But he's only putting ten shillings on for me', wailed Eggs.

'Faulty work', said Steak succinctly. 'Come and we'll watch the race, honey', she added, taking my arm.

Never, never shall I forget that race. When I am old and peevish, sans teeth, sans hair, and shod with elastic-sided boots, I shall be content merely with the memory of that race. When St Peter asks me my greatest display of charity and fortitude on earth, my answer will be that I refrained from choking Steak when King Rabbit won the Grantham Stakes.

When the barrier went up, the jockey seemed quite oblivious to the fact that I had four pounds on his mount. He appeared to go to sleep on the horse's neck. They wallowed round the bend behind everything else that had legs. The jockey seemed to be about as useful as a wart on the hip and I groaned aloud.

To this day, I believe the horse heard me. He laid his ears back, opened his mouth and accelerated. He threw his legs about in wild abandon. His hoofs touched the turf merely here and there. He flung himself along like a thing gone mad. His tail stood out. Like a chestnut bullet he sped past the field, past the favourite, past the winning post, and twice around the course before he could be pulled up. Doped, of course.

The great, beautiful, brave beast, may he live for a hundred years and die in a lucerne paddock surrounded by his progeny.

Hoarse with shouting, my hands sore from beating the railing, I assisted the almost unconscious Steak out of the crowd. The stricken punters were very, very, very quiet and the happy laughter of the bookmakers plunged the iron into their souls.

Thirty-three to one! Even now my hand trembles as I write.

One hundred and thirty-six pounds I collected, and sixty-eight for Steak. If horses have halos when they die, King Rabbit should look like a zebra. We were joined by the rest of the party. I wanted to go home. I was padded with notes.

L. W. LOWER (1904–1947)
Here's Luck

HOW M'DOUGAL TOPPED THE SCORE

A peaceful spot is Piper's Flat. The folk that live around—
They keep themselves by keeping sheep and turning up the ground:
But the climate is erratic, and the consequences are
The struggle with the elements is everlasting war.
We plough, and sow, and harrow—then sit down and pray for rain;
And then we all get flooded out and have to start again.
But the folk are now rejoicing as they ne'er rejoiced before,
For we've played Molongo cricket, and M'Dougal topped the score!

Molongo had a head on it, and challenged us to play
A single-innings match for lunch—the losing team to pay.
We were not great guns at cricket, but we couldn't well say no,
So we all began to practise, and we let the reaping go.
We scoured the Flat for ten miles round to muster up our men.
But when the list was totalled we could only number ten.
Then up spoke big Tim Brady: he was always slow to speak,
And he said—'What price M'Dougal, who lives down at Cooper's Creek?'

So we sent for old M'Dougal, and he stated in reply
That he'd never played at cricket, but he'd half a mind to try.
He couldn't come to practice—he was getting in his hay,
But he guessed he'd show the beggars from Molongo how to play.
Now, M'Dougal was a Scotchman, and a canny one at that,
So he started in to practise with a paling for a bat.
He got Mrs Mac to bowl to him, but she couldn't run at all,
So he trained his sheep-dog, Pincher, how to scout and fetch the ball.

Now, Pincher was no puppy; he was old, and worn, and grey;
But he understood M'Dougal, and—accustomed to obey—
When M'Dougal cried out 'Fetch it!' he would fetch it in a trice,
But, until the word was 'Drop it!' he would grip it like a vice.
And each succeeding night they played until the light grew dim:
Sometimes M'Dougal struck the ball—sometimes the ball struck him.
Each time he struck, the ball would plough a furrow in the ground;
And when he missed, the impetus would turn him three times round.

The fatal day at length arrived—the day that was to see
Molongo bite the dust, or Piper's Flat knocked up a tree!
Molongo's captain won the toss, and sent his men to bat,
And they gave some leather-hunting to the men of Piper's Flat.
When the ball sped where M'Dougal stood, firm planted in its track,
He shut his eyes, and turned him round, and stopped it—with his *back*!
The highest score was twenty-two, the total sixty-six,
When Brady sent a yorker down that scattered Johnson's sticks.

Then Piper's Flat went in to bat, for glory and renown,
But, like the grass before the scythe, our wickets tumbled down.
'Nine wickets down for seventeen, with fifty more to win!'
Our captain heaved a heavy sigh, and sent M'Dougal in.
'Ten pounds to one you'll lose it!' cried a barracker from town;
But M'Dougal said, 'I'll tak' it, mon!' and planked the money down.
Then he girded up his moleskins in a self-reliant style,
Threw off his hat and boots and faced the bowler with a smile.

He held the bat the wrong side out, and Johnson with a grin,
Stepped lightly to the bowling crease, and sent a 'wobbler' in;
M'Dougal spooned it softly back, and Johnson waited there,
But M'Dougal crying 'Fetch it!' started running like a hare.
Molongo shouted 'Victory! He's out as sure as eggs'.
When Pincher started through the crowd, and ran through Johnson's legs.
He seized the ball like lightning; then he ran behind a log,
And M'Dougal kept on running, while Molongo chased the dog.

They chased him up, they chased him down, they chased him round and then
He darted through a slip-rail as the scorer shouted 'Ten!'
M'Dougal puffed; Molongo swore; excitement was intense;
As the scorer marked down 'Twenty', Pincher cleared a barbed-wire fence.
'Let us head him!' shrieked Molongo. 'Brain the mongrel with a bat!'
'Run it out! Good old M'Dougal!' yelled the men of Piper's Flat.
And M'Dougal kept on jogging, and then Pincher doubled back,
And the scorer counted 'Forty' as they raced across the track.

M'Dougal's legs were going fast, Molongo's breath was gone—
But while Molongo chased the dog—M'Dougal struggled on.
When the scorer shouted 'Fifty!' then they knew the chase would cease;
And M'Dougal gasped out 'Drop it!' as he dropped within his crease.
Then Pincher dropped the ball, and, as instinctively he knew
Discretion was the wiser plan, he disappeared from view.
And as Molongo's beaten men exhausted lay around,
We raised M'Dougal shoulder-high, and bore him from the ground.

We bore him to M'Ginniss's, where lunch was ready laid,
And filled him up with whisky-punch, for which Molongo paid.
We drank his health in bumpers, and we cheered him three times three,
And when Molongo got its breath, Molongo joined the spree.
And the critics say they never saw a cricket match like that,
When M'Dougal broke the record in the game at Piper's Flat.
And the folk are jubilating as they never were before;
For we played Molongo cricket, and M'Dougal topped the score!

THOMAS E. SPENCER (1845–1910)

VICTOR TRUMPER BATS INCOGNITO

The Demon is now madder than a bull with a bee-sting on his muzzle. He snorts, he slathers, he scowls, he mutters. He digs holes now as he runs up. His arms swing over like the blades of a reaper and binder. He leaps nearly six feet in the air and the ball sizzles towards the young bloke's head.

'Duck!' yells the skipper.

Don't ask me how it happens, but the young bloke's bat is there and the ball streaks out past square leg for four.

'Didn't I tell you to duck!' yells the skipper.

'I'm sorry, but I didn't have time', says the young bloke. 'It was on me before I could do as you said.'

The next over of the Demon's somehow finds the young bloke taking the strike, and again the skipper tells him what to do and when to duck, and again the willowy young bloke does it different and then apologizes to the skipper, and all the while the runs mount up and up. The young bloke hits six fours and two sixes off the Demon in the over and the Demon and the rest of us can hardly believe our eyes. At the end of the over the Demon is frothing at the mouth, the skipper has decided to let the young bloke bat in his own way, and the rest of us are waking up to what we are seeing.

In the next over the willowy young cove does everything to the Demon except hit him over the head with the bat. He jumps yards down the wicket and smashes the ball back past the Demon or belts it high over the boundary. He goes back on his stumps and hooks the ball off his eyebrows to the leg boundary. He does late cuts and he does square cuts, he does pulls and he does glances. And the Demon, he bellows, he runs harder, he jumps higher at the crease, he swings his arms over faster. He boils in the sun, he sweats in bucketfuls, he gets glassy-eyed and he sways on his feet.

And the young bloke goes on. He drives, he cuts, he glances, he pulls, he hooks. It's a four off almost every ball and a sixer off every third.

In no time he has a hundred and then one hundred and fifty. The skipper, too, has got back his ruddy brown, and he, too, belts the Demon a little. And both of them slather the other bowlers.

Before long we have passed the other mob and we know we have seen a wizard batsman. When he hits a lolly and gets out we cheer him madly. It is only later that we realise we don't know his name.

DAL STIVENS (1911–   )
The Batting Wizard from the City

THE SCARLET PIMPERNEL

Clarrie Grimmet was known by more than one *nom de ballon*, among them 'The Fox' and 'The Gnome'. His team-mates called him 'Scarlet', not because he ever painted the town red, but as a contraction of 'The Scarlet Pimpernel'—in grateful acknowledgment of his many lone-hand exploits in rescuing the Australians from perilous situations with a coolness and ingenuity worthy of Sir Percy Blakeney. . . .

In England he bore the brunt of the attack in 1930 so admirably that his team-mate Fairfax thought him more important to the side than Bradman. Without going so far, the captain, Woodfull, told me that if the team had lost Bradman the remaining batting strength would have been capable of presentable scores, but if Scarlet had fallen by the wayside Australia's position would have been hopeless. Grimmet's deeds in 1930 were given comparatively little recognition until the hardy veteran fell ill for a couple of days. Australia's relief at his recovery was so great that one newspaper came out with a front-page heading: GRIMMET GETS UP FOR LUNCH.

On Australian turf he took 39 English wickets in nine Tests, and paid seven runs apiece more for them than in England, where his 67 wickets in 13 matches is the record for a bowler of either country.

RAY ROBINSON (1905–   )
Between Wickets

BRADMAN VERSUS BODYLINE

That innings of 103 was the only real setback Jardine suffered at Bradman's hands in his war of nerves against Australia's batsmen. Though Don was seldom dismissed for a low score all his other innings against bodyline were marked by an agitation which showed itself in overtones of rashness and an undertone of uneasiness, as if he were jittery—as he had ample cause to be. It was most evident in his retreats to a new line, wide of the leg stump. A more nervous short-leg fieldsman than Jardine might have felt concerned lest his toes be trodden on.

From his remote disadvantage-point Bradman indulged in swishful thinking by attempting slashing square-cuts and cover-hits. His bat, so often described as a flashing broadsword, was used more like a harpoon. If, instead of a bodyliner, the ball happened to be straight, Whaler Bradman trusted to luck that it would clear his foresaken stumps. . . .

A secondary factor was his haymaking off other bowlers before the bodyliners could cloud out the sunshine. In the third Test, after bumpers from Larwood in the first innings had struck Woodfull over the heart and Oldfield had been carried off with a head injury—casualties accidentally suffered under enemy action—Jardine did not consent to Larwood's appeals for the bodyline setting in the second innings until Australia's score was 75 (Bradman 46). Don then assailed Verity's bowling brilliantly and one of his threshing strokes, a six over long-on, struck a woman onlooker. I think Don was right in going for every run in the respites between bodyline, as there were few positive ways to combat Jardine's plans. There was something feverish in Bradman's brilliance. It was as if he had posted up one of those shop placards: *Great Fire Sale. Everything Must Go.* This time, he jumped down the wicket to almost every ball until Verity caught a hard drive to dismiss him for 66, made in only 77 minutes. On entering the dressing room Bradman was asked why he had not gone a little steadier. He replied frankly: 'Oh, I wanted to hit one bowler before the other hit me'. . . .

That stormy season left on Bradman's batmanship a scar which never completely faded. . . .

Counting everything in, Bradman is the greatest batsman I ever saw. I am grateful for him as he is, scar and all, and would never wish him to be a cricketing counterpart of Superman or some other indestructible character from an adventure strip who overcomes difficulties so easily that he forfeits all claim to credit for his deeds.

RAY ROBINSON (1905–   )
Between Wickets

POEMS, SONGS AND BALLADS

ARANDA SONG

This song of the Aboriginals in Central Australia pictures the bloodwood trees in blossom, circled by clouds of birds.

The ringneck parrots, in scattered flocks,
The ringneck parrots are screaming in their upward flight.

The ringneck parrots are a cloud of wings;
The shell parrots are a cloud of wings.

Let the shell parrots come down to rest, —
Let them come down to rest on the ground!

Let the caps fly off the scented blossoms!
Let the caps fly off the bloodwood blossoms!

Let the caps fly off the scented blossoms!
Let the blossoms descend to the ground in a shower!

The clustering bloodwood blooms are falling down, —
The clustering bloodwood blossoms, nipped by birds.

The clustering bloodwood blooms are falling down, —
The clustering bloodwood blossoms, one by one.

Translated from the Aranda by T. G. H. STREHLOW (1908–1978)

WANDERER'S LAMENT

A song of the Aboriginals who, when away from their tribal country, call upon it at sundown, since it is the giver of all and is sacred through the tribal heroes of the mythical Dreaming Time. If the native, since the coming of the white man, is separated from his country and tribe, his lonely life loses meaning and he welcomes death.

Poor fellow me,
Poor fellow me,
My country
It gave me
All that I see,
Gifts that I see,
All that I see,
Poor fellow me.

Once I was gay,
Once I was gay,
Once I was gay,
Poor fellow me.
Then came the day,
I went away,
Now I am grey,
Poor fellow me.

Now I'm alone,
Now I'm alone,
Now I'm alone,
Poor fellow me.
Nothing I own,
Spirit has flown,
Poor fellow me.

So let me die,
Peaceful I lie,
Let my shade fly,
Poor fellow me,
Poor fellow me.

W. E. HARNEY (1895–1962) *and* A. P. ELKIN (1891–   )
Songs of the Songman

JACK DONAHUE

A life that is free as the bandits' of old,
When Rome was the prey of the warriors bold
Who knew how to buy gallant soldiers with gold,
Is the life, full of danger,
Of Jack the bushranger,
Of brave Donahue!

If Ireland lies groaning, a hand at her throat,
Which foreigners have from the recreants bought,
Forget not the lessons our fathers have taught.
Though our Isle's full of danger,
And held by the stranger,
Be brave and be true!

I've left the old Island's hospitable shores,
The land of the Emmets, the Tones, and the Moores;
But Liberty o'er me her scalding tear pours,
And she points to the manger,
Where *He* was a stranger,
And perished for you.

Then hurl me to crime and brand me with shame,
But think not to baulk me, my spirit to tame,
For I'll fight to the last in old Ireland's name,
Though I be a bushranger,
You still are the stranger,
And I'm Donahue.

Old Bush Song

THE OVERLANDER

There's a trade you all know well—
It's bringing cattle over—
I'll tell you all about the time
When I became a drover.

I made up my mind to try the spec,
To the Clarence I did wander,
And bought a mob of duffers there
To begin as an overlander.

Chorus
Pass the wine cup round, my boys;
Don't let the bottle stand there,
For to-night we'll drink the health
Of every overlander.

When the cattle were all mustered,
And the outfit ready to start,
I saw the lads all mounted,
With their swags left in the cart.
All kinds of men I had
From France, Germany, and Flanders;
Lawyers, doctors, good and bad,
In the mob of overlanders.

From the road I then fed out
When the grass was green and young;
When a squatter with curse and shout
Told me to move along.
I said, 'You're very hard;
Take care, don't raise my dander,
For I'm a regular knowing card,
The Queensland overlander'.

.　.　.　.　.　.

The pretty girls in Brisbane
Were hanging out their duds.
I wished to have a chat with them,
So steered straight for the tubs.
Some dirty urchins saw me,
And soon they raised my dander,
Crying, 'Mother, quick! take in the clothes,
Here comes an overlander!'

In town we drain the wine cup,
And go to see the play,
And never think to be hard up
For how to pass the day.
Each has a sweetheart there,
Dressed out in all her grandeur—
Dark eyes and jet black flowing hair,
'She's a plum', says the overlander.

Old Bush Song

THE CREEK OF THE FOUR GRAVES

So went they forth at dawn; at eve the sun,
That rose behind them as they journeyed out,
Was firing with his nether rim a range
Of unknown mountains, that like ramparts towered
Full in their front; and his last glances fell
Into the gloomy forest's eastern glades
In golden gleams, like to the Angel's sword,
And flashed upon the windings of a creek
That noiseless ran betwixt the pioneers
And those new Appennines— ran, shaded o'er
With boughs of the wild willow, hanging mixed
From either bank, or duskily befringed
With upward tapering feathery swamp-oaks,
The sylvan eyelash always of remote
Australian waters.

CHARLES HARPUR (1813–1868)

ORARA

The strong sob of the chafing stream
    That seaward fights its way
Down crags of glitter, dells of gleam,
    Is in the hills to-day.

206

But, far and faint, a grey-winged form
   Hangs where the wild lights wane—
The phantom of a bygone storm,
   A ghost of wind and rain.

The soft white feet of afternoon
   Are on the shining meads,
The breeze is as a pleasant tune
   Amongst the happy reeds.

The fierce, disastrous, flying fire,
   That made the great caves ring,
And scarred the slope, and broke the spire,
   Is a forgotten thing.

The air is full of mellow sounds,
   The wet hill-heads are bright,
And down the fall of fragrant grounds
   The deep ways flame with light.

HENRY KENDALL (1839–1882)

FAITH

Faith shuts her eyes,
   Poor self-deceiver!
The last god dies
   With the last believer.

VICTOR DALEY (1858–1905)

LOST AND GIVEN OVER

A mermaid's not a human thing,
An' courtin' sich is folly;
Of flesh an' blood I'd rather sing,
What ain't so melancholy.
Oh, Berta! Loo! Juanita! Sue!
Here's good luck to me and you—

Sing rally! ri-a-rally!
The seas is deep; the seas is wide;
But this I'll prove whate'er betide,
I'm bully in the alley!
I'm bull-ee in our al-lee!

The Hoogli gal 'er face is brown;
The Hilo gal is lazy;
The gal that lives by 'Obart town
She'd drive a dead man crazy;
Come, wet your lip, and let it slip!
The *Gretna Green's* a tidy ship—
Sing rally!
The seas is deep; the seas is blue;
But 'ere's good 'ealth to me and you!
Ho, rally!

The Lord may drop us off our pins
To feed 'is bloomin' fishes;
But Lord forgive us for our sins—
Our sins is most delicious!
Come, drink it up and fill yer cup!
The world it owes us bite and sup,
And Mimi, Ju-ju, Sally;
The seas is long; the winds is strong;
The best of men they *will* go wrong—
Hi, rally; ri-a-rally!

The Bowery gal she knows 'er know;
The Frisco gal is silly;
The Hayti gal ain't white as snow—
They're whiter down in Chili.
Now what's the use to shun the booze?
They'll flop yer bones among the ooze
Sou'-west-by-sou' the galley.
The seas is green; the seas is cold;
The best of men they must grow old—
Sing rally! ri-a-rally!

E. J. BRADY (1869–1952)

O DESOLATE EVES

O desolate eves along the way, how oft,
despite your bitterness, was I warm at heart!
not with the glow of remember'd hearths, but warm
with the solitary unquenchable fire that burns
a flameless heat deep in his heart who has come
where the formless winds plunge and exult for aye
among the naked spaces of the world,
far past the circle of the ruddy hearths
and all their memories. Desperate eves,
when the wind-bitten hills turn'd violet
along their rims, and the earth huddled her heat
within her niggard bosom, and the dead stones
lay battle-strewn before the iron wind
that, blowing from the chill west, made all its way
a loneliness to yield its triumph room;
yet in that wind a clamour of trumpets rang,
old trumpets, resolute, stark, undauntable,
singing to battle against the eternal foe,
the wronger of this world, and all his powers
in some last fight, foredoom'd disastrous,
upon the final ridges of the world:
a war-worn note, stern fire in the stricken eve,
and fire thro' all my ancient heart, that sprang
towards that last hope of a glory won in defeat,
whence, knowing not sure if such high grace befall
at the end, yet I draw courage to front the way.

CHRISTOPHER BRENNAN (1870–1932)
from *The Wanderer*

THE LAND I CAME THRO'

The land I came thro' last was dumb with night,
a limbo of defeated glory, a ghost:
for wreck of constellations flicker'd perishing
scarce sustain'd in the mortuary air,
and on the ground and out of livid pools
wreck of old swords and crowns glimmer'd at whiles;
I seem'd at home in some old dream of kingship:
now it is clear grey day and the road is plain,
I am the wanderer of many years
who cannot tell if ever he was king
or if ever kingdoms were: I know I am
the wanderer of the ways of all the worlds,
to whom the sunshine and the rain are one
and one to stay or hasten, because he knows
no ending of the way, no home, no goal,
and phantom night and the grey day alike
withhold the heart where all my dreams and days
might faint in soft fire and delicious death:
and saying this to myself as a simple thing
I feel a peace fall in the heart of the winds
and a clear dusk settle, somewhere, far in me.

CHRISTOPHER BRENNAN (1870–1932)
from *The Wanderer*

NEVER ADMIT THE PAIN

Never admit the pain,
Bury it deep;
Only the weak complain,
Complaint is cheap.

Cover thy wound, fold down
Its curtained place;
Silence is still a crown
Courage a grace.

MARY GILMORE (1865–1962)

211

SONG OF THE RAIN

Night,
And the yellow pleasure of candle-light . . .
Old brown books and the kind fine face of the clock
Fogged in the veils of the fire—its cuddling tock.

The cat,
Greening her eyes on the flame-litten mat;
Wickedly wakeful she yawns at the rain
Bending the roses over the pane,
And a bird in my heart begins to sing
Over and over the same sweet thing—

Safe in the house with my boyhood's love,
And our children asleep in the attic above.

HUGH McCRAE (1876–1958)

LET YOUR SONG BE DELICATE

Let your song be delicate.
   The skies declare
No war—the eyes of lovers
   Wake everywhere.

Let your voice be delicate.
   How faint a thing
Is Love, little Love crying
   Under the Spring.

Let your song be delicate.
   The flowers can hear:
Too well they know the tremble,
   Of the hollow year.

Let your voice be delicate.
  The bees are home:
All their day's love is sunken
  Safe in the comb.

Let your song be delicate.
  Sing no loud hymn:
Death is abroad . . . oh, the black season!
  The deep—the dim!

SHAW NEILSON (1872–1942)

TUMULT OF THE SWANS

What else had I come to find,
driven by that travail's needs,
but the black swans sailing out
beyond the shaking spear of reeds?
Looking back from where I climbed,
secret lay the still lagoon
holding double tree and cloud,
swans and the solitary moon.
If the land I crossed was dumb,
ravaged, stark with fire's scars,
sudden, in green flames of scrub,
rose the blood-proud waratahs.
Savage was the place where night
cried in winds about my ears,
where the honey-eaters still
sang clinging to the grass-tree spears:
blending song with song where day
died behind the ridge's stones,
leaving earth and sky for one
wind-torn tumult of the swans.

ROLAND ROBINSON (1912–   )

EYRE ALL ALONE

Edward John Eyre led an expedition from Adelaide in June 1840 northwards to reach the centre of the continent. Blocked by bogs around Lake Torrens, he moved to Fowler's Bay to attempt an east-west crossing to Western Australia with a reduced party of the overseer Baxter and three Aboriginals in February 1841. In April Baxter was shot by two of the Aboriginals, who deserted Eyre. With Wylie, the remaining Aboriginal, Eyre pressed westward by the shores of the Great Australian Bight. After great hardships in the desert and a rescue by a French whaler, Eyre finally reached Albany. His trans-continental expedition is a stirring epic of courage in Australian exploration.

Wylie, where have you sprung from, what do you say?
I must go to a rare country with this stranger,
Cross an inhuman acre to sleep and forget.
O my warm gentle desert!—a squall threatens.
Well, Baxter, here you lie, bleeding and inert,
Across the yellow moon is drawn a curtain.
Your Sleep is in a manner mine, I tell you, but a thin
Merciful moonshine turns away from our window:
After her, after her, tramping, taking wing . . .
Or, dolt, poltroon, breathe so my brain tingles
To monotonous urgent lifelines of our path,
So, before God, we are again together.
You are dead. And two other parts of man have fled.
Is there life in my slack fingers to cross the ledger?
That game left foot will always somehow limp,
My friend, lie spotless there and very simple.
Your pain and your great patience in the dream
Are working oddly over the Bight and gleaming.
Transfixed in fear and loneliness I burn.
Maimed my brain, maimed my limbs. And a journey—
Daybreak, snigger of dawn. I am alone.
Walk, walk. From dubious footfall one
At Fowler's Bay the chosen must push on
Towards promised fondlings, dancings of the Sound.
Fourth plague, of flies, harries this bloodless ground.
Cliff and salt balance-wheel of heathen planet
Tick, twinkle in concert to devise our minute.
But something on foot, and burning, nudges us
Past bitter waters, sands of Exodus.

FRANCIS WEBB (1925–1973)
Eyre All Alone

THE TOMB OF
LT. JOHN LEARMONTH, A.I.F.

'At the end on Crete he took to the hills, and said he'd fight it out with only a revolver. He was a great soldier. . . .'

One of his men in a letter.

This is not sorrow, this is work: I build
A cairn of words over a silent man,
My friend John Learmonth whom the Germans killed.

There was no word of hero in his plan;
Verse should have been his love and peace his trade,
But history turned him to a partisan.

Far from the battle as his bones are laid
Crete will remember him. Remember well,
Mountains of Crete, the Second Field Brigade!

Say Crete, and there is little more to tell
Of muddle tall as treachery, despair
And black defeat resounding like a bell;

But bring the magnifying focus near
And in contempt of muddle and defeat
The old heroic virtues still appear.

Australian blood where hot and icy meet
(James Hogg and Lermontov were of his kin)
Lie still and fertilise the fields of Crete.

Schoolboy, I watched his ballading begin:
Billy and bullocky and billabong,
Our properties of childhood, all were in.

I heard the air though not the undersong,
The fierceness and resolve; but all the same
They're the tradition, and tradition's strong.

Swagman and bushranger die hard, die game,
Die fighting, like that wild colonial boy
Jack Dowling, says the ballad, was his name.

He also spun his pistol like a toy,
Turned to the hills like wolf or kangaroo,
And faced destruction with a bitter joy.

His freedom gave him nothing else to do
But set his back against his family tree
And fight the better for the fact he knew

He was as good as dead. Because the sea
Was closed and the air dark and the land lost,
'They'll never capture me alive', said he.

.   .   .   .   .   .

That's courage chemically pure, uncrossed
With sacrifice or duty or career,
Which counts and pays in ready coin the cost

Of holding course. Armies are not its sphere
Where all's contrived to achieve its counterfeit;
It swears with discipline, it's volunteer.

I could as hardly make a moral fit
Around it as around a lightning flash.
There is no moral, that's the point of it,

No moral. But I'm glad of this panache
That sparkles, as from flint, from us and steel,
True to no crown nor presidential sash

Nor flag nor fame. Let others mourn and feel
He died for nothing: nothings have their place.
While thus the kind and civilised conceal

This spring of unsuspected inward grace
And look on death as equals, I am filled
With queer affection for the human race.

JOHN MANIFOLD (1915–   )

BEGINNINGS

Not to have known the hard-bitten,
tight-lipped Caesar
clamped down on savage Britain;
or, moving closer,
not to have watched Cook
drawing thin lines across
the last sea's uncut book
is my own certain loss;

as too is having come late,
the other side of the dark
from that bearded, sedate
Hargrave of Stanwell Park,
and so to have missed, some bright
morning, in the salty, stiff
north-easter, a crank with a kite—
steadied above the cliff.

Beginnings once known
are lost. Perpetual day,
wheeling, has grown
each year further away
from the original strength
of any action or mind
used, and at length
fallen behind.

One might give much
to bring to the hand
for sight and touch

cities under the sand,
and to talk and trade
with the plain folk met
could we walk with the first who made
an alphabet.

But more than to look back
we choose this day's concern
with everything in the track,
and would give most to learn
outcomes of all we found
and what next builds to the stars.
I regret I shall not be around
to stand on Mars.

ROBERT D. FITZGERALD (1902–   )

FIVE BELLS

Time that is moved by little fidget wheels
Is not my Time, the flood that does not flow.
Between the double and the single bell
Of a ship's hour, between a round of bells
From the dark warship riding there below,
I have lived many lives, and this one life
Of Joe, long dead, who lives between five bells.

Deep and dissolving verticals of light
Ferry the falls of moonshine down. Five bells
Coldly rung out in a machine's voice. Night and water
Pour to one rip of darkness, the Harbour floats
In air, the Cross hangs upside-down in water.

Why do I think of you, dead man, why thieve
These profitless lodgings from the flukes of thought
Anchored in Time? You have gone from earth,
Gone even from the meaning of a name;

Yet something's there, yet something forms its lips
And hits and cries against the ports of space,
Beating their sides to make its fury heard.

Are you shouting at me, dead man, squeezing your face
In agonies of speech on speechless panes?
Cry louder, beat the windows, bawl your name!
But I hear nothing, nothing . . . only bells,
Five bells, the bumpkin calculus of Time.
Your echoes die, your voice is dowsed by Life,
There's not a mouth can fly the pygmy strait—
Nothing except the memory of some bones
Long shoved away, and sucked away, in mud;

And unimportant things you might have done,
Or once I thought you did; but you forgot,
And all have now forgotten—looks and words
And slops of beer; your coat with buttons off,
Your gaunt chin and pricked eye, and raging tales
Of Irish kings and English perfidy,
And dirtier perfidy of publicans
Groaning to God from Darlinghurst.[1]

KENNETH SLESSOR (1901–1971)

SLEEP

Do you give yourself to me utterly,
Body and no-body, flesh and no-flesh,
Not as a fugitive, blindly or bitterly,
But as a child might, with no other wish?
Yes, utterly.

Then I shall bear you down my estuary,
Carry you and ferry you to burial mysteriously,
Take you and receive you,

[1] An inner area of Sydney.

Consume you, engulf you,
In the huge cave, my belly, lave you
With huger waves continually.

And you shall cling and clamber there
And slumber there, in that dumb chamber,
Beat with my blood's beat, hear my heart move
Blindly in bones that ride above you,
Delve in my flesh, dissolved and bedded,
Through viewless valves embodied so—

Till daylight, the expulsion and awakening,
    The riving and the driving forth,
Life with remorseless forceps beckoning—
    Pangs and betrayal of harsh birth.

                                    KENNETH SLESSOR (1901–1971)

CHILD WITH A COCKATOO

Portrait of Anne, daughter of the Duke of Bedford, by S. Verelst.

'Paid by my lord, one portrait, Lady Anne,
Full length with bird and landscape, twenty pounds
And framed withal. I say received. Verelst.'

So signed the painter, bowed, and took his leave.
My Lady Anne smiled in the gallery
A small, grave child, dark-eyed, half turned to show
Her five bare toes beneath the garment's hem,
In stormy landscape with a swirl of drapes.
And, who knows why, perhaps my lady wept
To stand so long and watch the painter's brush
Flicker between the palette and the cloth
While from the sun-drenched orchard all the day
She heard her sisters calling each to each.
And someone gave, to drive the tears away,

221

That sulphur-crested bird with great white wings,
The wise, harsh bird—as old and wise as Time
Whose well-dark eyes the wonder kept and closed.
So many years to come and still, he knew,
Brooded that great, dark island continent
Terra Australis.

        To those fabled shores
Not William Dampier, pirating for gold,
Nor Captain Cook his westward course had set
Jumped from the longboat, waded through the surf,
And clapt his flag ashore at Botany Bay.
Terra Australis, unimagined land—
Only that sulphur-crested bird could tell
Of dark men moving silently through trees,
Of stones and silent dawns, of blackened earth
And the long golden blaze of afternoon.
That vagrant which an ear-ringed sailor caught
(Dropped from the sky, near dead, far out to sea)
And caged and kept, till, landing at the docks,
Walked whistling up the Strand and sold it then,
The curious bird, its cynic eyes half closed,
To the Duke's steward, drunken at an inn.
And he lived on, the old adventurer,
And kept his counsel, was a sign unread,
A disregarded prologue to an age.
So one might find a meteor from the sun
Or sound one trumpet ere the play's begun.

ROSEMARY DOBSON (1920–   )

LOOK OUT TO WINDWARD....

Look out to the windward of this morning
And count its colours with me, strain to the green
Of the earth's light burden. For I know this country
As a continuing weight upon the heart, and drawn
Brutally fine along her bone of rock.
So count her birds and colours while we may.

We read, and are as jealous of this land
As a young man watchful of each gleam in eyes
Which turn to older musings. What we seek
Is not these shifts of movement and of light
But, deeper down, the strata that define
The good and evil pulsing in her soil.

Yet even the summer sun will not lay bare
The bones of a continent. Watch how this last
Of winter greens her further from our sight.
Although I know to-night's emerging stars
Will shake and scorch the air, my words are blown
Like birds in a half-gale, and no one hears.

And what can I know in her, except a Word
Grown dull with tongues, grown weary of being denied?
Till death is a night wind falling, the eyes of faith
Go dry and burning, like a drought-brown season
Vaunting over green; and our hearts become
A shifting landscape under those great stars.

                          VINCENT BUCKLEY (1926–   )

ARIEL

Frost and snow, frost and snow:
The old ram scratches with a frozen toe
At silver tussocks in the payable mist
And stuffs his belly like a treasure-chest.

His tracks run green up the mountain-side
Where he throws a shadow like an elephant's hide;
He has tossed the sun in a fire of thorns,
And a little bird whistles between his horns.

'Sweet-preety-creature!' sings the matchstick bird,
And on height and in chasm his voice is heard;
Like a bell of ice on the crack of the frost
It rings in the ears of his grazing host.

223

'Sweet-preety-creature!' While all is as still
As the bird on the ram on the frozen hill,
Oh the wagtail warms to his tiny art
And glaciers move through the great beast's heart.

DAVID CAMPBELL (1915–1979)

WOMAN TO MAN

The eyeless labourer in the night,
the selfless, shapeless seed I hold,
builds for its resurrection day—
silent and swift and deep from sight
foresees the unimagined light.

This is no child with a child's face;
this has no name to name it by:
yet you and I have known it well.
This is our hunter and our chase,
the third who lay in our embrace.

This is the strength that your arm knows,
the arc of flesh that is my breast,
the precise crystals of our eyes.
This is the blood's wild tree that grows
the intricate and folded rose.

This is the maker and the made;
this is the question and reply;
the blind head butting at the dark,
the blaze of light along the blade.
Oh hold me, for I am afraid.

JUDITH WRIGHT (1915–   )

MEDITATION ON A BONE

A piece of bone, found at Trondhjem in 1901, had the following runic inscription (about A.D. 1050) cut on it: *I loved her as a maiden; I will not trouble Erlend's detestable wife; better she should be a widow.*

Words scored upon a bone,
Scratched in despair or rage—
Nine hundred years have gone;
Now, in another age
They burn with passion on
A scholar's tranquil page.

The scholar takes his pen
And turns the bone about,
And writes those words again.
Once more they seethe and shout,
And through a human brain
Undying hate rings out.

'I loved her when a maid;
I loathe and love the wife
That warms another's bed:
Let him beware his life!'
The scholar's hand is stayed;
His pen becomes a knife

To grave in living bone
The fierce archaic cry.
He sits and reads his own
Dull sum of misery.
A thousand years have flown
Before that ink is dry.

And, in a foreign tongue,
A man, who is not he,
Reads and his heart is wrung
This ancient grief to see,
And thinks: When I am dung,
What bone shall speak of me?

A. D. HOPE (1907–   )

THE FIRE ON THE SNOW

Stewart's radio verse play describes Captain Scott's expedition to the South Pole 1910–1912, ending with the death of Scott, Wilson, and Bowers in their tent on the return journey.

SCOTT: One night I walked to the cliffs alone, and the moon
   Was pure and burning on those frozen spires and crags,
   So that they leapt like flames. The ice was blazing.
   And the hut, when I came back, was a red island,
   A ship at sea, a fire of human beings,
   Warm and secure. But that was years ago.
   I remember the march to the Pole beginning; sledges,
   Dogs, ponies, the happy cavalcade,
   The long swinging easy marches, the feeling
   Of songs and banners.
   I remember the black flag that told us about Amundsen,
   That fatal day.
WILSON: We shouldn't have cared.
SCOTT: But we did,
   And the Pole was ghosts and ruins, and the snow on our mouths
   Was ashes, ashes. And Evans crumbled away,
   And the Soldier after him.
                 How am I justified,
   Wilson, how am I justified for Oates and Evans,
   And Bowers . . . and you?
WILSON: All of us chose to do it,
   Our own will brought us, our death on the ice
   Was foreseen by each of us; accepted. Let your mind be at peace.
   I have seen this death as the common fate made clearer,
   And cleaner, too, this simple struggle on the ice.
   We dreamed, we so nearly triumphed, we were defeated
   As every man in some great or humble way
   Dreams, and nearly triumphs, and is always defeated,
   And then, as we did, triumphs again in endurance.
   Triumph is nothing; defeat is nothing; life is
   Endurance; and afterwards, death. And whatever death is,
   The endurance remains like a fire, a sculpture, a mountain
   To hearten our children. I tell you,

226

Such struggle as ours is living; it lives after death
Purely, like flame, a thing burning and perfect.

SCOTT: There was something else. I can't remember now;
   I am tired. Death is very near me.
                         Wilson,
There is something else, something to do with me.
Moonlight on ice. Wilson—
                 Wilson!
                     Agony.
Two dead men; and a dying man remembering
The burning snow, the crags towering like flame.
                         DOUGLAS STEWART (1913–   )
                              The Fire on the Snow

228

TRADITIONS AND BELIEFS

THE RINGER

Never allow the thoughtless to declare
That we have no tradition here!

. . . . . .

Australia's wells are deep and full,
But every shallow thinker looks afar,
And says, 'There is no water here;
The windlasses are new'.
And yet tradition ranges through our land!
For here the Ringer strode in seven-league boots,
Or shears, or pride, or courage, moving eager on,
Till he out-swam the seas, out-climbed the mountain tops,
Made servant of the air—and dared—and dared—
And, daring, out-paced time.

MARY GILMORE (1865–1962)

DREAMING OF THE FISH-WOMAN, INTABIDNA

This myth, related by Tjonba of the Arranda tribe, gives a clear description of the 'fish-woman' who is the narrator's totemic ancestress.

The fish-woman Intabidna travelled from Loowarra the big water-hole. She went past the running water Etmungarra. Across the big plain Ilduraba, which is dotted with little round stones, she went. These stones are quadda, the eggs that the fish-woman left. She came from the south and she was travelling towards Indareya, which is Hermansburg Mission.

As Intabidna travelled she sang. She sang: 'I see that claypan far ahead of me. I think there is water there. No more. That water has gone away'. That water was vanishing water, mirage.

She travelled on and came on Uratanga, a big water. It can't dry. It can never finish. It is quick-sand. A big sand-hill is there. The white-man calls it Salt-hole.

229

At the place Uratanga a mob of blacks made a big V-shaped weir out of bushes. They made this fish-trap called Unjeea. They caught a big mob of fish. One big fish they could not catch, it was too cunning. That fish was the woman-fish. She was woman, Kunga. She had a woman's head, breasts, arms and body. Her body ended in a fish tail.

The old man called out: 'Hey! that one is Intabidna the woman-fish. She runs away!'

The woman-fish went back to her own country Louwarrkrurka. That woman-fish was my grandmother. Her name was Palabultjura.

ROLAND ROBINSON (1912–   )
The Feathered Serpent

A NEW BRITANNIA

This precocious expression of an ardent nationalism was written as early as 1823 by a patriot who, born in Norfolk Island in 1792, was one of the very first of the native-born Australians.

And, oh, Britannia! shouldst thou cease to ride
Despotic Empress of old Ocean's tide—
Should thy tamed lion—spent his former might—
No longer roar, the terror of the fight;
Should e'er arrive that dark, disastrous hour,
When, bowed by luxury, thou yield's to power;
When thou, no longer freest of the free
To some proud victor bend's the vanquished knee;
May all thy glories in another sphere ·
Resume, and shine more brightly still than here;
May this, thy last-born infant then arise,
To glad thy heart, and greet thy parent eyes;
AND AUSTRALASIA FLOAT, WITH FLAG UNFURLED,
A NEW BRITANNIA IN ANOTHER WORLD!

WILLIAM CHARLES WENTWORTH (1790–1872)
Australasia

WALTZING MATILDA[1]

Once a jolly swagman camped by a billabong
    Under the shade of a coolibah tree;
And he sang, as he watched and waited while his billy boiled:
    'Who'll come a-waltzing Matilda with me?'

Chorus
Waltzing Matilda, Waltzing Matilda,
    Who'll come a-waltzing Matilda with me?
And he sang as he watched and waited while his billy boiled:
    'Who'll come a-waltzing Matilda with me?'

Down came a jumbuck to drink at that billabong,
    Up jumped the swagman and grabbed him with glee;
And he sang as he shoved that jumbuck in his tucker-bag,
    'You'll come a-waltzing Matilda with me!'

Chorus
Waltzing Matilda, Waltzing Matilda,
    You'll come a-waltzing Matilda with me;
And he sang as he shoved that jumbuck in his tucker-bag:
    'You'll come a-waltzing Matilda with me!'

Up came the squatter, mounted on his thoroughbred,
    Up came the troopers—one—two—three!
'Whose that jolly jumbuck you've got in your tuckerbag?
    You'll come a-waltzing Matilda with me!'

Chorus
Waltzing Matilda, Waltzing Matilda,
    You'll come a-waltzing Matilda with me:
'Whose that jolly jumbuck you've got in your tucker-bag?
    You'll come a-waltzing Matilda with me!'

Up jumped the swagman and sprang into the billabong,
    'You'll never catch me alive!' said he,
And his ghost may be heard as you pass by that billabong,
    'You'll come a-waltzing Matilda with me!'

[1] Carrying a swag.

Chorus
Waltzing Matilda, Waltzing Matilda,
  You'll come a-waltzing Matilda with me!
And his ghost may be heard as you pass by that billabong,
  'You'll come a-waltzing Matilda with me!'

A. B. ('BANJO') PATERSON (1864–1941)
Folk Version

A VIRGIN CONTINENT

It is not in our cities or townships, it is not in our agricultural or mining areas, that the Australian attains full consciousness of his own nationality; it is in places like this, and as clearly here as at the centre of the continent. To me the monotonous variety of this interminable scrub has a charm of its own; so grave, subdued, self-centred; so alien to the genial appeal of more winsome landscape, or the assertive grandeur of mountain and gorge. To me this wayward diversity of spontaneous plant life bespeaks an unconfined, ungauged potentiality of resource; it unveils an ideographic prophecy, painted by Nature in her Impressionist mood, to be deciphered aright only by those willing to discern through the crudeness of dawn a promise of majestic day. Eucalypt, conifer, mimosa; tree, shrub, heath, in endless diversity and exuberance, yet sheltering little of animal life beyond half-specialised and belated types, anachronistic even to the Aboriginal savage. Faithfully and lovingly interpreted, what is the latent meaning of it all?

Our virgin continent! how long has she tarried her bridal day! . . . The mind retires from such speculation, unsatisfied but impressed.

Gravely impressed. For this recordless land—this land of our lawful solicitude and imperative responsibility—is exempt from many a bane of territorial rather than racial impress. She is committed to no usages of petrified injustice; she is clogged by no fealty to shadowy idols, enshrined by Ignorance, and upheld by misplaced homage alone; she is cursed by no memories of fanaticism and persecution; she is innocent of hereditary national jealousy, and free from the envy of sister states.

Then think how immeasurably higher are the possibilities of a Future than the memories of any Past since history began.

TOM COLLINS (JOSEPH FURPHY) (1843–1912)
Such is Life

THE GREAT AUSTRALIAN DREAM

Where is Australia, singer, do you know?
  These sordid farms and joyless factories,
Mephitic mines and lanes of pallid woe?
  Those ugly towns and cities such as these
With incense sick to all unworthy power,
And all old sin in full malignant flower?
No! to her bourn her children still are faring:
  She is a Temple that we are to build:
For her the ages have been long preparing:
  She is a prophecy to be fulfilled!

All that we love in olden lands and lore
  Was signal of her coming long ago!
Bacon foresaw her, Campanella, More,
  And Plato's eyes were with her star aglow!
Who toiled for Truth, whate'er their countries were,
Who fought for Liberty, they yearned for her!
No corsair's gathering ground, or tryst for schemers,
  No chapman Carthage to a huckster Tyre,
She is the Eldorado of old dreamers,
  The Sleeping Beauty of the world's desire!

She is the scroll on which we are to write
  Mythologies our own and epics new:
She is the port of our propitious flight
  From Ur idolatrous and Pharaoh's crew.
She is our own, unstained, if worthy we,
By dream, or god, or star we would not see:
Her crystal beams all but the eagle dazzle;
  Her wind-wide ways none but the strong-winged sail:
She is Eutopia, she is Hy-Brasil,
  The watchers on the tower of morning hail!

BERNARD O'DOWD (1866–1953)
The Bush

THE BUSH ETHOS

From the beginning, then, outback manners and *mores*, working upwards from the lowest strata of society and outwards from the interior, subtly influenced those of the whole population. Yet for long this was largely an unconscious process recorded in folklore and to some extent in popular speech, but largely unreflected in formal literature. Towards the end of the nineteenth century, when the occupation of the interior had been virtually completed, it was possible to look back and sense what had been happening. Australians generally became actively conscious, not to say self-conscious, of the distinctive 'bush' ethos, and of its value as an expression and symbol of nationalism. Through the trade union movement, through such periodicals as the Sydney *Bulletin*, the *Lone Hand*, or the Queensland *Worker*, and through the work of literary men like Furphy, Lawson or Paterson, the attitudes and values of the nomad tribe were made the principal ingredient of a national *mystique*. Just when the results of public education acts, improved communications, and innumerable other factors were administering the *coup de grâce* to the actual bushman of the nineteenth century, his idealised shade became the national culture-hero of the twentieth. Though some shearers are now said to drive to their work in wireless-equipped motor-cars, the influence of the 'noble bushman' on Australian life and literature is still strong.

RUSSEL WARD (1914–   )
The Australian Legend

THE MEN FROM OUTBACK

In that country, and in the other parts of Australia like it, in the pastoral industry and at the diggings, the ideal of the Australian is still being made—the standards of pluck, hardiness, unaffectedness, loyalty, truthfulness, hospitality, on which the rest of Australia consciously forms its ideal. In other words, Australians invariably reserve their greatest admiration for the man from outback; and perhaps that, as far as one can tell to-day, is likely to be the great value of this outside country to Australia. It is true it produces wool, meat, tallow, skins, perhaps ultimately a little soap and some glue. But in the course of that great pastoral industry it produces something far more valuable to the country than all the rest, and that is—men . . .

In guessing at the future of Australia—which of course is still a guess—it seems essential to remember that the Australian, one hundred to two hundred years hence, will still live with the consciousness that, if he only goes far enough back over the hills and across the plains, he comes in the end to the mysterious half-desert country where men have to live the lives of strong men. And the life of that mysterious country will affect Australian imagination much as the life of the sea has affected that of the English.

C. E. W. BEAN (1879–1968)
The Dreadnought of the Darling

MATES

Looked at in an abstract point of view, it is quite surprising what exertions bushmen of new countries, especially mates, will make for one another, beyond people of the old countries. I suppose want prevailing less in the new countries makes men less selfish, and difficulties prevailing more make them more social and mutually helpful. . . .

There is a great deal of this mutual regard and trust engendered by two men working thus together in the otherwise solitary bush, habits of mutual helpfulness arise, and these elicit gratitude, and that leads on to regard. Men under these circumstances often stand by one another through thick and thin; in fact it is a universal feeling that a man ought to be able to trust his own mate in anything.

ALEXANDER HARRIS (1805–1874)
Settlers and Convicts

GORDON'S CREED

'Question not, but live and labour
Till yon goal be won,
Helping every feeble neighbour,
Seeking help from none;
Life is mostly froth and bubble,
Two things stand like stone:
KINDNESS in another's trouble,
COURAGE in your own'

ADAM LINDSAY GORDON (1833–1870)

236

THE LANDSCAPE WRITERS

The folklore element in Australian literature is not lost. It continues, taking different forms, and renewing itself from time to time from its communal source. As fiction branched away from its source, the folklore element found a new medium in what has been called the 'landscape school of writing'. The Australian scene became itself a sufficient subject. Writers went back and picked up themes they had overlooked in their absorption in daily life. In the descriptive or landscape writing there is a conscious return to origins, a Back to Bool Bool festival. As group writing gave way to more individual performance, the folklore element found in this form a new medium. The movement away from origins was thus countered by a return to them in a different vehicle. The landscape writers return to explore a world which, no sooner had we adopted it as ours, began to perish in the face of improved communications.

Much of it is touched with nostalgia for a lost world, however rough and difficult. Nearly all these books—and their name is legion—are stories of travel by varying means from aeroplanes, cars, caravans, bicycles, to shanks' pony. They are in the nomadic tradition so strong in Australian writing. The paths of these articulate travellers criss-cross the continent.

Their books in general, in number and popularity, eclipse all other forms of writing in Australia to-day. Even in the present difficult state of Australian publishing and writing, in its search for publication the descriptive book, almost alone, finds a ready response and audience. In many individual specimens of the genre it is difficult to see, in cold blood, where their immense power to attract lies. Some are not well-written, and in matters of accuracy are not exactly like Caesar's wife. But in bulk these books do build into something significant and among them are books with a genuine freshet within them. Varied though their approach may be, together they give a romantic vision of a world with which many men secretly or openly want to identify themselves, the unique Australian world that is the possession and kingdom of our imagination. We, a small people, can say: 'We have this strange, this antique, still virgin world; it is ours'. They are wonder books, bringing to the reader the marvels and curiosities of a very old country, 'the cenotaphs of species dead elsewhere'; the riddle of the dark races and their customs that are often vestiges of something forgotten long ago: the skills of the bushman born of sheer necessity, the folklore and magics that grow up in the void; old wives' tales on a grand

and perturbing scale. Another aspect of their appeal is that they usually have homeliness to recommend them, familiar incidents, oft-repeated family jokes. There is a pleasure in reading about droving, boundary-riding, teamwork, fencing and tank-sinking, the familiar pleasure of watching men-at-work that is illustrated in any street where the steamroller is busy or the water-main under repair. Familiar and unfamiliar, nostalgic and complaining, interpretative, scientific, mysterious or point blank plain—the landscape books have their charm. They are about us, even if we are townsmen, knowing no more of Australia than the face of the city in which we live. There is always more to say, a different light to throw on country that may be as flat as water from horizon to horizon. Immensity and rarity act as magnifying lens to every incident.

FLORA ELDERSHAW (1897–1956)
The Landscape Writers

THE BLOKE

I have been looking up the Oxford Dictionary, and find that the word 'bloke'—like most other words, if the truth were told—is of uncertain origin. But even if that high authority had told me that it was derived from the French 'blauque'—or the Welsh 'bwlloc'—I should have remained unconvinced. Nobody can persuade me that it came to England from outside; I am certain that the splendid monosyllable first took shape in an English brain. It is as English as Dickens. It is the most satisfying of the many English efforts to find a substitute for the inexpressive 'man' or 'person'. We do not like saying that any one is a 'a curious man'; we say he is a queer chap, or a rum cove, or a quaint customer, or a weird bird, or a funny sort of feller—the list is endless. 'Bloke' is the best of them all—the ugliest, the most undignified, the most disrespectful, and yet somehow the most expressive of them all. It is slang at present; but like all really good slang words, it will become standard English—the future Virgil will begin his epic with 'Arms and the Bloke I sing'—and finally it will become stale and colourless; meanwhile—well, it is good enough for me! . . .

I heard the word magnificently used the other day by a lift-boy. There were four of us in the lift, besides the boy; three common, vulgar people, and a dignified citizen, attired in a frock-coat and a silk hat, who looked as if he had just attended a civic reception, or been given a knighthood; and who signified his desire to ascend to the third floor. When the lift reached the second floor, one of the vulgar persons got out, and the frock-coated citizen stalked out after him. Some lift-boys, I fear, would have felt a secret glee, and allowed him to find out his mistake for himself; but this particular boy, though undistinguished in appearance, had a considerate heart. What did he do? With great presence of mind he shifted the chewing-gum to the left cheek, said 'Hi! bloke', and beckoned the errant one back with a jerk of his thumb. The citizen came back, looking a little red. Evidently he was not used to being so addressed in public. As for me, I wanted to shake the lift-boy's hand; it would have considerably astonished him if I had yielded to the impulse. He was not conscious of having said anything remarkable; he did not know that neither Shelley nor Keats had ever uttered a more perfect phrase. I suppose if he had been French, and if there had been lifts in the days of Robespierre, he would have said 'Hola! citoyen!' something like that. And how pitifully weak it would have been. For the person in the frock-coat did not need to be reminded that he was a citizen. He was only too conscious of that; it was quite plain that he knew himself for a pillar of society. What he did need to be reminded of was the fact that he and the lift-boy were two specimens of the species bloke. The boy, with his two curt monosyllables, uttered more of the essential truth than some long treatises on democracy do. For democracy does not mean representative government or manhood suffrage, or any other piece of machinery. Democracy is a mental attitude. Democracy means a belief in equality. It is based on the conviction that we are all blokes.

WALTER MURDOCH (1874–1970)
The Bloke

YOUNG DEMOCRACY

Unknown, these Titans of our Night
Their New Creation make:
Unseen, they toil and love and fight
That glamoured Man may wake . . .

. . . They teach and live the Golden Rule
Of Young Democracy: —

'That culture, joy and goodliness
Be th' equal right of all:
That Greed no more shall those oppress
Who by the wayside fall:

That each shall share what all men sow:
That colour, caste's a lie:
That man is God, however low—
Is man, however high.'

BERNARD O'DOWD (1866–1953)

THE CONTRIBUTION OF THE HORSE

Absence of backward breeds abolished the flunkey class; the transformation of the peasant element was the contribution of the horse. No man can remain a peasant and go a-horse. Willy-nilly the blood saddle horse will limber him out of his peasant characteristics. This four-footed brother cannot supply what Nature has omitted, and liven dunces into intelligence, but he can change their bovine peculiarities into those of jockeys or caballeros of sorts.

Horses! Horses!

The whole population took to horse. Wishes were horses from the 'forties onward . . .

The stodginess of the yokels from Europe was swiftly massaged into something more flexible. The bumpkin was exercised towards a swagger. The galoot, for good or ill, was transformed into a stockrider, a jockey, a spieler, a drover, a horse-breaker, a horse-coper, a horse-breeder—a caballero of one kind or another. He plodded no more on foot. Only derelicts walked.

The man at one with light horses may be a brave dashing gentleman at large, a cavalry officer at heel, a soulless undersized simian or any of the intermediate grades, but he ceases to be a peasant. Australia has remained a peasantless Commonwealth, a peonless community.

MILES FRANKLIN (1879–1954)
All That Swagger

240

AUSTRALIAN ENGLISH

Australian English tells us many things. In the first place, it makes it quite evident that our environment is vastly different from that of Britain. As we etch in the details of this environment with words that Australians have either invented or borrowed from abroad and converted to their own use, we become aware that a distinct picture is emerging which has no more than a vague English counterpart; *bush, outback, backblocks, never-never, gibber plains, gully, scrub, creek, station, run, billabong, bombora, channel country, Red Heart* and so on.

. . . For some reason, the Australian seems to have a notable capacity for linguistic invention. I believe that this flair tells us quite a lot about the Australian character. Not only does it assure us of the Australian's sharp-witted innovation and adaptability, which have been features of his life since the earliest days of settlement in this country, but it betrays his restless discontent with the orthodoxies of the English language. This latter point may well be one of some significance, for it is quite clearly a rebellion against established authority. Innovation is justified (and inevitable) when the environment of one linguistic community differs from that of another, but here we seem to be confronted with novelty for novelty's sake.

This work-making exuberance extends into many remote corners of our speech. Consider, for example, such common expressions as *stockwhip, stock route, tucker, pigroot, bushranger, duffing, southerly buster, dinkum, brumby, bowyangs, barracking, googly, guiver, nitkeeper, shanghai, smoodge, bombo, slygrog, skerrick, waltzing matilda, Rafferty's rules* and *johnhop.* And such phrases as to *poke borak, bald as a bandicoot, no good to gundy, put the hard word on, home on the pig's back, to go hostile, do a perish, rough as bags* and *send her down, Hughie!*

It is important to remember that these expressions are not casual neologisms, used once and then forgotten. Most of them have been long-established as part of the linguistic currency of Australia. Not only do they remind us that, in spite of English and American influences, we have preserved an identity of our own, but they suggest that the spirit of linguistic rebellion runs deep.

SIDNEY J. BAKER (1912–1976)
Language and Character

THE LITERARY TRADITION

There was, in truth, nothing to hold people to the country until the dreams of men who had been born in it and conceived a mystical faith in its future with their first impressions gave it a spiritual core . . . The first signs of a new people's birth can be felt more truly in those oral songs and stores (the folk balladry and lore) than in any land-laws or government proclamations.

And in the more conscious writing that followed there was a fixing of the features that by then had become characteristic of Australian life. From the sketches of countless occasional writers of the eighties and nineties, as well as from the more permanent work of Lawson and Furphy, a special type emerged—a laconic but sociable fellow with his own idiom and his own way of looking at things. He had humour of a dry sardonic kind, a sensitive spirit with a tough covering, initiative and capacity that were qualified by 'near enough' standards of achievement. His mental horizons were comparatively narrow, but his sympathies were broad. What little he had read of Biblical or secular history he liked to reduce to the homely terms of his experience. In his approach to life he was realistic; he had no impulse to romanticise it, like the American backwoodsman or cowboy; yet there was a streak of idealism in his nature that expressed itself in his sentiment about mateship and in political movements that made for equality.

It was through the eyes of many versions of this national figure that the writers of the eighties and nineties viewed the Australian scene. They established the type—the Joe Wilsons, the Clancys, and the Tom Collinses—and at the same time they fixed the habit of regarding it as the literary norm. This gave their work, whatever its absolute value, a special quality: perhaps it might be called a democratic quality . . . The writer's values were those of the people he brought into his stories, for his experience was likely to have been the same as theirs; Lawson had carried his swag and shared the life of the shearing-shed, Furphy had been a bullock-driver; and they were not rendered self-conscious by the necessity of making concessions to an outside audience.

A tradition of democratic writing was thus established, and it has not been lost, for it is strongly marked in the Australian novel and short story of to-day.

VANCE PALMER (1885–1959)
The Legend of the Nineties

243

THE WILD COLONIAL BOY

'Tis of a wild Colonial boy, Jack Doolan was his name,
Of poor but honest parents he was born in Castlemaine.
He was his father's only hope, his mother's only joy,
And dearly did his parents love the wild Colonial boy.

Chorus
Come, all my hearties, we'll roam the mountains high,
Together we will plunder, together we will die.
We'll wander over valleys, and gallop over plains,
And we'll scorn to live in slavery, bound down with iron chains.

He was scarcely sixteen years of age when he left his father's home
And through Australia's sunny clime a bushranger did roam.
He robbed those wealthy squatters, their stock he did destroy,
And a terror to Australia was the wild Colonial boy.

In sixty-one this daring youth commenced his wild career,
With a heart that knew no danger, no foeman did he fear.
He stuck up the Beechworth mail coach, and robbed Judge MacEvoy,
Who trembled, and gave up his gold to the wild Colonial boy.

He bade the Judge 'Good morning', and told him to beware,
That he'd never rob a hearty chap that acted on the square,
And never to rob a mother of her son and only joy,
Or else you may turn outlaw, like the wild Colonial boy.

One day as he was riding the mountain side along,
A-listening to the little birds, their pleasant laughing song,
Three mounted troopers rode along—Kelly, Davis, and FitzRoy.
They thought that they would capture him—the wild Colonial boy.

'Surrender now, Jack Doolan, you see there's three to one.
Surrender now, Jack Doolan, you daring highwayman.'
He drew a pistol from his belt, and shook the little toy.
'I'll fight, but not surrender', said the wild Colonial boy.

He fired at Trooper Kelly, and brought him to the ground,
And in return from Davis received a mortal wound.
All shattered through the jaws he lay still firing at FitzRoy,
And that's the way they captured him—the wild Colonial boy.

Old Bush Song

TRADE UNIONISM IN THE BUSH

Unionism came to the Australian bushman as a religion. It came bringing salvation from years of tyranny. It had in it that feeling of mateship which he understood already, and which always characterised the action of one 'white man' to another. Unionism extended the idea, so a man's character was gauged by whether he stood true to union rules or 'scabbed' it on his fellows. The man who never went back on the union is honoured to-day as no other is honoured or respected. The man who fell once may be forgiven, but he is not fully trusted. The lowest term of reproach is to call a man a 'scab'.

Experience has taught that the man who sells himself to the employer at a time of strike is a man of weak character, if not worse. At many a country ball the girls have refused to dance with them, the barmaids have refused them a drink, and the waitresses a meal.

Unionists have starved rather than accept work under other conditions. Hundreds of men have worn their boots and clothes to tatters seeking work upon union terms; and not finding it, have gone without for a year—remaining penniless, but independent and proud that they had not degraded themselves. It was such men who made the union a success, and enabled it to hold its own against well-organised capitalism aided by friendly governments. Men imbued with such a spirit put the cause above personal self-interest. They needed no prompting—no exciting by fiery orators—but stood loyal to principle, no matter what the consequences might be. Rough and unpolished many of them may be; but manly, true, and 'white' all the time, and the movement owes them much.

W. G. SPENCE (1846–1926)
Australia's Awakening

245

THE RADICAL CARDINAL

The association between the Roman Catholic Church and the Labour movement has been a distinctive feature of Australian life. It derived from the predominantly working-class character of the Church's adherents, bond or free, during the first half-century of Australian history and the tradition of revolt against British rule brought out by the Irish, priest or layman.

The dismissal of an officer unionist by a steamship company in Melbourne provided the spark for an industrial conflagration. A great maritime strike began on August 16, 1890. A wave of strikes and lock-outs swept through all the eastern states, involving all key industries, the seamen, wharf labourers, coal miners, southeastern pastoral workers (1890), the silver-lead miners of Broken Hill (1891), and the shearers and bush-workers of Queensland (1891 and 1894). The issue was fundamentally economic liberalism versus unionism. The workers opposed reductions in wages and stood for collective bargaining and the '*closed shop*'. The employers wanted '*freedom of contract*' in the full sense of classical economics and avowed their intention of smashing the Australian unions.

The great Christian social leader and champion of the strikers was Cardinal Moran, Archbishop of Sydney. . . .

His first pronouncement on the strike, which was made in an interview with the press on September 13, 1890, caused alarm and consternation among the wealthy class of the colony. Unionism was for them synonymous with socialism. The Cardinal supported the principle of unionism, endorsed the claims of the strikers, and urged conciliation and compromise, with the first step to be taken by the shipowners. . . .

But the Cardinal was not content with merely expressing his views on the strike. He took the initiative in meeting the leaders in Sydney. A deputation representing the strikers had an interview lasting an hour and a half with the Cardinal at St Mary's Cathedral. . . .

On the Saturday following the Cardinal's meeting with the Labour Defence leaders, a great strike procession was held in Sydney in which eight thousand men marched through the city to the Domain Gardens to hold a mass meeting. As the marchers passed the buildings of associations in sympathy with their cause, there was an outburst of feeling among the unionists. The most remarkable demonstration took place outside St Mary's Cathedral in honour of Cardinal Moran. As the marine officers approached the residence, they called for 'Three Cheers for the Cardinal', and all the

246

societies and unions took up the cheering as they passed along to the
Domain.

JAMES G. MURTAGH (1908–1971)
Australia: The Catholic Chapter

FACES IN THE STREET

They lie, the men who tell us, for reasons of their own,
That want is here a stranger, and that misery's unknown;
For where the nearest suburb and the city proper meet
My window-sill is level with the faces in the street—
   Drifting past, drifting past,
   To the beat of weary feet—
While I sorrow for the owners of those faces in the street.

And cause I have to sorrow, in a land so young and fair,
To see upon those faces stamped the marks of Want and Care;
I look in vain for traces of the fresh and fair and sweet
In sallow, sunken faces that are drifting through the street—
   Drifting on, drifting on,
   To the scrape of restless feet;
I can sorrow for the owners of the faces in the street.

In hours before the dawning dims the starlight in the sky
The wan and weary faces first begin to trickle by,
Increasing as the moments hurry on with morning feet,
Till like a pallid river flow the faces in the street—
   Flowing in, flowing in,
   To the beat of hurried feet—
Ah! I sorrow for the owners of those faces in the street.

The human river dwindles when 'tis past the hour of eight,
Its waves go flowing faster in the fear of being late;
But slowly drag the moments, whilst beneath the dust and heat
The city grinds the owners of the faces in the street—
   Grinding body, grinding soul,
   Yielding scarce enough to eat—
Oh! I sorrow for the owners of the faces in the street.

And then the only faces till the sun is sinking down
Are those of outside toilers and the idlers of the town,
Save here and there a face that seems a stranger in the street
Tells of the city's unemployed upon their weary beat—
    Drifting round, drifting round,
    To the tread of listless feet—
Ah! my heart aches for the owner of that sad face in the street.

And when the hours of lagging feet have slowly dragged away,
And sickly yellow gaslights rise to mock the going day,
Then, flowing past my window, like a tide in its retreat,
Again I see the pallid stream of faces in the street—
    Ebbing out, ebbing out,
    To the drag of tired feet,
While my heart is aching dumbly for the faces in the street.

And now all blurred and smirched with vice the day's sad end is seen,
For where the short 'large hours' against the longer 'small hours' lean,
With smiles that mock the wearer, and with words that half entreat,
Delilah pleads for custom at the corner of the street—
    Sinking down, sinking down,
    Battered wreck by tempests beat—
A dreadful, thankless trade is hers, that Woman of the Street.

But, ah! to dreader things than these our fair young city comes,
For in its heart are growing thick the filthy dens and slums,
Where human forms shall rot away in sties for swine unmeet
And ghostly faces shall be seen unfit for any street—
    Rotting out, rotting out,
    For the lack of air and meat—
In dens of vice and horror that are hidden from the street.

I wonder would the apathy of the wealthy men endure
Were all their windows level with the faces of the Poor?
Ah! Mammon's slaves, your knees shall knock, your hearts in terror beat,
When God demands a reason for the sorrows of the street,
    The wrong things and the bad things
    And the sad things that we meet
In the filthy lane and alley, and the cruel, heartless street.

248

I left the dreadful corner where the steps are never still,
And sought another window overlooking gorge and hill;
But when the night came dreary with the driving rain and sleet,
They haunted me—the shadows of those faces in the street,
 Flitting by, flitting by,
 Flitting by with noiseless feet,
And with cheeks that scarce were paler than the real ones in the street.

Once I cried: 'O God Almighty! if Thy might doth still endure,
Now show me in a vision for the wrongs of Earth a cure'.
And, lo, with shops all shuttered I beheld a city's street,
And in the warning distance heard the tramp of many feet,
 Coming near, coming near,
 To a drum's dull distant beat—
'Twas Despair's conscripted army that was marching down the street!

Then, like a swollen river that has broken bank and wall,
The human flood came pouring with the red flags over all,
And kindled eyes all blazing bright with revolution's heat,
And flashing swords reflecting rigid faces in the street—
 Pouring on, pouring on,
 To a drum's load threatening beat,
And the war-hymns and the cheering of the people in the street.

And so it must be while the world goes rolling round its course,
The warning pen shall write in vain, the warning voice grow hoarse,
For not until a city feels Red Revolution's feet
Shall its sad people miss awhile the terrors of the street—
 The dreadful, everlasting strife
 For scarcely clothes and meat
In that pent track of living death—the city's cruel street.
HENRY LAWSON (1867–1922)

IN THINGS OF THE MIND

September 25th, 1929. 'The trouble about this country', said Will Dyson last night, 'is its mental timidity. Physical courage—yes, I suppose it's got its share of that, perhaps a little more than its share, but put it face to face with a new idea and it goes all of a tremble. For years we've been boasting that we're youthful and adventurous. It's all boloney. In things of the mind we show about as much spirit as a suburban old maid'.

And he began to lay the blame on our intellectuals. They hadn't the courage of their convictions. . . .

The intellectuals, with their old-maidish modesty and diffidence, had let the country become a backwater, a paradise for dull boring mediocrities, a place where the artist or the man with ideas could only live on sufferance. It wasn't a question of what outsiders thought, but of the condition of Australia itself. Was it ever to fill its empty mental spaces and become a country fit for adults?

An evening of conflict, with Dyson less witty than usual, more inclined to use sword than rapier, slashing out wildly at other people and perhaps at himself. More than a hint of frustration in him. As Furnley Maurice pointed out afterwards, his charge of mental timidity might easily make a boomerang sweep. In London he won fame by his dash in attacking the whole world of political and social humbug; his dazzling cartoons became known throughout Europe; men like Shaw, Wells, Orage and Chesterton gave homage to him. Yet here, on the home ground, how muffled his attack has been! In four years hardly a line or a word that would penetrate this skin of mediocrity or pretentiousness. Is it that some power has gone out of him or are the odds here too heavy?

NETTIE PALMER (1885–1964)
Fourteen Years

THE DAY'S A PUP

A long argument. I will summarise it, in the hope of making clear the causes, as I see them, which lead to Easy Optimism: Sunshine; a spirit of leap before you look, called forth by 'Give-it-a-go'; and a youthful self-confidence which does not know what the other fellow is doing and does not want to find out.

I may be wrong in settling the parentage of Easy Optimism, but I am sure of its eldest child—Improvisation. Australians have a genius for this. It is their strength and their weakness. The selector who stops a leak in the roof of his humpy with an old opossum skin is true to type. So are the men who built Parliament House in Canberra. (They said it would do all right for fifty years. Then they'd build another.) But improvisation and precision cannot go together. Australians, indeed, show an indifference to precision that almost amounts to dislike. 'What's the worry?' they say; 'the day's a pup'. This easy-going casualness, this habit of making things do, is probably a survival of the early days when things had to do. Conditions have changed but not the attitude of mind. I could give examples which touch life at many points. . . .

This improvisation has another side, however, which no one in decency could fail to mention. It brings out resource and initiative. If such a person as the average Australian could exist—for how can any one, even from the members of his own family or his own town pick on one single representative who would embody the characteristics of the rest?—he would not be my first choice if I wanted an organiser. He is, as his poet boasts,

> Product of the present only,
> Thinking nothing of the past.

But if I were in a tight corner he is the best man in the whole world to get me out of it. And he would succeed, if resource, good humour, and sheer unmatchable bravery could do the job. I am not quoting second-hand opinions. I am saying what I found myself. If I had not met these qualities I should not be alive and writing about them.

THOMAS WOOD (1892–1950)
Cobbers

A SURPRISING REVELATION

From mid-1942 onwards, Australian air-crews were operating from bases in Britain . . . Over 7,000 Australian lads gave their lives in Britain's three years of air-assault upon Germany.

Here was rather a surprising revelation. That young Australians would make superb fighter-pilots could have been foreseen. But in fact most of them served in heavy bombers; and the reputation they earned was the opposite of what had been expected, at any rate by the British—who seem

251

to have imagined that Australians would be irresponsible dare-devils, reckless, careless and slap-dash. Yet actually those Australian pilots and navigators won an outstanding name—for what? For care and thoroughness, for meticulous attention to detail, for their passion for getting everything just exactly right. They became recognised as being among the most trustworthy, the most conscientious, the most responsible of navigators and pilots. To many observers they seemed to be much more adult than British young men of their age.

This was consistent, however, with the characteristic which older Australians were revealing at home in the fields of science and industry. They were mastering new techniques with astonishing rapidity and thoroughness; they were finding out new and more efficient methods of production which older industrial countries had taken decades to discover; they were continually inventing and improving and improvising. Australians —perhaps to their own astonishment—found that they excelled, not only as young pathfinders and pilots flying through the night to destroy cities in Europe, but also as scientists in their laboratories, and as technologists and technicians working in the factories of Australia. In both cases their secret was the combination of initiative, enterprise, and unorthodoxy, with a tremendous thoroughness, a scrupulous attention to detail. It was a newly-revealed characteristic of the more intelligent sections of the Australian people. But there was no doubt about it.

A. E. MANDER (1894–   )
The Making of the Australians

IRONY IN FURPHY'S *SUCH IS LIFE*

Furphy's literary modernism is made even clearer through the central importance of the Ironic to his design. Its play is seldom absent for long. It pops out intriguingly in the turn of the incidental comment—'that integrity which springs from the certainty of being ultimately found out', 'the indescribably weary step of the station man when the day is warm and the boss absent'; such phrases have a relish of Jane Austen, if due allowance is made for the influence of Furphy's masculine temperament, and for the slower rhythm of the Riverina drawl. He is constantly inventing detail for the sake of an ironic savour:

Should I first walk across to B——'s and get Dick L—— to shift some of my inborn ignorance re Palestine?

252

I decided on the latter line of action, and followed it with—Well, at all events, I have the compensating consciousness of a dignity uncompromised, and a nonchalance unruffled, in the face of Dick's really interesting descriptions of South-eastern Tasmania.

But irony is more than the book's flavouring spice. It is the key to the whole unusual design. The idea of Tom Collins as the book's unifying factor rests on the ironically unexpected results which his interventions produce. . . .

To find among his contemporaries an irony comparable with Furphy's, one must go to Samuel Butler—a writer plainly prophetic of the twentieth century approach; and of the two, Furphy is the greater ironist. Butler's is used in the service of a certain timidity—as a pair of water-wings to float him over those depths of life which he is plainly a little afraid. Furphy's is bedded in a philosophic humanism, suggesting the depths by its effect of echo. It reflects a sane and bold attitude—undenying of the nobilities, but ready to face the facts. Incidentally, it has a notably Australian character. It is no accident, I believe, that Furphy and Lawson were among the first writers to rediscover the structural value of irony in the writing of fiction. It came, as the great technical inventions in art usually come, from the quality of the writers' experience of life.

A. A. PHILLIPS (1900–   )
The Australian Tradition

THE COMMON MAN

The aggressive insistence on the worth and unique importance of the common man seems to me to be one of the fundamental Australian characteristics. Nor is it obviously related to the doctrine of Rousseau. It is a local development. Australia is perhaps the last stronghold of egalitarian democracy. The great Australian literary philosopher of the common man is Tom Collins.[1] Collins lacked fluidity, but he had vigor, originality, and independence, which are vastly more important. He was an adventurer of the mind as well as an adventurer of the body. He was a speculative materialist and he was a great writer.

C. HARTLEY GRATTAN (1902–1980)
Australian Literature

[1] The pseudonym of Joseph Furphy.

THE PAINTINGS OF GRUNER

Gruner's pictures provide an *Australian's hypothesis of Australia.* He can show Australians themselves, no less than immigrants, how Australia shall be viewed henceforth. Gruner's lucent but faint Australian purple and his dry-refracting Australian subtle blue is as distinctive an example of artistic creativeness as was Turner's misty London blue or flaming Venice sunset red. Gruner, the greatest Australian landscape painter, has shown in his work how the Spirit of a Place creates and is created by the artist. He sees Australia lyrically, the only true realism is his—that which constructs a country as a vision to be attained, as a country that is loved. In proof of this love, there are his pictures, a reality: Australia becomes real in its own culture and by its own aesthetic. Once you have seen a painting by Gruner, you can never again believe that the Australian landscape is drab or colourless.

P. R. STEPHENSEN (1901–1965)
The Foundations of Culture in Australia

LIFE'S TESTAMENT VI

I worshipped, when my veins were fresh,
A glorious fabric of this flesh,
Where all her skill in living lines
And colour (that its form enshrines)
Nature had lavished; in that guess
She had gathered up all loveliness.
All beauty of flesh, and blood, and bone
I saw there: ay, by impulse known,
All the miracle, the power,
Of being had come there to flower.
Each part was perfect in the whole;
The body one was with the soul;
And heedful not, nor having art,
To see them in a several part,
I fell before the flesh, and knew
All spirit in terms of that flesh too.

But blood must wither like the rose:
'Tis wasting as the minute goes:
And flesh, whose shows were wonders high,
Looks piteous when it puts them by.
The shape I had so oft embraced
Was sealed up, and in earth was placed—
And yet not so; for hovering free
Some wraith of it remained with me,
Some subtle influence that brings
A new breath to all beauteous things,
Some sense that in my marrow stirs
To make things mute its ministers.
I fall before the spirit so,
And flesh in terms of spirit know—
The Holy Ghost, the truth that stands
When turned to dust are lips and hands.

WILLIAM BAYLEBRIDGE (1883–1942)

DITHYRAMB IN RETROSPECT

I was carried to a font.
Stranger fingers marked my front.
   Significant, no doubt, the rite
   that day was day and night was night
   yet it could not make me see.
   Lifeless was that sorcery.
Then I sought a font in Toil,
smeared my sweaty brows with Soil.
   Still by fingers strange 'twas done,
   though the fingers were my own.

Then I sought a font in Fire;
leapt I Armageddon's pyre.
   Iron set on me his hand:
   but 'twas still a stranger brand.
Then a passion smote my heart
with a devastating dart.
   Still I could in no wise see.
   Darkness ever compassed me.

With my pain I face the Sky
When my planet there must ply . . .
   And the fingers of the wind
touch me with my Very Wand.
Straightway know I power to see
   what the light has hid from me.

By the Wind that walks the Night
I am baptised into sight.

PETER HOPEGOOD (1891–1967)

THIS LAND

Give me a harsh land to wring music from,
brown hills, and dust, with dead grass
straw to my bricks.

Give me words that are cutting-harsh
as wattle-bird notes in dusty gums
crying at noon.

Give me a harsh land, a land that
swings, like heart and blood,
from heat to mist.

257

Give me a land that like my heart
scorches its flowers of spring,
then floods upon its summer ardour.

Give me a land where rain
is rain that would beat high heads low.
Where wind howls at the windows

and patters dust on tin roofs
while it hides the summer sun
in a mud-red shirt.

Give my words sun and rain,
desert and heat and mist,
spring flowers, and dead grass,
blue sea and dusty sky,
song-birds and harsh cries,
strength and austerity
that this land has.

IAN MUDIE (1911–1976)

258

FIRST LINES OF POEMS

INDEX OF AUTHORS

263

ACKNOWLEDGEMENTS

The publishers gratefully acknowledge the co-operation of the following authors, owners of copyrights and publishers who have given permission for poems, prose extracts, dramatic passages, and photographs to appear in this book. While every care has been taken to trace and acknowledge copyright, the publishers tender their apologies for any accidental infringement where copyright has proved untraceable.

MRS P. M. I. ALEXANDER for the poem 'Song for Lovers' by T. Inglis Moore.

ANGUS & ROBERTSON PUBLISHERS for prose extracts from the following works: 'Donalbain McCree and the Sin of Anger' from *Tales of Parramatta and India* by Ethel Anderson, edited by John Douglas Pringle; *The Dreadnought of the Darling* by C. E. W. Bean; *Henry Lawson, By His Mates* by J. Le Gay Brereton; 'The Old Miner' from *Short Shift Saturday and Other Stories* by Gavin Casey; *Man-Shy* and *Dusty* by Frank Dalby Davison; *All That Swagger* and *Up The Country* by Miles Franklin; *Prosper the Commonwealth* by Sir Robert Randolph Garran; *Capricornia* by Xavier Herbert; *The Great Australian Loneliness* by Ernestine Hill; *Crusts and Crusades* by W. M. Hughes; *Riverslake* by T. A. G. Hungerford; *Flynn of the Inland* by Ion L. Idriess; *The Magic Pudding* by Norman Lindsay; *Here's Luck* by L. W. Lower; 'The Bloke' from *Collected Essays* by Walter Murdoch; *Working Bullocks* by Katharine Susannah Prichard; *Flying Fox and Drifting Sand* by Francis Ratcliffe; *Jonah* by Louis Stone; *The Battlers* and *Tiburon* by Kylie Tennant; and for the following poems: 'The Land I Came Thro'' and 'O Desolate Eves' from *Selected Poems* by Christopher Brennan; 'Windy Gap' and 'Ariel' from *Selected Poems* by David Campbell; the extract from 'At The Play' from *The Sentimental Bloke* by C. J. Dennis; 'Child With Cockatoo' from *Selected Poems* by Rosemary Dobson; 'Beginnings' from *Southmost Twelve* by Robert D. Fitzgerald; 'Nationality', 'Marri'd', 'Eve-Song', 'Never Admit The Pain', 'The Ringer', and 'The Waradgery Tribe' from *The Passionate Heart and Other Poems*, and 'Old Botany Bay' from *The Singing Tree* by Dame Mary Gilmore; 'Boomerang' from *Poems of Discovery* by W. Hart-Smith; 'Meditation on a Bone' from *Collected Poems 1930–1970* by A. D. Hope; 'Dithyramb in Retrospect' from *Circus At World's End* and 'Austral Pan' by Peter Hopegood; 'Giovanni Rinaldo, P.O.W.' from *Pools of the Cinnabar Range* by Flexmore Hudson; 'New Guinea' from *Collected Poems* by James McAuley; 'Song of the Rain' from *Poems* by Hugh McCrae; 'Mokie's Madrigal' from *The Ballad of Bloodthirsty Bessie* by Ronald McCuaig; 'Elegy for My Sad-Faced Uncle' by Ray Mathew; 'Freeman' from *Poems 1940–1955* by Ernest G. Moll; 'Tangmalangaloo' from *Around the Boree Log* by John O'Brien; 'From the Gulf' from *Fair Girls and Gray Horses* by William H. Ogilvie; 'Clancy of the Overflow',

'The Man From Snowy River' and 'Waltzing Matilda' from *The Collected Verse of A. B. Paterson* (reprinted by permission of the copyright owner and Angus & Robertson Publishers); 'Argument' from *Battle Stations* by John Quinn; the extract from 'Five Visions of Captain Cook' and the extract from 'Five Bells', and 'Sleep' from *Kenneth Slessor—Selected Poems*; 'Eyre All Alone—April 29th' from *Francis Webb: Collected Poems*; and 'Woman to Man' by Judith Wright from *Judith Wright: Collected Poems 1942–1970*.

AUSTRALIAN WAR MEMORIAL for prose extracts from *The Official History of Australia in the War of 1914–1918* by C. E. W. Bean; and the extract from *Australia in the War of 1939–1945* by Gavin Long and D. P. Mellor.

MS S. BAKER for the extract from *The Australian Language* by Sidney J. Baker.

MR H. N. BLOCKSIDGE for the poem 'Life's Testament' by William Baylebridge.

PROFESSOR VINCENT BUCKLEY for his poem 'Look Out to Windward'.

THE BULLETIN for the poems 'Air Shaft' and 'Advice from a Nightwatchman' by Ian Healy.

CHATTO & WINDUS LTD, LONDON for the extract from *Australian Accent* by John Douglas Pringle.

MRS CHARLES CHAUVEL for the extract from *Walkabout* by Charles and Elsa Chauvel.

THE LADY COWPER for the extracts from *Georgiana's Journal* and *My Father and My Father's Friends* by Hugh McCrae.

CURTIS BROWN (AUST) PTY LTD, SYDNEY for the prose extracts from *Southern Steel* by Dymphna Cusack; *The Timeless Land* by Eleanor Dark; *The Flesh and the Spirit* by Douglas Stewart; 'The Batting Wizard from the City' from *The Gambling Ghost and Other Tales* by Dal Stivens; and the poem 'My Country' by Dorothea Mackellar.

MR P. M. DRAKE-BROCKMAN for the extract from *The Fatal Days* by Henrietta Drake-Brockman.

EDWARDS & SHAW PTY LTD for the prose extract from *The Feathered Serpent* and the poem 'Tumult of the Swans' by Roland Robinson; and the extract from the poem 'The Traveller' from *Thirty Poems* by John Thompson.

THE EQUITY TRUSTEES and the EDWARD VANCE PALMER ESTATE for the extract from *A. G. Stephens* by Vance Palmer.

ERNEST BENN LTD, ENGLAND for the extract from *Australia* by W. K. Hancock.

MRS J. G. EWERS for the extract from *With the Sun on My Back* by John K. Ewers.

MR H. H. FINLAYSON for the extract from his book *The Red Centre*.

HUTCHINSON GROUP (AUST) PTY LTD for the extract from *We of the Never-Never* by Mrs Aeneas Gunn.

JOHN FARQUHARSON LTD for the extract from *Plaque with Laurel* by Marjorie Barnard and Flora Eldershaw.

LANSDOWNE PRESS and MR JOHN O'GRADY for the extracts from *They're a Weird Mob* and the poem 'Integrated Adjective' by John O'Grady (Nino Culotta).

MRS RUTH LOCKWOOD for the poem 'Wanderer's Lament' by W. E. Harney and A. P. Elkin from *Songs of the Songman*.

LONGMAN CHESHIRE for the extract from *The Australian Tradition* by A. A. Phillips.

LOTHIAN PUBLISHING CO. PTY LTD for the following poems: 'Lost and Given Over' from *The Ways of Many Waters* by E. J. Brady; the extract from the poem 'The Victoria Market Recollected in Tranquillity' from *Poems* by Furnley Maurice; 'Let Your Song Be Delicate' and 'Love's Coming' from *Collected Poems* by Shaw Neilson; 'Australia' and the extracts from the poems 'The Bush' and 'Young Democracy' from *Collected Poems* by Bernard O'Dowd.

MRS MARGOT LUDOWICI for the extracts from *Literary Memories* and the *Preface to Gordon's Poems* by A. G. Stephens.

MR ALAN MARSHALL for the extract from his work *They Were Tough Men on the Speewah*.

MS MARY ANNE HUGHES MAUERMANN for the extract from *Australian Literature* by C. Hartley Grattan.

MEANJIN for the prose extracts from *The Landscape Writers* by Flora Eldershaw; *Going Through* by John Morrison; *Fourteen Years* by Nettie Palmer; and the poems 'Bullocky' and 'South of My Days' from *The Moving Image* by Judith Wright.

MELBOURNE UNIVERSITY PRESS for prose extracts from the following works: *Men Were My Milestones* by A. R. Chisholm; *The Outside Track* by George Farwell; *National Portraits* and *The Legend of the Nineties* by Vance Palmer; and *Memories of Myrtle Bank* by John Rowland Skemp.

MRS RENEE MUDIE for the poem 'This Land' by Ian Mudie.

OXFORD UNIVERSITY PRESS for prose extracts from the following works: *Sources of Australian History* by C. Manning Clark; *The Australian Legend* by Russel Ward; and *Cobbers* by Thomas Wood.

PERMANENT TRUSTEE CO. LTD for the poem 'Emus' by 'E' (Mary Fullerton).

THE POLDING PRESS for the extract from *Australia: The Catholic Chapter* by James G. Murtagh.

RIGBY PUBLISHERS LTD for the poem 'Bert Schultz' from *Man in a Landscape* by Colin Thiele.

MRS ROHAN RIVETT for the extract from *The Migrant and the Community* by Rohan Rivett.

MR RAY ROBINSON for the extracts from his work *Between Wickets*.

MR ALEX W. SHEPPARD and MR A. E. MANDER for the extract from *The Making of the Australians* by A. E. Mander.

THE SOCIETY OF AUTHORS, LONDON (literary representative of the Estate of John Masefield) for the extract from *Gallipoli* by John Masefield.

THE STREHLOW RESEARCH FOUNDATION for the translation by T. G. H. Strehlow of the poem 'Aranda Song'.

266

TESSA SAYLE (LITERARY & DRAMATIC AGENTS) for the extract from *Big Red* by Henry G. Lamond.

UNIVERSITY OF QUEENSLAND PRESS for the poem 'The Tomb of Lt. John Learmonth A.I.F.' from *Collected Verse* by John Manifold.

WILLIAM HEINEMANN LTD, LONDON for the extract from *The Fortunes of Richard Mahony* by Henry Handel Richardson.

Acknowledgement is gratefully made to the National Library of Australia for the use of photographs and illustrations from their collection.

Page   7   Transport—Shipping Hobson's Bay Railway Pier, Sandridge, C. Nettleton's *Views of Melbourne and Suburbs*.

Page 18   A bush selector's hut in Gippsland, Caire collection.

Page 27   Andamooka Station, lent by Mrs Gordon 1977.

Page 44   Experiences of a pioneer squatter, *Sydney Mail* (21 November 1885).

Page 67   On the road to our selection, cartoon by A. Vincent, *On Our Selection* by A. H. Davis (Steele Rudd), from the *Bulletin*.

Page 84   Cattle branding, Emerald, Queensland, Album 259—*Queensland Farming and Pastoral Industry*.

Page 86   Overland with cattle, *Illustrated Sydney News* (16 October 1865).

Page 107   Interior of shearing shed at Walla, Riverina District, 1901.

Page 113   Bullock teams, Michael Kerry collection.

Page 128   Sunday in the bush, *Town and Country Journal* (10 January 1874).

Page 163   Strayed from the picnic, *Australasian Sketcher* (25 December 1875).

Page 173   Sheep washing plant, Michael Kerry collection.

Page 177   Rural Views: Katoomba, New South Wales, S. M. Maule collection.

Page 204   Pioneers: A night encampment of Bushmen, *Illustrated Australian News* (25 April 1864).

Page 207   Agriculture, *Queensland Farming and Pastoral Industry*, c. 1890.

Page 215   Kalgoorlie, Western Australia, 'Happy Thought', Ray Miller album.

Page 228   'Shepherding' in Australia, *Illustrated Australian News* (25 May 1864).

Page 235   Shepherd's hut on the Moira Station, near the Murray, Victoria, *Illustrated Australian News* (25 January 1869).

Page 243   Bridges: Rustic bridge near Darlington, Victoria.

Page 257   Yandilla: Effects of black soil in wet weather, *Yandilla Queensland* album.